T0247812

The
Hidden
Globe

The

Hidden
Globe

How Wealth Hacks the World

Atossa Araxia Abrahamian

RIVERHEAD BOOKS • NEW YORK • 2024

RIVERHEAD BOOKS
An imprint of Penguin Random House LLC
penguinrandomhouse.com

Portions of chapter 7, "Ad Astra," were previously published in slightly different
form as "How a Tax Haven is Leading the Race to Privatise Space" in
The Guardian (2017). Portions of chapter 11, *Terra Nullius*, were published in
slightly different form as "The Dream of Open Borders Is Real—in the High
Arctic" in *The Nation* (2019), and very small portions of chapter 3, "White
Cube, Black Box," appeared as "Inside the New 'Fortress' in New York City
That's Housing Millions of Dollars of Art" in *Artsy* and *Longreads* (2018).

Other small portions of the work were published in slightly different form on
the author's blog, *Terra Nullius*.

LIBRARY OF CONGRESS CATALOGING-IN-PUBLICATION DATA
Names: Abrahamian, Atossa Araxia, author.
Title: The Hidden Globe : How Wealth Hacks the World /
Atossa Araxia Abrahamian.
Description: New York : Riverhead Books, 2024.
Identifiers: LCCN 2024027757 | ISBN 9780593329856 (hardcover) |
ISBN 9780593329870 (ebook) | ISBN 9780593854099 (international edition)
Subjects: LCSH: Wealth. | Income distribution. | Rich people—Psychology. |
Boundaries—Economic aspects.
Classification: LCC HC79.W4 A27 2024 | DDC 305.5/234—dc23/eng/20240710
LC record available at https://lccn.loc.gov/2024027757

Printed in the United States of America
1st Printing

Book design by Alexis Farabaugh

Law makes long spokes of the short stakes of men.

—WILLIAM EMPSON, *LEGAL FICTION* (1928)

Contents

Introduction   *1*

1: City of Holes   *11*

2: Good Fences   *33*

3: White Cube, Black Box   *49*

4: In the Zones   *81*

5: Hacking the World   *113*

6: The City and the City   *133*

7: Ad Astra   *159*

8: Titanic   *195*

9: Excised   *233*

10: Laos Vegas   *259*

11: Terra Nullius   *287*

Acknowledgments   *313*

Notes on Sources   *315*

The
Hidden
Globe

Introduction

I began this book about the world on a lifelong hunch: there was something strange about the place where I grew up.

That place is the Swiss city of Geneva, though its location doesn't tell the whole story. Geneva hosts the United Nations, the World Health Organization, and hundreds more international organizations and NGOs that employ thousands of diplomats, consuls, expatriate workers, and their families. There are more multinational companies there than I can count. Nearly half of Geneva's population has a non-Swiss nationality. Without outsiders, the city would be nothing.

I am, and will always be, a part of this world apart—a place defined by a certain placelessness. I went to international schools, where the history we were taught had little to do with the battles that had been fought steps from the playground. My parents' jobs at the UN—my father was an economist at the organization's Conference on Trade and Development, and my mother, a conference interpreter for its secretariat—compounded the feeling of being a little elsewhere. My classmates seemed to move every few years, which made it feel like I was always moving, too, without my ever actually leaving. These feelings of rootlessness inspired my first book, *The Cosmopolites*, an investigation into the global passport market—the legal, above-board acquisition of citizenship documents. If you could buy a passport like a pair of sneakers, how much could it mean, really?

But there was another, less obvious reason for my unease with Geneva. It had to do with the rules: who made them, who followed them, and the places and people to whom they didn't apply. As a teen, I watched the children of diplomats enjoying the functional immunity that came with their parents' station by just walking away when the police caught them speeding or smoking pot in the park after dark. Duty-free shopping was another perk: if you fall into a certain employment category as a foreigner, the world is your airport. Near the UN, in a nondescript commercial building and down a steep flight of stairs, there is a special shop that lets you avoid sales tax on everything from boxer shorts to La Mer moisturizer. ("Easily one of the world's most bizarre retail experiences," reads one online review. "Where else can you spend thousands of euro on a watch and in the same transaction buy a microwaveable TV dinner?")

Diplomats, I discovered, were only the visible tip of Geneva's special cases. On the city's main drag, private banks stored information that even the Swiss government couldn't access, about the secret accounts of deposed monarchs and the ill-gotten gains of multinational evaders and avoiders. And a short walk from the pool where I learned to swim stood the Geneva Freeport, a cordoned-off warehouse that operated outside Swiss customs regulations. Conceived centuries ago to allow merchants to store grain, the freeport is where oligarchs now stash art, wine, jewels, and other luxury items.

On one hand, Geneva's composition epitomizes a familiar kind of internationalism: the tangible, imperfect, often lovely kind that brings people of the world together in one place at one time, in peace. But there is something else at work here—something you can't see, but whose influence on the world around it is as potent as the globalism of flesh and blood. I call it the spectral economy: the distant, disparate, yet astonishingly lucrative transactions that happen not *in* Geneva, but *from* Geneva. The city is full of conduits, or entrepôts, for a capitalism that is run remotely. It functions less as a place where things happen than as a portal to other worlds. And it turns out there are many more places like it. This book is about these places.

When I started writing *The Hidden Globe*, I sought to understand how my city got this way: how its infamous dullness squared with its endless repository of secrets. I also wanted to understand why I, a citizen of Geneva, felt so drawn to those other nowheres: city-states like Singapore and Dubai, Caribbean tax shelters, island offshore centers, airport bars, hotel lobbies, diplomatic compounds, and customs depots. These locales aren't everyone's idea of a good time, but to me they have always felt familiar, as though they share a common logic with my hometown.

It was only after leaving Geneva for New York that I began to piece the bigger picture together in my mind. I started to understand how spaces defined by surprising or unconventional jurisdiction—embassies, freeports, tax havens, container ships, Arctic archipelagoes, and tropical city-states—were the lifeblood of the global economy and a defining part of our daily lives.

Take world trade. Notwithstanding its brute physicality, shipping relies on the abstract technicalities that create special economic zones, grant control of ports to foreign corporations, allow landlocked nations to sell flags of convenience, and create loopholes for shipping firms to hire cheap onboard labor. The transactions that fund the movements of these goods—the silent transfer of unholy sums on screens—don't necessarily follow a straightforward geography either. The routes that people, money, and things take to cross the globe do not trace the crow's flight. Their paths are twisted, halting, and circuitous—and intentionally so.

In the United States alone, there are 193 active "foreign-trade zones" exempt from federal customs duties. They employ around 460,000 people (the population of Palm Springs!) and see hundreds of billions of dollars' worth of merchandise, from car parts to pharmaceuticals, move into and out of them over the course of a year, to be stored, altered, or assembled. In a world made up of 192 countries, at last count, there are an estimated 3,000 of these carve-outs. In China, the World Bank estimates that special economic zones have contributed 22 percent of the country's GDP, 45 percent of total national foreign direct investment, and 60 percent of exports.

Or look to culture, even. Billions of dollars' worth of artwork is believed to be kept in special warehouses exempt from national customs duties, along with cases of wine, piles of gold, and boxes of jewels. The harm here is two-fold: not only is nobody present to admire, study, and understand these sequestered Monets and Picassos, but their owners may be hiding them for more nefarious reasons, like avoiding taxes or dodging a lawsuit.

These freeports inspired the Christopher Nolan film *Tenet*. *Tenet* is an action movie full of shootouts and car chases whose plot hinges on the idea that time is not always linear (which—spoiler alert—matters a great deal in a shootout or a car chase). The movie takes place almost entirely offshore: on yachts, on wind farms, and in these warehouses, which are geographically "in" a country but enjoy a fictitious extraterritorial status.

In his choice of settings, the director happened upon something more profound than the film might let on: The hidden globe can suspend time and place. It upends our sense of where we are.

My growing interest in these weird jurisdictions coincided with what appeared to be a geopolitical sea change. Donald Trump had just been elected president in the United States and was talking a big game about ending "globalism." Narendra Modi, Victor Orbán, Jair Bolsonaro, and Rodrigo Duterte had won elections in India, Hungary, Brazil, and the Philippines on overtly nationalist platforms. The British were gearing up to pass Brexit, while European nations struggled to reconcile their purported commitments to human rights with large numbers of asylum seekers showing up at their borders. Pundits proclaimed that the era of freewheeling globalization was coming to an end, and nationalist politicians fed those pundits what they wanted in the form of racism, xenophobia, and the occasional trade tariff.

In the pages of the *Financial Times* and *The Economist*, on CNBC, and in dozens more websites and publications, columnists waved farewell to Davos Man. The nation-state was back, baby!

The tenor of these public conversations—and in particular, the binary between nationalism and globalism that was taking shape—vexed me. Having grown up in Geneva, with its many enclaves, I knew that you could be in two places at once: on Swiss soil, but under foreign jurisdiction; bound by some Swiss laws, but immune from others. On a much bigger scale, it seemed obvious that being part of a nation, territorially or otherwise, did not preclude participation in the global economy. That was precisely why Geneva was so full of international organizations. You had to be *somewhere*.

I also noticed that the so-called anti-globalists in the news had an awfully, well, global way of doing things. Donald Trump ran hotels and golf courses all around the world, as well as having a thing for foreign women. His high-profile entourage, too, seemed always to have one foot out the door. Peter Thiel, the libertarian investor turned conservative donor, was revealed to have bought himself New Zealand citizenship at the precise time he was embracing Trump's America First ideology. Steve Bannon, often made out in the press to be Trump's mastermind, was consorting *with nationalists from other countries* to globalize his vision for closed borders—from an Italian castle. Shortly before the 2017 World Economic Forum—the Trump administration's first—I emailed the organization to ask how many times the members of his delegation had attended. The answer stunned me. Although energy secretary Rick Perry had attended only once before, Secretary of State Rex Tillerson had been to Davos three times. Elaine Chao, overseeing the Department of Transportation, was preparing for her fifth visit. And Robert Lighthizer, the secretary of trade, had fifteen notches on his ski poles.

Politicians are not known for being particularly consistent in their beliefs. But the chasm between what these men and women represented and what they actually did—not just in their personal lives, but with their money, and professionally—seemed to reveal more than opportunistic hypocrisy. It suggested that the system we all live in is made for this: to reconcile closed borders with the capitalist maxim of free trade.

As I began to understand these contradictions more clearly, I identified the places set aside to reconcile them so that everyday life could carry on: the places above, beneath, and sometimes within nations, in special jurisdictions that are largely hidden away, and in laws that stretch so far beyond a country's borders that they are physically out of reach. These places also let politicians keep talking about their borders and tariffs and walls without losing out on business. This game of hopscotch, the economist Ronen Palan argues in his prescient 2003 book, *The Offshore World*, offers states "a politically acceptable, albeit awkward, way of reconciling the growing contradictions between their territorial and nationalist ideology . . . and their support for capitalist accumulation on a global scale."

These places are not exactly secrets, but they are far-flung and disparate enough to seem at first glance like discrete oddities, rather than a network or a system. That is one of the reasons they remain so hidden in plain sight.

We tend to think of ourselves as citizens, or at least residents, of a nation. After all, the lessons most of us encountered in school included a map of the world divided by lines into countries. Each country, we learned, has a government; and each government rules over its land and its things and its people. The idea of one land, one law, one people, and one government is dominant, powerful, and often accurate. It forms the basis for much of national and international law.

The hidden globe is a kind of transfiguration of this map, an accretion of cracks and concessions, suspensions and abstractions, carve-outs and free zones, and other places without nationality in the conventional sense, stretching from the ocean floor to outer space. The hidden globe is a mercenary world order in which the power to make and shape law is bought, sold, hacked, reshaped, deterritorialized, reterritorialized, transplanted, and re-imagined. It is state power catapulted beyond a state's borders. It is also a state's selective abdication of certain powers within its remit: enclaves filled not by lawlessness but by different, weirder laws.

The concept of the *loophole* originated in the seventeenth century to describe the small vertical slits in a castle wall through which archers could fire without risking enemy exposure. Its modern meaning has not changed all that much, only the archers are lawyers, consultants, and accountants—and the fortress, the state itself.

The desire to carve out exceptions is not new: communities have always set places apart for the purpose of contemplation, ritual, and worship. The Celts called these "thin places," where the distance between heaven and earth was said to be shorter.

Today, our elsewheres and nowheres aren't places of offerings, but places of evasion. They remind us of the *newness* of our world of bordered, independent states—a mold whose contents began to set only after decolonization—and its vulnerability to more powerful forces.

Capitalists, forever pursuing profit, regard liminal and offshore jurisdictions as frontiers. This book is as much about these modern frontiersmen as it is about their battlegrounds. But theirs is no freewheeling regime of open borders. While the existence of the hidden globe might appear to challenge the myth of the meaningful, unified nation, the nation is too sticky and politically expedient a concept to do away with entirely. In fact, the hidden globe can empower the most xenophobic and exclusionary nationalism. And these policies are not just the domain of the political right. Whether Republican or Democrat, conservative or liberal, the regimes behind them aim to bring the right people in and keep the wrong ones out.

By enabling nationalist immigration policies, the hidden globe thus circumscribes the lives of the world's most disenfranchised people: there are detainees languishing in offshore prisons in the Caribbean and the Pacific, impoverished workers processing goods for export in duty-free industrial zones across the Global South, sailors and asylum seekers stuck on vessels they cannot leave for lack of papers. When a person can't stay home and is unwanted abroad, they might end up in a third space: neither here nor there.

Seeing these spaces for what they are changed the way I saw the world, and I think it will change the way you see it too.

In the chapters that follow, you will learn how my hometown of Geneva and its nation, Switzerland, laid the foundation for the world we live in, through the people and wars and laws that shaped it. You'll discover how this model inspired other states to push their borders farther and farther afield—onto the high seas, down to the ocean floor, and even into deep space. You'll visit secret warehouses, virtual courtrooms, and legal black holes controlled by Western democracies and their allies. You'll spend time in a free zone for goods, and think through whether we should be building free zones for people too.

The individuals I profile—who, I should add, took the time to share their worldview, their methods, and their ideals—are but a sample of a much larger group operating in the context of world-historical forces. I am grateful for their participation and am not here to judge their choices. But I do hope that my position on the hidden globe's impact is clear. When the wealthiest citizens hide their money instead of paying taxes, towns and municipalities make do with less, which means worse schools, roads, infrastructure, and health care. When that money ends up in offshore centers, or is funneled through them westward, inequality grows. At a time when money is disproportionately transferred from poor countries to rich ones, and not the other way around, we need to think about the mechanisms that make that happen. When 90 percent of goods travel by ships that can easily evade responsibility for carbon emissions or labor practices, our seafood ends up being processed by slaves, and our appliances come with a side of pollution.

A permanent refugee population anywhere casts a pall on our countries' commitments to human rights and basic decency. For those of us in nominally democratic states, it casts a pall on us all.

I also want to make clear that resorting to nationalism is not the solution. To know where any of us stand—politically, economically, even physically—we need to stare deep into the cracks between borders. Only there can we see our true reflection in this world—and start to build a better one.

1.

City of Holes

Cities, like dreams, are made of desires and fears, even if the thread of their discourse is secret, their rules are absurd, their perspectives deceitful, and everything conceals something else.

—ITALO CALVINO, *INVISIBLE CITIES*

Welcome to Geneva: the capital of the hidden globe. It is a city of exceptions, a state of Swiss cheese. For centuries, its vaults and hiding holes have shielded people from persecution and revolution, taxation and litigation. Since the Renaissance, it's been a haven for people on the run, as well as their money, their ways of life, and their political beliefs.

Communists and capitalists, Protestants and Catholics, arms dealers and peacemakers, exiled monarchs and penniless refugees have all spent time in Geneva, patronizing the same cafés and chocolate shops, taking strolls along the same picturesque stretch of lake, communicating with one another in fragments of languages from around the world. Geneva has always been neutral territory: if not apolitical then mostly nonpartisan. But what brings us here is also a matter of metaphysics.

Above, beneath, and within this city are dozens of smaller cities, each encased in special dispensations, all playing by slightly different rules. Some are the size of a suitcase. Some are as big as a town. A fortune of vaults, warehouses, consulates, embassies, missions, international organizations, nuclear research facilities, and trading desks—all of them hiding in plain sight—give Geneva the fractal aspect of a Magic Eye book. Walk by quickly and you'll see wallpaper. Stare harder, and constellations float up from between the lines.

It took me a long time to see Geneva in all its dimensions. The face it shows the world is so solid, so rooted, so heavy, it seems eternal. Its old city, *la vieille ville,* feels to me as much a part of the natural landscape as the mountains that surround it, as integral to the region's topography as the Rhône and Lac Léman (aka Lake Geneva). If you read Mary Shelley's *Frankenstein,* set in Geneva more than a century ago, you'll notice that the roads, neighborhoods, and embankments have held on to their old names.

The old town's narrow passageways might even sound the way they used to. Several times a day, on the dot and to the minute, dozens of bells still ring out in tune from St. Peter's Cathedral. Clémence, the bass bell of the carillon, was installed in 1407. She is twelve feet tall, weighs more than six tons, and keeps us in check with her scolding knell. The bell's vibrations bore deep into the ground, where beneath the cathedral, the exhumed bones of a warrior chief from the first century BC have been preserved.

St. Peter's was built high up on a hill in the twelfth century and grew over the years to command the cobblestones with its spiny zinc spire and its glowing stained glass. During the Protestant Reformation, the sixteenth-century movement that united many Europeans against the excesses of the Roman Catholic Church, St. Peter's Gothic facade was stripped of all adornments and refashioned in a neoclassical style. The religious reformers—led in Geneva by John Calvin—embraced austerity to an extreme. Along with imposing strict moral codes, the Calvinists banned art—even religious art—as encouraging idolatry.

The cathedral's colorful windows made the cut. An altarpiece, *The Mi-*

raculous Draught of Fishes, did not. But one of its panels was saved from destruction and now sits on permanent display at a nearby museum.

The painting, by the Basel artist Konrad Witz, is a remarkable artifact: by many accounts, it is the first in European history to depict a recognizable topographical landscape rather than an imagined or biblical scene. Witz was working in the early 1440s, when Geneva was mostly countryside, but he must have been inspired by something bigger when he stared at Lac Léman. The panel explicitly positions the lake as a place where the sacred meets the profane. It anticipates the city's role as a mediator between the material and the spectral. It is also a painting about faith: in God, of course, but also in money and in the importance of not asking too many questions.

The piece depicts a group of five apostles in a rowboat near shore, two of them holding oars, the three others pulling on a net bursting with writhing fish. It's immediately apparent that the scene is not set on the Sea of Galilee, where the Bible story is said to have occurred, but someplace closer to the artist's home: he paints alps, hedges, warehouses, a dock. The countryside is a lush green, so Witz was probably working in the spring or summer, and big white clouds hang heavy above the water. A low mountain, the Salève, with a telltale peak in the background—the white cap of Mont Blanc—gives his precise location away. Witz was likely painting the Léman from the right bank of Lake Geneva.

The men are dressed in knee-length tunics of red, white, and black. They're staring at the sky, stunned at their good fortune: after a disappointing day on the water, the story goes, they followed Jesus's advice, cast their nets out one last time, and were richly rewarded. St. Peter is shown, too, wading arms outstretched toward Jesus. The resurrected Christ receives him dressed in a bright red robe, beaming beatifically in the shallows.

Witz was doing something previously unthinkable by painting the physical world as it was. But his painting is somehow otherworldly, and it's not because of the men, the mountains, or even the miracle. While Witz is meticulous in his treatment of shadow and light, only the figure of Christ casts no reflection onto the water.

By omission, Konrad Witz offers an early glimpse of the other, metaphysical Geneva: one where the laws of man and of nature don't always apply.

Over the last half century, at the very site of Witz's miracle, wealth has replaced God. By night, the logos of luxury—Rolex, Breitling, Zenith—light up the sky. Staring back from the lake's surface is a city equal and opposite to that on the ground: a city as evasive as Geneva is knowable, as fluid and placeless as Geneva is real.

Lac Léman still has plenty of fish: perch, to be precise, which restaurants fry and serve with tartar sauce and lemon. But the real money comes from that spectral economy it plays ghostly host to, swaddled in security, neutrality, secrecy laws, and tax exemptions.

The canton of Geneva has only about half a million residents, with barely two hundred thousand living in the city proper, but more than one third of the world's grain is traded from desks here. More than half the bags of coffee in the world pass "through" Switzerland, most of them via firms in and around Geneva, in much the same fashion. The country didn't get its first Starbucks until 2001; a few months later, the company began purchasing its coffee through a Swiss affiliate. There are other jurisdictions, including Singapore, that offer comparable or lower taxes to these kinds of companies. But with a bank on every corner and an insurance company at every turn, Geneva has been too convenient for them to give up.

Geneva has long been a hub for oil—if you can call it a "hub" when the barrels never actually turn up there. Until a few years ago, between 50 and 60 percent of Russian crude was traded from Switzerland, mostly Geneva, according to the research nonprofit Public Eye. When the Swiss Parliament reluctantly voted to join the EU's sanctions regime against Russia after

Vladimir Putin's invasion of Ukraine, some of that business decamped to Dubai—a jurisdiction inspired by, if not directly modeled on, Geneva's patchwork of tax incentives, discretion, and professional know-how, to the point that oil traders have begun calling it "the new Geneva." (Oil rich as the UAE is, 90 percent of its trades were likewise conducted without oil present.)

Switzerland is landlocked. That is no impediment to its being home to some of the biggest shipping companies in the world, which charter and manage vessels from Geneva while shrouding their beneficial (de facto) owners in layers of corporate secrecy. When asked why the maritime industry has converged so far from the seashore, the Swiss litigator Mark Pieth says that the government simply does not regulate what a boat does, unless it is one of just twenty-seven ships flying the Swiss flag. You don't need water to float.

This way of positioning itself in the world is Geneva's greatest contribution to the way we all live now: in an age of exceptions, where the *where* and *when* don't matter as much as *who, how much*, and *why*. It's a world where wealth travels in abstract form: numbers on a screen, trades on a terminal. It's a world in which borders are drawn not just around places but also around people and things.

In theory, enclaves with special rules can be used for more than money-making. During the First World War, the French surgeon general, Georges Saint-Paul, was so horrified by the conflict's toll on civilians that he proposed establishing islands of safety, which he called Geneva Zones: a little Switzerland in every nation. These zones would distinguish themselves from ordinary camps for displaced persons by being established during peacetime, in anticipation of welcoming the most vulnerable civilians should war break out. Importantly, they would be under the control of the host nation's government, not some supranational body. The hope was that even during conflict, warring parties would abstain from attacking them. (This seems especially naïve today: humanitarian zones established to shelter non-combatants during conflicts in Bosnia, Rwanda, and Iraq, to name just a few, ended up becoming targets.)

Georges Saint-Paul founded the Association des Lieux de Genève, or the Geneva Zones Association, in 1931 in Paris before moving it to Geneva in 1937. He died before he got a chance to put his plans into action. Still, Geneva Zones seem to have gained some traction on the other side of the earth: the idea inspired a Jesuit priest, Father Robert Jacquinot de Besange, to establish similar safe zones in Shanghai that did save half a million Chinese citizens during the Second Sino-Japanese War. (In a curious territorial twist, the zones were, like Geneva itself, adjacent to the city's French-controlled concession.) Copycats cropped up in other Chinese cities, including Shenzhen, which would become famous for its free economic zones, and in Spain during its civil war. In this time of great upheaval, with few prospects for actual peace and no international agreements on the rights of refugees, the idea of the enclave was an appealing way to split the difference and save lives.

Today, the heir to Saint-Paul's idea is an organization called the International Civil Defense Organization (ICDO). The registered international body does provide relief for civilians in wartime, and has operated in politically sensitive places like Cuba, North Korea, and the Caucasus, but only after Russia's Ministry of Emergency Situations signed off on the missions. The organization is almost entirely funded by the Russian state, to the tune of $140 million per year. Until 2012, it was headed by a Russian diplomat whom Margaret Thatcher had expelled from the UK in 1985 for allegedly threatening national security. A Swiss television report found that today, aid contracts serve to enrich the Russian defense minister, who personally helps select the contractors receiving relief funds. The ICDO's head paid himself more than the UN's secretary general. The organization operates out of a stone mansion in the Geneva neighborhood of Petit Lancy, overlooking a park full of tall oaks, graceful willow trees, and, in front of its terrace, three incongruous palms: a reminder that strange things can take root here.

The contrast between the city's body and its soul is often just as perplexing. One of Geneva's hundreds of asset management firms provides ultrahigh-net-worth individuals "assistance in opening accounts worldwide" using its "next-generation financial platform." Their money begets money, which in turn begets money, which plays peekaboo with the taxman wherever it goes. All of this from a big stone house in an old town built centuries before "platform" and "net worth" meant anything other than a ground, a weight.

Across the street, a wealth management consultant claims to do much the same thing in English, French, and Russian. If you have ever dreamed of relocating to low-tax Mauritius in any capacity—corporate, professional, personal—there is a family firm on the same block that has specialized in such matters since the late 1990s.

Never mind that Geneva and Mauritius have little to do with each other in the physical world. They are part of an invisible firmament that binds a most unlikely constellation of places.

Swiss banks have historically been ground zero for this fractured atlas. For years they operated like black holes, taking money from nearly anyone, anywhere, and making it disappear. Much of this was legal: what was *illegal*, under Swiss law, was to disclose a bank account's real owner to anyone. As recently as 2015, whistleblowers have been convicted for doing so. As of this writing, Swiss banks hold $8.6 trillion in their portfolios, with more than $2 trillion in the hands of private individuals. By contrast, the country's nominal gross domestic product is $700 billion, or about a tenth of that sum. The asymmetry stems from the fact that much of the wealth in these banks—from garden-variety certificates of deposit to exotic derivatives—belongs to complete strangers to the country.

The University of California, Berkeley, economist Gabriel Zucman found in 2008 that just a third of foreign securities held by private Swiss banks belonged to people who were Swiss, with the remaining two thirds in entities held by foreigners. French, German, Saudi, and Emirati citizens are particularly faithful clients, but the bankers also manage funds of unknown or unclear provenance, whose contents might have shape-shifted from African mine to suitcase of cash to Caribbean trust to numbered account.

What's more, much of the money is just making a pit stop on a journey longer than time. "This pattern epitomizes what offshore financial centers do," writes Zucman. "Swiss banks essentially help foreigners invest out of Switzerland." The banks are not so much safe houses as they are conduits.

During the Second World War, the Nazi Reichsbank famously sold what today amounts to $20 billion worth of gold to the city's banks and bankers while the Swiss insisted they weren't taking sides. The fallout was sensational: an investigation by the U.S. State Department, endless press coverage, a high-profile commission for reparations, and apologies from the highest ranks of industry. In its wake, Swiss neutrality (and banking) became a punch line. But the humiliation was apparently not enough.

After the Arab Spring revolutions of the early 2010s, it transpired that Swiss financial institutions, many of them with branches in Geneva, were sitting on millions of dollars in assets belonging to the heads of state of Egypt, Syria, Tunisia, and Libya. That was on top of fortunes linked to dictators from Nigeria, the Philippines, and the former Soviet Union. Much of this money is still frozen in deanonymized accounts totaling $5 billion, as of 2015.

The banks have made retroactive efforts to block access or dole out restitution, but this work can take years. The embarrassments made an impact: a partial rollback of the country's bank secrecy laws following pressure from other countries has made it somewhat more difficult for large foreign fortunes to vanish from view.

But the scandals keep piling up: the most powerful people in Malaysia, Kazakhstan, Russia, and Ukraine have all turned out to have lakeside pieds-à-terre, if not for themselves then for a trust or a fund or an investment vehicle linked to an entity connected to their person. More recently, a Texan tech billionaire named Robert Brockman was indicted in the United States for using a Geneva bank (among others) to evade a record-breaking $2 billion in U.S. taxes. Public Eye counted 13,600 shell companies in the city of Geneva, some mere letterboxes, some nominally staffed, many acting as portals through which clients could siphon money farther and farther offshore.

Geneva's courthouse, the Palais de Justice, stands directly across from St. Peter's Cathedral. A converted convent, it has been open to lawyers and plaintiffs—but not the public, save for on designated dates—since 1860. In addition to local crimes and misdemeanors, the court routinely hears cases related to far-flung infractions: mining concessions in Guinea, corruption in Venezuela, bribery in Ivory Coast and the Republic of the Congo. These cases reveal how successfully Geneva has woven itself into the fabric of the world and its money by convincing firms to establish a corporate presence there: sometimes real, sometimes fake, and often somewhere in between.

So many things pass through Geneva. Most of them don't touch the ground.

It was not far from here, on the banks of Lac Léman, that Mary Shelley conjured up her famous monster.

In 1816, Shelley (then still Mary Godwin) was summering in a villa a couple of miles north of the city with her lover, Percy Bysshe Shelley, and her pregnant stepsister, Claire Clairmont. Lord Byron, who was sleeping with Clairmont, had set up the next door down. The group was supposed to be on holiday, but the weather got in the way: a freak volcano eruption in Indonesia's Mount Tambora earlier in the year had killed ten thousand people, and the migrating ash blanketed much of the globe. It blocked out the sun over Europe, causing crop failures, famine, a deadly typhoid outbreak, and political unrest. As far away as Geneva, "incessant rain often confined us for days to the house," Mary recalled of this "year without summer." The group told ghost stories to pass the time; or at least, they tried. Mary was plagued by writer's block, "that blank incapacity of invention," until one night, a vision came to her.

"I saw the hideous phantasm of a man stretched out," she later wrote, "and then, on the working of some powerful engine, show signs of life. . . .

"The idea so possessed my mind, that a thrill of fear ran through me, and I wished to exchange the ghastly image of my fancy for the realities around," she wrote. "I see them still; the very room, the dark parquet, the closed shutters, with the moonlight struggling through, and the sense I had that the glassy lake and white high Alps were beyond."

The chimera became one of literature's most unforgettable figures: an eight-foot-tall giant, composed entirely of corpses plucked from different places, who would roam the earth in search of revenge, friendship, and a mate. The monster was brought to life by Victor Frankenstein, citizen of Geneva.

In ordinary times, the lakeside inspires no such monsters. It's pleasant, with temperatures rarely dipping below freezing. But the winter months are dark and close and damp, and occasionally the bone-chilling bise, the north wind, sharpens the chill. Then, come spring, a hot, dry foehn—the Alpine Santa Ana—is said to spike psychotic breaks, migraines, and car wrecks. It isn't that Genevans believe in wind spirits per se; they aren't a superstitious lot. They blame nature because they believe themselves to be in control. Irrationality can only be a function of meteorology.

From the embankment, one of four pedestrian bridges will lead you across the lake. On its west side, some of the most significant events in diplomatic history have taken place: conventions on world war and peace, international laws, crimes, and punishments. A long, scenic quay named after Woodrow Wilson leads to a grand old sandstone palace also bearing his name. Next to the palace is a separate Hotel President Wilson and, inside it, the most expensive hotel suite in the world. It has twelve bedrooms and a Steinway grand, and it rents for $81,000 per night.

Genevans consider themselves in Wilson's debt. He was instrumental in founding the League of Nations, which put Geneva on the map—even though it failed abjectly at its mandate to keep peace, and even though Wilson's own country refused to join. Princeton University has removed the former president's name from its school of international affairs on account of his overt racism. Genevans—or at least Genevan hoteliers—don't seem to mind.

In 1946, the United Nations took over from the League, moved into the building intended for it, and brought into the world a multitude of sister agencies—the World Trade Organization, the World Health Organization, the World Intellectual Property Organization, and a dozen more intergovernmental bureaucracies, regulating everything from telecommunications to refugee resettlement.

It was through their membership in these organizations that nation-states—the building blocks of the world we live in—came into their own. Empires were split up into countries, ex-colonies recognized as independent, and each national unit bestowed with sovereign equality: one land, one country, one government, one vote at the UN.

How ironic, then, that Switzerland did not join the UN until 2002. And how fitting that its buildings enjoy legal inviolability from the police. Several thousand members of the Geneva workforce have a degree of diplomatic immunity, exempting them from certain taxes and, in some cases, criminal prosecution. Diplomats carry precious documents around in diplomatic pouches, also cloaked in protections accorded to them by international conventions. Even their cars are exempt from parking tickets and speeding violations. Some have bulletproof exteriors and tinted windows. All of them bear the telltale license plates: CD, for *corps diplomatique.*

Geneva's international organizations deal in this parallelism too. The UN has its own postage stamps, different ways of taxing income, and uniquely dysfunctional labor rules that largely prevent workers from striking, suing, or unionizing. And there's the strange little duty-free shop. I remember visiting it on Friday evenings after school, inevitably bumping into a colleague of my father's or a schoolfriend's parent between the perfume aisle and the candy. Geneva's small worlds exist as if suspended, like the subject of a nuclear physics experiment at CERN—which occupies a sprawling campus at Geneva's northwest border, part of it in France, part of it in Switzerland, much of it buried underground.

Mary Shelley wrote a book about a man, a monster, and the places they tried to hide. But Frankenstein is also the story of a city: itself a chimera, made of disparate parts, animated by hubris and greed and a touch of the supernatural.

In his essay on the notion of the uncanny, founder of psychoanalysis Sigmund Freud notes that the German term *heimlich*—meaning "homelike, familiar, enjoyable"—is frequently also used to mean its exact opposite. "In general we are reminded that the word *heimlich* is not unambiguous, but belongs to two sets of ideas, which without being contradictory are yet very different," Freud explains. "On the one hand, it means that which is familiar and congenial, and on the other, that which is concealed and kept out of sight."

(Un)*heimlich* is Geneva. (Un)*heimlich* is the hidden globe. You could walk by these places ten times a day without thinking twice about what— or where—they really are. I would know; I did it for eighteen years. And had I not left, I probably would still be doing it.

So I write this first from memory—or rather, from impressions of a memory—and from afar. Then I go back to retrace my steps and retouch, resmell, resee. It's only backward that I can find the words to convey not the concrete reality of Geneva, or the Swiss state, but the power above and beyond the sixteen thousand square miles that Switzerland occupies in the heart of Europe.

It all started with bodies.

There were no big banks then, no international organizations, not even paper money. It was a time before capitalism, nationalism, or imperialism as we now know them.

In fact, when the Old Swiss Confederacy began its life as an alliance of cantons, Switzerland looked like "a patchwork of overlapping jurisdictions, ancient customs, worm-eaten privileges and ceremonies, irregularities of custom, law, weights and measure," the historian Jonathan Steinberg writes in *Why Switzerland?* A "fantastic array of tiny republics, prince-bishoprics, princely abbeys, counties, free cities, sovereignty cloisters and monasteries, free valleys, overlapping jurisdictions, guilds, oligarchies and city aristocracies" characterized the territory.

In other words, if Switzerland had a body politic, not even Dr. Frankenstein could have stitched it together—but none of this was unusual. The Holy Roman Empire, which the Old Swiss Confederacy was part of, was similarly chaotic: nominally one ruler's land, the empire included myriad governing units, including duchies, marquisates, kingdoms, abbeys, city-states.

This is worth remembering as we contemplate the contemporary "weirdness" of the hidden globe. For those of us who learned geography and history from a world map, it might seem unusual to have parallel or overlapping systems of taxation, policing, and immigration within one state. But the reason for that owes more to nationalist mythology than historical facts. The nation-state, the historian Claire Vergerio writes, did not suddenly become the "only legitimate unit of the international system" after the 1648 Treaty of Westphalia. In fact, the so-called Westphalian ideal of one land, one people, one government did not really look that way until decolonization. Nationalism has "rewired our collective imagination into the belief that this has been the normal way of doing things since 1648," Vergerio writes.

One thing that has not changed is that rulers can wield power over their people. And long before they took the form of a nation, the Swiss figured out how to monetize their ability to make rules, laws, and armies.

The kernel of the Swiss Confederation emerged in 1291, when the cantons of Uri, Schwyz, and Unterwalden warded off attacks from their neighbors and formed an alliance to ensure their future protection. They shared a common enemy in the Hapsburg Empire, and by 1315 tensions among the imperial rulers and the cantons led Leopold I to invade the Swiss with an army of eight thousand men—and to suffer a surprising loss.

His opponents' secret weapon? Tightly packed, square infantries armed with eighteen- to twenty-foot pikes.

With these tactics, the Swiss won huge victories for the next century and a half, defeating Austrian and Burgundian armies four to thirty-six times their size. By the late 1400s, the alliance of territories grew to eight self-governing regions held together by pacts and treaties. With success, their reputation for ruthlessness spread throughout Europe, and before long, their unique tactical formations would become not only feared and respected but exported, in the form of trained warriors.

In retrospect, the cantons' burgeoning mercenary trade might best be understood through supply and demand. Switzerland was, at the time, unrecognizably poor, with a population that had grown to overburden the arable land and resources of the Alpine regions. Neighboring monarchies (notably the French) had domestic problems that made forming their own militias tricky. Lords couldn't trust their peasants not to mutiny, and kings didn't trust the lords either, for fear they'd challenge their power. Enter the Swiss. "To resolve the problems of overpopulation in this infertile land (where there was no public spending to improve agriculture) the heads of the ruling families thought up an ingenious solution: they sold their compatriots to foreign governments," writes the Swiss politician, intellectual, and activist Jean Ziegler in *Switzerland: The Awful Truth*.

At first, the mercenaries from the cantons were independent contractors: free "lancers" who were often paid late and enjoyed few workplace protections. In the absence of prospects at home, they made the most of military life and took part in the requisite looting, drunkenness, and womanizing. By the seventeenth century, the mercenary economy had become more formalized, with recruiters, middlemen, managers, and codes of conduct. The men enjoyed all the advantages of Swiss backing—training, equipment, a salary—without actually fighting for their country.

Men of a canton would serve together as a unit, emigrating abroad to fight and returning home seasonally. Being unattached, they carried with them the promise of neutrality. Mercenaries harbored no resentment toward the sovereigns who used them to bolster their power against feudal lords. Nor did they hold rancor for these lords.

The men weren't considered to be within the jurisdiction of the contracting party but, rather, carried their home law on their backs, like belligerent snails. Their employers liked the arrangement. "These armed corps were completely independent, with their own regulations, their own judges and their own flags," reads a history issued by the Vatican, which to this day employs Swiss soldiers to guard the papal palace. "The orders were given in their own language, German, by Swiss officers, and they remained under the law of their Cantons: in short, the regiment was their fatherland, and all these customs were confirmed in similar agreements made in later years."

Military recruiters played a key role in this trade. They'd canvass poor parts of the confederation and draw up agreements loaning out young men to foreign militias. By the end of the eighteenth century, seventy thousand men from the cantons were a permanent element in foreign armies; they fought for everyone from the French Crown to the Dutch East India Company, warding off enemies, traveling abroad, and ultimately playing a small but significant role in helping to colonize the subcontinent.

As for the people they were fighting: "In the bourgeois challenge to absolutism and the class wars of independence," historian V. G. Kiernan writes, "the citizen soldier and civilian militia fought the mercenary, who was identified with the old, the reactionary, and the repressive arm of the king." The animus was not mutual; for the mercenaries, war was all business. Being guns for hire, they had no stake in local people's livelihoods, their families, their lives. The mercenaries didn't even speak their language. And as they were paid at a higher rate than a local recruit, they did not risk developing fellow feeling based on social class or bonds forged through church or trade. They got the job done, and then they left, leaving no widows and no orphans, and requiring no pensions, medical care, or lodging.

The result of this market for bodies is that the lives of poor men from the cantons became products. "Soldiers had become a standardized market-like product, a 'commodity,'" writes historian John Casparis. The commodification—or was it dehumanization?—of the men reached the point that they were traded like cattle. Cheese was becoming a major Swiss export, but the towns that produced the famous Gruyères, raclettes, and Emmentals needed a steady supply of salt to make them, and in the landlocked hinterlands there was none to be found. So the cantons bartered with the French Crown. Like the Roman soldiers from whom the expression came, the mercenaries became, quite literally, worth their salt. They were essentially how Swiss foreign policy was conducted.

And they did serve their country, in their way. The mercenary business brought an influx of cash and raised employment rates. By one estimate, 4 percent of the population in the fifteenth, sixteenth, and seventeenth centuries emigrated as mercenaries, with the proportion falling to 1 or 2 percent by the end of the eighteenth. The sons of the upper classes were commissioned as officers. Lieutenants made five times more than soldiers; captains, fifteen times more. But the lowest-ranking men were virtually indentured servants, living like today's construction workers in Dubai or domestic workers in Singapore. The money wasn't great, they enjoyed no social status, and they frequently died on the job, in battle or from disease.

But sending young men to die for someone else was a convenient way of maintaining domestic stability. Better to unleash indigent young men's aggression abroad than have to confront their demands at home. "Obviously, the service of the Bourbon King of Naples was a better place to see a turbulent young Obwaldner than at the gates of Basel, and no doubt the acceptance of compromise owes much to the export of the uncompromising," writes Jonathan Steinberg.

The mercenariat, then, served the nascent confederation well. It maintained social stability, created jobs, kept young men out of trouble, and ensured that bigger and more aggressive armies would gain more from leaving the Swiss alone than from attempting to dominate them.

The canton of Geneva, then an independent city-state, did not join the Swiss Confederation until later, but it understood the lesson: there are fortunes to be made by being an efficient and indiscriminate neighbor.

There are two more characters that can help us understand Geneva's ways: the preacher and the banker.

In the early 1400s, Geneva was an independent diocese at the crossroads of Southern and Northern Europe. It wasn't a particularly big town, but the Medicis of Florence—the world's wealthiest and most prominent trading family—opened a bank on what is now Geneva's main drag. (If you go there today, you'll find a Hermès boutique.) The Medicis chose Geneva because of its location and its thriving market in textiles and other luxuries. "It was an entrepôt, a place of exchange, and it was a city that served the different regions around and countries in early modern European territories," the historian Helena Rosenblatt told me. Little did they know that banking would overtake textiles, or any material goods for that matter, by orders of magnitude.

In 1541, a very different figure turned up in the Old Town: John Calvin, a French lawyer and Protestant theologian who would come to lord over Geneva from his perch in the church. He, too, would leave his mark on Geneva's marketplace.

Calvin was part of the Protestant Reformation, whose leaders—among them, Martin Luther—wanted a greater focus on Scripture as the word of God at a time when the Catholic popes were growing corrupt and losing credibility. Genevans aren't particularly religious anymore, but reminders of the Reformation are everywhere. In 1909, to celebrate John Calvin's four hundredth birthday, sculptors even carved his sixteen-foot likeness out of Geneva's city walls. He's still there, looming over a narrow pool where, throughout my childhood, every spring ducklings would hatch and cheep for bits of bread. The city's motto is etched into the wall as well: *Post tenebras lux*. After darkness, light.

There are other Protestant figures in the walls—the Scottish reformer John Knox, local leaders Théodore de Bèze and Guillaume Farel, and a man known as William the Taciturn. Even in this sullen company, Calvin was hard-core. There was no art, theater, or fun in Calvin's Geneva, and harsh punishments were doled out to those who broke rules and made noise. Still, his message praising worship and hard work was appealing to poor and working people because it implied that their personal behavior might reflect how well (or poorly) God saw them.

To be clear, Calvin made no causal link between working hard, making money, and being saved; salvation was preordained (by God) and unknowable (to man). But a person's dedication to God through their earthly work, or their calling, still mattered.

In 1904, the sociologist Max Weber published a book arguing that Calvin's ideas morphed into a valorization of work and wealth accumulation as goods in and of themselves. This obsession with industriousness, Weber wrote in *The Protestant Ethic and the Spirit of Capitalism*, was a way of channeling the deep anxieties that Calvinism inspired about mortality. There were two worlds: life on earth, and life beyond it. There was no surefire path to heaven. In the absence of answers, Weber wrote, Calvinists embraced the possibility that material success was a sign of God's favor. This, he argues, became a foundational principle of capitalism, helping account for the material success of Protestant groups beyond Geneva and throughout the entire world.

(Swiss bank secrecy might also be derivative of Calvinist thought, but for reasons as political as they are self-serving: it could shield Protestant exiles and citizens from the powerful Catholic Church. "Long ago we gave refuge to Protestants when Protestantism was illegal in much of Europe. Later, it was illegal to be a Jew. We consider a man's financial affairs to be just as sacred, and as important, as his soul or body. Why should we not give sanctuary to persecuted money, as well as souls?" a Bernese banker told *The Atlantic* in 1965.)

Calvinism also altered Geneva's demographics. The religious conflicts that tore through Europe in the early modern period played a formative role in Geneva's identity as a haven for people, ideas, things, and money. When, in 1685, the French king Louis XIV revoked the Edict of Nantes, which had previously guaranteed Protestants equal treatment under his rule, many turned up in Geneva—where some wound up working as financial advisers to the very same king who'd thrown them out. (Geneva's largest private bank, Pictet, is still run by a descendant of one of the king's bankers.) They kept their transactions secret too: the king could not be known to be transacting with heretics.

Just as neighboring cantons exported fighters, Geneva exported its bankers. The most notable was Jacques Necker, the son of a theologian and the father of author Madame de Staël, who got his start speculating on grain, and investing the proceeds in the French East India Company as it plundered its overseas territories. Switzerland was not an imperial power in the conventional sense, but it was imperialism adjacent: its bankers played a significant role in the financing of these chartered companies. At the same time, mercenaries from the cantons helped the company-states win important battles abroad.

Necker grew independently wealthy through his financial dealings, working his way into a top finance post in Paris under Louis XVI. As the monarchy's proto-CFO, Necker was tasked with raising funds—and fast.

There were wars to finance and Marie Antoinette to entertain. Necker's origins served him well. His compatriots in Geneva came up with money-making schemes—schemes in which Necker himself would become complicit.

To finance public works, the French state had long sold annuities that paid out until the buyer's death. An annuity, also known as a *rente*, is a financial product that promises to pay the bearer, or the owner of the annuity, a set amount of cash in regular installments. The idea is that the seller of the rente can obtain a large sum of money immediately, while the buyer can guarantee a steady stream of cash, plus interest, over a set period.

When the French got into the annuity business, quite a bit before Necker turned up, the size of these repayments initially depended on the buyer's age: a seventy-year-old investing a hundred pounds might be promised ten pounds per year, because he was likely to die sooner than a client half that age, who might receive only five pounds per year, on account of his greater life expectancy. The investment was a gamble for both parties, but it was calibrated to make everyone feel the bet was worth making.

Around 1760, the French changed their terms of service. The state started selling products that paid a fixed sum to all buyers, regardless of age, on the reasoning that the averages would work in their favor in the long run. Geneva's financiers quickly figured out that there was nothing preventing them from buying annuities in a client's name and taking a cut of the proceeds.

In 1774, a vaccine against smallpox significantly raised childhood survival rates, so a local banker, in consort with his family doctor, sought to acquire legal personhood from those most likely to live a long time: the vaxed and relaxed young daughters of the Swiss bourgeoisie. The "Thirty Demoiselles of Geneva," as they were known, formed the basis for lucrative annuity contracts. Bankers bought the bonds in the girls' names and paid out the proceeds regularly to investors of all ages, and their heirs.

The bankers did not stop there. A wholesome life was very well and good, but this was still Calvin's town: there was no telling upon whom God would smile. So they reduced the risk of betting on a single girl by bundling their "heads" into tranches of ten, twenty, thirty, or more, and settling on a rate of return based on averages. They would then sell off shares of these bundles to speculators. (Sound familiar?)

Facing pressure from the monarchy to increase returns, Jacques Necker turned to this "financial wizardry" of his compatriots to keep the cash-strapped French state afloat. This infusion of cash breathed new life into the program. Marc Cramer, the Swiss historian who uncovered the scheme, wrote that while Necker did not invent the annuities, "it was he who, having dug them out of the depths of the Comptroller's filing cabinets . . . made the most immoderate use of them."

The Genevese rentes helped France borrow what today would amount to billions of dollars, some of which went to finance the American Revolutionary War. Meanwhile, Geneva's demoiselles, having become a sought-after product on the financial markets, were rewarded with money for their upkeep. The scheme outlived the French Revolution and paid out until 1797, when the state went broke. All but three of the demoiselles lived past the age of sixty.

The link between the military recruiter in rural Toggenburg, the Calvinist preachers, and Geneva's early experiments with financial entrepreneurship is not a straight one. It may not even be a line. The world and its money changed dramatically between the Middle Ages and the Renaissance, and to draw equivalences is probably unwise.

But there's a confluence of worldview, I think, that unites selling off citizen-soldiers and the fashioning of securities out of the life expectancy of little girls. It's the spirit of the thing: a process of abstraction through which a body becomes a bond. It's the essence of speculation, the metaphysics of globalization. You could even call it a calling.

2.

Good Fences

Switzerland . . . is not an ordinary nation-state: it was created,
by both internal and external forces, *against* the nation-state
at a strategic moment of history. Switzerland is a unique
construct—an international mercenary state, first of feudal
militarism, and now of world capital.

—JON HALLIDAY

In early 1964, Jean Ziegler, then a young Swiss politician, received a
phone call from a man claiming to represent Ernesto "Che" Guevara,
the Cuban revolutionary and minister of industry. Che would be in Geneva in March for a UN conference on trade policy, and some comrades had
suggested Jean might be his chauffeur during his stay. Was Ziegler available
for the gig?

Today, in his ninth decade of life, Ziegler is Switzerland's most notorious
public intellectual. That's because, over the course of writing some thirty
books, serving for close to three decades in the Swiss Parliament, and relentlessly crusading for left-wing causes in his free time, Ziegler has made a career of unsparing criticism of his home country and its outsize influence on
the rest of the world.

In the sixties, though, he was just another eager young leftist, waiting for
his chance to change the world.

Ziegler, like Che, was born into a family of upper-middle-class professionals. And, like Che's, his travels around the world had radicalized him against what he perceived to be a capitalist, imperialist, and racist system. Everywhere he went, he saw its ravages: in the Belgian Congo, whose hungry children haunted him long after he went home; in Algeria's bloody wars of independence against the colonial French; and in annexed Cyprus, where the British had deprived citizens of their right to self-determination for decades.

Ziegler heard the echoes of oppression closer to home, too, in the deracinated commodity exchanges through which speculators bet on the price of food and fuel; and in the bank vaults mere steps from his home, where kleptocrats siphoned away their countries' natural resources.

For centuries, the Swiss had prided themselves on keeping blood and money apart. In Ziegler, they spawned an iconoclastic figure who forced them to reckon with the moral cost of their separation.

"Blood may not run down the walls of the UBS headquarters," he told me one afternoon in June 2021. "But it's as if it did: the relative well-being of Swiss people is financed by death, fear, and famine. This is Ali Baba's cave: the world's haven. That's unique to Switzerland."

We were speaking at Ziegler's home in the small village of Russin, a few miles outside Geneva. He and his wife live a short walk up a steep hill from a commuter train on the Chemin de Croix-de-Plomb, or Lead Cross Road: a fitting address for a Catholic convert waging a lifelong battle against the spirit of capitalism.

Ziegler was wearing gray sweatpants and a stained white shirt when he greeted me at the door, and offered me whisky, more whisky, and wine before conceding to pour me a glass of water while I waited on an upholstered yellow couch by the terrace door. The house was spacious and unfussy. It hung over a steep vineyard with a view of the lake. Every surface in the living room was piled with books, potted flowers, or photographs of his family. "I hope you don't mind that I'm barefoot," he said. "I took a tumble recently," he added, pointing to his bandaged forehead, "and it's more comfortable this way."

Ziegler is an old man now, but he still speaks French with the Swiss-Germanic cadence of his childhood. His frame is hunched and much thinner than it once was, and while his tendency to repeat himself might appear another symptom of his age, the truth is that he's always presented himself that way: persistent, ideological, dogmatic.

When he was born, in the canton of Berne in 1934 to a local judge and a homemaker, Ziegler's path was all but preordained. He would study hard, become a lawyer, and raise a family in their German-speaking town of Thun. But although his childhood was happy and comfortable enough, from an early age he had a sense that something was off. He fought with his father bitterly when he first learned of a long-standing Swiss tradition of "placing" children from poor families to work in wealthier households, often in abusive and neglectful conditions. He refused to accept his father's justification: that God had willed it so.

Ziegler nonetheless began his political life as a conservative; he was even an active member of a student group formed in 1819 to promote Swiss national unity. But his restlessness got the best of him, so he left his hometown and moved to Bern to read law. He passed the bar exam but found he was more drawn to sociology, which he then studied in Paris at the Sorbonne in the mid-1950s, before returning home to finish his PhD. Between lectures, Ziegler befriended Jean-Paul Sartre and Simone de Beauvoir, and over the course of smoke-filled, wine-drenched evenings in Sartre's mother's flat, the couple turned him on to Marxism and encouraged him to report on the Algerian war for their magazine, *Les Temps Modernes*.

Beauvoir took it upon herself to edit Ziegler's awkward Swiss–German–French into a more polished and literary prose. She also urged him to ditch his given name, Hans, and become Jean, which she judged a more dignified byline.

It was Jean that Ziegler went by when he joined the French Communist Party, and as Jean that he was expelled over his support for Algerian independence. But it was as Hans that he provided material support to the causes he loved: carrying suitcases of cash over the French–Swiss border for the Front de Libération National to deposit in Geneva, and "losing" his passport (with the aim of lending it to a comrade) a few too many times to pass himself off as innocently absent-minded.

During this period, Ziegler also started spending time with a Jesuit priest and Resistance hero named Michel Riquet. The priest's commitment to helping the poor left such a strong impression that Ziegler converted. "It was in Paris that [Ziegler] broke definitively with his bourgeois past: a Protestant turned Catholic, a Swiss German turned cosmopolitan Francophile, and, to top it off, a conservative who veered left," writes his biographer and former student, Jürg Wegelin.

Upon his return to Switzerland—first Bern, then Geneva—Ziegler quickly found a job in corporate law. He hated it. Among his clients was Investor Overseas Service, a firm that sold mutual funds door-to-door and would collapse spectacularly under the weight of its own grift. He quit to continue his studies in sociology at Columbia University but got homesick in New York and made every effort to leave.

Close to a hundred job applications landed him a gig as a journalist covering world affairs for a Cuban newspaper. That was how he first met Che: reporting on the revolution from the Habana Libre hotel in 1959. But it wasn't until a two-year stint working for the United Nations that he embraced socialism in earnest.

In 1961, Ziegler responded to a classified ad seeking French speakers to accompany a British civil servant on a mission to what is today the Democratic Republic of Congo. The country had just become independent, but a coup backed by Belgium (which wanted to keep mining concessions) and the United States (which wanted to squash communism) deposed the elected president, Patrice Lumumba, and installed Mobutu Sese Seko in his stead.

Mobutu was your archetypal kleptocrat: a ruthless, fiercely anti-communist megalomaniac hell-bent on enriching himself and his cronies while the Congolese people suffered. He nationalized industry but put the country's resources in the hands of friends and family, leaving ordinary citizens little to show for their country's vast mineral wealth. He talked a big game about Congolese identity and made a point of purging all signs of Belgian rule, yet had an airport runway specially built so he could charter a Concorde to Paris to go shopping. His first wife, who died young in a private clinic just outside Geneva, was named Marie-Antoinette.

Ziegler was staying in a gated hotel in what is now Kinshasa, ensconced behind high walls snared with barbed wire, where every day hungry local children would gather and beg for leftover food. One day, Ziegler watched as the compound's guards violently dispersed the children and sent them away bruised and bleeding. It broke his heart to see them treated that way, simply for being born in the wrong place at the wrong time, and for being hungry. His voice cracked as he recalled the incident as though it had happened just yesterday.

When Ziegler then learned that Mobutu had siphoned off unthinkable sums of money from his country and deposited them in Swiss banks, the political started to feel personal—intensely personal. "I saw children in terrible, terrible conditions there," he told me. "And knowing that Mobutu, who came to Geneva with this blood money that caused so much death in his country, was enabled by the Swiss oligarchy—that's what motivated me."

By the time Ziegler met Che and his associates in Geneva a couple of years later, in their berets and olive-green uniforms, he was all in. Over the next two weeks, he ingratiated himself with the Cubans, driving them to Mont Blanc, translating what Spanish he could, and making himself available at all hours of the day. The revolutionaries brought the jungle with them to the staid city, sleeping in shared rooms in hammocks, drinking, smoking, and staying up all night arguing. Ziegler joined in, and on their last evening he gathered up the courage to ask Che to take him back to Cuba so he could join the revolution.

It was a clear night, and from their room on the eighth floor of the Hotel InterContinental, they could see the lake, illuminated then as now with fluorescent signs for luxury watches.

Che gestured out over the water. "Here is where you were born, and here lives the monster's brain," Ziegler remembers him saying. "It is here," he continued, "that you must fight."

It was probably just a throwaway line intended to dissuade a scrawny dilettante from getting himself killed. But Ziegler took it to heart. He knew there was something about the way Switzerland operated that made it uniquely useful to the forces of capitalism: not as a lead actor, but as an enabler working from behind the scenes.

Some years later, Ziegler would use the term "secondary imperialism" to define his country's modus operandi. This was not the first-order French, British, or, later, American imperialism with boots on the ground and armies on call. It was a more discreet kind of influence that intervened in its wake: a cabal of multinational firms and financiers who kept poor countries dependent on Western (mostly American) goods, guns, and money.

The Swiss enabled these practices by offering access to favorable regulations and financing, and a reputable, orderly, and neutral business environment: good rules, good laws. It was, in a sense, the mercenary trade by another name. The Swiss weren't sending bodies abroad to fight someone else's war of conquest. But in Ziegler's reading, they were providing a launching pad for a modern corollary. "Once I saw what was going on," he told me, "I couldn't *not* denounce it."

Switzerland: The Awful Truth was published in 1976. Part economics textbook, part Marxist screed, part investigative report, Ziegler's thesis, which he stands by to this day, is that Switzerland's role in the world is that of accomplice—handmaiden, of sorts—to capitalism.

Following Weber, he blames Calvinism for his compatriots' propensity to hide, launder, and coddle wealth from all over the world. "In Switzerland, the handling of money has a quasi-sacramental character," Ziegler wrote. "Holding money, accepting it, counting it, hoarding it, speculating and receiving, are all activities which, since the first influx of Protestant refugees to Geneva in the sixteenth century, have been invested with an almost metaphysical majesty."

Ziegler then lays into Swiss banks and pharmaceutical companies, trade groups and multinationals, implicating the firms and the individuals behind them in everything from drug trafficking to human rights abuses abroad. "It is hard to imagine a human activity that is not financed by a [financial institution] in Geneva, Zurich, Basel or Lugano," he wrote.

The transgressors included the banks that welcomed suitcases of cash from dictatorships in Portugal and the Dominican Republic; the real estate agencies that helped Gulf sheikhs and Guatemalan colonels buy lakeside apartments in which to hide; and subsidiaries of the American firms Dow Chemical and Honeywell, who oversaw the international sales of napalm and land mines. (Ziegler also blamed Switzerland for providing the Bolivian army with the rifle that killed Che in 1967, notwithstanding the likelihood that Che's own gun, a SIG KE7, was Swiss-made itself.)

The claims Ziegler made in this and subsequent books landed him nine defamation lawsuits in five jurisdictions over the course of the following decades (Swiss defamation law is more liberal, for plaintiffs, than its U.S. counterpart). All told, he has been assessed damages of 6.6 million Swiss francs (CHF), equivalent to almost 7.5 million U.S. dollars, penalties that have essentially bankrupted him, at least on paper.

Ziegler has done more than point fingers at morally unscrupulous industries. He identifies his country's famed political neutrality as a massive money-making asset in itself, a structural advantage in commerce and diplomacy that allows the Swiss elite to create safe spaces for capital and capitalists to thrive, no matter where they come from or what they believe. From there, the Swiss sweeten the deal with special concessions that go beyond what its European neighbors might offer: today, that might include a tax deduction for research and development costs in the pharmaceutical industry; special warehouses that are designated as outside customs territory, where wealthy people can store high-value objects like art and wine; a tendency not to hold firms based in Switzerland accountable for pollution and labor abuses abroad; and, of course, the country's strict laws against disclosing bank information.

Plenty of countries mobilize their capacities as recognized nation-states— the ability to wage war (or not), collect taxes (or not), pass laws (or not), and police their borders (selectively)—as means to bring in money. But Ziegler's argument has always been that his country punches far above its weight class, to everyone's detriment. That, he writes, makes it "a defensive association, not a nation-state in the usual sense."

The result is that, while maintaining the facade of an ultra-populist, referendum-driven direct democracy, the Swiss government is utterly beholden to global capital. It is also remarkably nimble. When voters decided in a 2019 national referendum to overhaul their country's tax system and do away with preferential tax rates for multinationals, individual cantons took matters into their own hands and cut taxes locally: in Basel, corporate tax rates fell from 20 percent to 13, while Geneva's tax increases were essentially symbolic, growing from a baseline of 11.6 to 13.9 percent.

As Ziegler likes to put it: the Swiss have "fences" to render wealth untouchable. The word he employs is telling. In French, as in English, *receleur* and *fence* are double-entendres that can refer either to a physical barrier or to a recipient of stolen goods. The fence is both the border and the banker, the moat and the middleman.

The fence—not the cuckoo clock, not fondue, certainly not brotherly love—is the nation's contribution to the world we live in. If you know where to look, you will see little Switzerlands anywhere you go.

. . .

An enduring assumption about taxes in Switzerland (and its fellow tax havens) is that the country lowered rates in order to attract business. That narrative has it backward: in the early twentieth century, France and Germany began to impose progressive income and inheritance taxes on their populations for the first time—taxing greater wealth at higher rates—while Switzerland did not. News got out through a deliberate advertising campaign targeting the rich: the University of Lausanne historian Sébastien Guex writes that the banks printed "brochures, circulars, personalized letters, and advertising in newspapers, and sent representatives who approached their clientele in person." It worked: according to Guex, half Switzerland's gross domestic product (and between 2 and 2.5 percent of French wealth alone) arrived in Swiss banks through fiscal osmosis.

Other states, among them Luxembourg and the Netherlands, followed the same playbook with some success, but the Swiss, writes the economic historian Christophe Farquet, were particularly aggressive in defending their newly forged haven. Theirs was a strategy of active obstruction, whether by adopting federal policies that precluded negotiations with other governments that might have held tax cheats accountable, by letting the Swiss banks "self-regulate," or simply by refusing to crack down on the practice. The Swiss also benefited from a federal system that encouraged cantons to compete not only with foreign entities but with one another—and to provide clients with plenty of options.

In 1934, Switzerland adopted its now infamous (and finally somewhat neutered) bank secrecy legislation. The line you're likely to hear about its origins—one that even Ziegler is wont to repeat—is that it was conceived to shield foreigners from persecution for taking money out of their home countries: some German Jews, sensing trouble brewing, did so, and Germany had begun to punish such capital flight with the death penalty. But the historian Peter Hug discovered that this explanation was revisionist propaganda constructed in the 1960s by Credit Suisse. In fact, the secrecy law was the result of an existential scandal.

In 1932, the French police were tipped off about a secret meeting in an apartment on the Champs-Élysées, during which the head of Basel's commercial bank was giving tax advice—of an unquestionably shady variety—to members of French high society. It transpired that the Basel bank's some two thousand tax-averse French clients included bishops, generals, newspaper publishers, a dozen senators, a minister, the wife of a famous perfumer, and the industrialist Armand Peugeot. Their wealth, all of it undeclared, amounted to no less than one fifth of Swiss GDP.

The bankers returned hundreds of millions of francs to the French, realizing that such incidents would cause clients to lose confidence and take their business elsewhere. Not two years later, the Swiss Parliament made disclosing the owner of a numbered account a federal crime, thus sealing their nascent banking industry from sight for the greater part of the next century. Under the new law, you didn't need a victim to bring a criminal complaint; in the absence of a plaintiff, charges could be brought by the state itself.

In 2014, forty-seven of the world's governments entered a deal requiring automatic exchanges of clients' account information. Under international pressure, Switzerland finally joined in, but it had already won. Over the course of the twentieth century, the country anticipated and accommodated the increasingly footloose nature of wealth by transforming itself from a (non)state into a kind of black hole straddling globalization and regulation, as Farquet puts it. The cash, gold, bonds, and other securities that found their way to Bern or Geneva enjoyed the advantages of being both somewhere safe and nowhere visible at the same time. The fact that tax evasion—that is, deliberately making false declarations about wealth or income—is prosecuted in Switzerland as a civil, not a criminal, offense could not have hurt either. And as unrest spread throughout Europe, the Swiss bankers could always depend on their biggest commercial asset: their political neutrality.

Switzerland's wiles and neutral status meant that it was able to ride out the Second World War with relatively few disruptions. But that calm came at a steep moral cost that Ziegler remembers firsthand and has spent much of his career coming to grips with. He tells this story in *The Swiss, the Gold, and the Dead*, a damning portrait of the Swiss banking establishment's complicity with the Nazis. While Ziegler was not the first person to reveal how the country functioned as Hitler's personal and political piggybank, the story had more clout coming from a Swiss politician, and it became an international bestseller. Its publication, in 1997, was also timed perfectly. In the late nineties, the World Jewish Congress (WJC) was in the process of suing Swiss banks on behalf of Holocaust survivors and their heirs, contending that the bankers were making it difficult for rightful owners to obtain access to their accounts (subsequent audits confirmed this, and the WJC settled with the banks for $1.25 billion). The United States had thrown its weight behind the suits, and during the course of the hearings, revisited probably the most sordid moment in Swiss history.

The economics of the arrangement worked like this: During the war, the Swiss acquired 1.7 billion Swiss francs' worth of gold bars and coins (then still the world's reserve currency) from Germany, which included assets plundered from deported Jews, amounting to a full third of the world's known gold production during that time. The Nazis received Swiss francs in return, which they could then transact with freely to buy munitions and other military supplies at a time when sanctions and a weak currency were hobbling their buying power. The central banks of the countries selling arms to the Germans would then use those francs to buy gold from the Swiss: a full-circle transaction.

"Switzerland functioned to [Hitler's] entire satisfaction as the Third Reich's bank vault," Ziegler writes, noting that the führer himself had an account at the Union Bank of Switzerland (UBS). (Hermann Göring opted for "smaller cantonal banks, whose confidentiality and loyalty he could fully trust.") The last shipment of Nazi gold arrived in Bern just weeks before Hitler's suicide, and it was only in March 1945—a couple of months before V-E Day—that Switzerland promised to stop buying German gold, and to identify and freeze German bank assets.

As if this were not enough, the country's dismissive behavior toward Jewish refugees—demanding that most, if not all, arrive with special designations on their passports, then turning many away at the border—ensured that while it emerged from the war physically unscathed, the nation was in moral and ethical tatters.

If Geneva had once been a haven for those fleeing persecution—Protestants during the Reformation, but also Russian anarchists and communists in the late nineteenth century, and Europeans fleeing military drafts or violence during World War I—by the 1950s, it was clear that this largesse extended to money much more than to bodies.

There's always a price to pay for breaking with national character. Ziegler is ninety years old, and he is still paying.

In 1990, he was sued by six different parties for allegedly defamatory statements in his book *Switzerland Washes Whiter*, in which he accused Swiss banks of taking money from drug dealers and other criminals.

In some cases—as, for example, when he called the husband of a prominent Swiss politician a "vulture" for his involvement in a drug money–laundering operation—Ziegler was found guilty of defamation. Because his publisher, Seuil, was French, the trial took place in Paris, where a court fined him 13,000 French francs. (The husband still wound up being charged with fraud in a subsequent lawsuit, and the politician ultimately resigned.)

In others—notably, when he accused a famous hotelier of "trafficking in petrol and cotton"—a Swiss court found his work to have suffered from inaccuracy and a lack of evidence (the hotelier he was accusing went bankrupt shortly thereafter, this time for unrelated reasons).

Ziegler wound up losing his parliamentary immunity—which shields elected officials from certain types of prosecution—and being ordered to pay hundreds of thousands of francs in fines. For years, security guards were stationed near his house. "The threats are very precise," he told the *Los Angeles Times*. "They always say something like, 'Yesterday your son was here, you were there.' It's a kind of psychological destabilization." Ziegler's wife, Erica, an art historian, holds the deed to their house so that it can't be taken from them, he told me, and his book royalties are still being garnished.

In 1998, Ziegler was called to testify before the U.S. Congress on the role of Swiss banks during the Second World War. "The ordinary Swiss people were deeply hostile to the mass murderers in Berlin. They hated Adolf Hitler and refused any dealings whatsoever with him and his cronies," he said. "Unfortunately, this was not the case for some of the members of the ruling class, namely the directors of the Swiss National Bank, board members of commercial banks, and some members of the Swiss government." For his remarks, a group of conservatives in Switzerland accused him of criminal treason, arguing that his "malicious lies, fabrications, calumny and boundless exaggerations" threatened state security. The charge claimed he was "provoking or assisting activities against the security of the state by foreign organizations or their agents." The "agents" in question included Alfonse D'Amato, a U.S. senator working on behalf of "Jewish organizations," they claimed, though the suit went nowhere.

Ziegler's reputation also suffered in his own circles. His battle for tenure at Geneva University was a drawn-out affair tarred with charges of academic unseriousness and plagiarism. He emerged from these battles victorious, but not until faculty called on the city government to weigh in on his behalf. Among fellow left-wing activists, his association with Muammar Gaddafi likewise left a stain, although Ziegler eventually denounced the Libyan dictator. And Ziegler continues to defend morally fraught causes, including the current Cuban regime—even as he himself has made ample use of a freedom of speech Cubans do not enjoy.

He has countered, repeatedly, that that sort of freedom doesn't mean anything if there are hungry children and sick people on the streets. From 2000 to 2008, Ziegler served as the UN's Special Rapporteur on the Right to Food, and during his tenure made a habit in meetings of brandishing photos of a child suffering from malnutrition to make his case. (He also carries copies of the Universal Declaration of Human Rights and a document about world hunger.) Much of his recent work concerns the right to food.

"I always assumed it was like a flame going out, but [hunger] is a violent, awful affliction," he says. "Children are a marvel," he goes on. "And what an outrage that every five seconds a child dies of hunger."

It struck me that after a lifetime of observing the mechanics of capitalism, Ziegler still seemed spellbound by the ingenuity, cynicism, and malevolence of its enablers. "The fact that this tiny country of only forty-two thousand square kilometers, of which only sixty percent is habitable, with a population of fewer than ten million, is such a powerful offshore center—that twenty-seven percent of the world's offshore fortunes are managed in or from Switzerland—it's just astonishing," he told me. His moral outrage seemed compounded with wonder. I could relate.

I asked Ziegler if it had all been worth it, and if he felt he'd made a dent in the system he spent so long fighting. After all, bank secrecy was not what it used to be; money laundering, while by no means eradicated, is at least now a criminal offense; and Swiss banks are on the defensive.

Shortly before Ziegler and I met, twenty of the world's richest nations had agreed to a global minimum tax on corporate profits. Since 2016, international news headlines had been full of reports of tax cheats, fraudsters, and money launderers using remote locations to hide their wealth: the Panama Papers, the Pandora Papers, SwissLeaks, LuxLeaks. Ziegler's most prominent heirs, it seems, are not just left-wing activists, but also nonpartisan data journalists reporting for organizations like the International Consortium of Investigative Journalists and the Organized Crime and Corruption Reporting Project.

The prominence of these types of stories is proof that left-wing activists like Ziegler have influenced public debates about justice, fairness, and inequality, and that awareness of the hidden globe's havens is growing. But it's not yet clear what impact these campaigns will have on actual wealth inequality and on the world's poor.

Ziegler, for one, thinks his country will abide by the letter, but not the spirit, of the law.

"It's true that Switzerland, under pressure, has signed the international agreement on the automatic transfer of bank information," Ziegler told me. "If a Frenchman opens an account in Switzerland, the French authorities are immediately informed." He continued: "But the government and the banks repeat this lie that Switzerland is finished as a tax haven, when it's completely false. If you're rich, richer than rich, there is in Geneva an army of lawyers who do nothing but open offshore accounts for clients. . . . If the money is in the hands of a banker, he's obligated to know where it came from. Lawyers are exempt from the requirement." (In 2023, the Swiss Federal Council proposed to end this exemption. The country's parliament will vote on the matter in 2024.)

In short, Ziegler still sees the hidden globe as clearly as the material one. Perhaps more. Then he repeated a Zieglerism that's been in heavy rotation at least since his testimony before Congress: "Switzerland is a beautiful country without any raw materials. Its raw material is money, mostly foreign money, from wherever it comes.

"At least we made them uncomfortable," he went on. "Besides, I couldn't have lived my life any other way."

Before I went back down the hill, Ziegler took me out onto his terrace under a light summer rain. In better weather, he said, you'd be able to see the white peak of Mont Blanc from here.

"Nicolas Pictet lives just twenty meters away," Ziegler remarked impishly, gesturing toward a nearby house. "The president of the biggest private bank."

I asked him what it was like to be a famous Swiss leftist living mere feet from Switzerland's capitalist number one.

Ziegler kept a straight face, but I felt him vibrate with pleasure.

"Our relationship is ironic."

3.

White Cube, Black Box

KAT Do you know what a freeport is?

PROTAGONIST A storage facility for art that's been acquired—

KAT But not yet taxed. . . .

PROTAGONIST The clients can view their investments—without importing them, so they avoid paying tax.

NEIL Sort of a transit lounge for art?

KAT Art, antiques, anything of value, really.

PROTAGONIST Anything?

KAT Anything legal. . . .

PROTAGONIST But it's not unlike the Swiss banking system. Opaque.

—CHRISTOPHER NOLAN,
SCENE FROM *TENET* (2020)

On a steamy day in August 1995, a retired Italian customs cop named Pasquale Camera was driving home after lunch about an hour and a half south of Rome when he lost control of his beige Renault and went careening into the railing on the side of the highway. When the police arrived to investigate the accident, paramedics had already pronounced him dead at the scene; his car had flipped over, and without his seat belt he hadn't stood a chance.

The traffic police also found, in the glove compartment of Camera's car, photographs of vases, sculptures, and various other artifacts that looked like they could be antiques. By chance, the local chief had previously worked on a team that specialized in tracking down looted antiquities, so he called his former colleagues in Rome. Incredibly, they had been on Camera's trail for months.

The photos got the police a search warrant, which led to a raid of Camera's apartment, which turned up a chart of the names of people in the antiques trade, along with their locations. That analog piece of evidence, laid out neatly in Camera's handwriting, led investigators down a rabbit hole of museum robbers, art dealers, collectors, and shell companies hidden in offshore jurisdictions.

The probe had every feature of an archaeological dig, only instead of excavating dirt and rocks to find buried treasure, investigators sifted through layer upon layer of fictitious corporate entities before landing in a Geneva storage room leased by an art dealer named Giacomo Medici. On the fourth floor of a steel-gray warehouse, a trove of illegally obtained Greek, Roman, and Etruscan antiquities—some looted from archaeological digs in Italy, some with Sotheby's labels dangling from them—were arranged on shelves and in boxes, like apples and bananas in a supermarket.

"All the cupboards were shelved—and each and every one of the shelves was packed—crowded, teeming, overloaded with antiquities: with vases, statues, bronzes; with candelabra, frescoes, mosaics; with glass objects, faience animals, jewelry, and still more vases," write Peter Watson and Cecilia Todeschini in their book on the heist, *The Medici Conspiracy*. There were also invoices, checks, letters, and IOUs. "It was clear that the outer room was where Medici received prospective buyers, and where objects for sale were displayed in secure and discreet circumstances. It was equally clear . . . that Medici had never expected anyone to come calling here—everything was just lying around, with no attempt at concealment."

The warehouse in question was not your average mini storage. It was the Geneva Freeport: a place where, since 1888, goods have entered the building and remained there, perhaps even for lifetimes, accruing value, hiding from scrutiny, evading taxes, even changing hands, all without leaving the confines of the warehouse. The warehouse had stood largely unnoticed in a nondescript commercial district of Geneva for years, until all of a sudden, it found itself at the center of spectacular highway accidents, unscrupulous millionaires, a team of cops called the "art squad," and real-life tomb raiders.

The investigation reached halfway across the world, prompting the Italian authorities to seek stolen artworks in museums from Boston to Toledo, Ohio. It ensnared figures linked to institutions as far away as the Metropolitan Museum of Art and the Getty. It also led the Swiss to regulate the storage of ancient artifacts and empower the police to conduct inspections of the warehouse. The Medici affair turned the lights on, if briefly, in this cloistral corner of the hidden globe.

But as quickly as it began, the scandal faded from memory and the freeport returned to obscurity. The lights wouldn't be back on for more than a decade.

Freeports are all around us. Known interchangeably as foreign-trade zones, free-trade zones, or free economic zones, they are designated areas, often but not always near an airport, seaport, or border, where goods can enter a country and be kept there without being subject to that country's trade tariffs or other tax regulations. They can be stand-alone warehouses or industrial sites, entire districts, or one floor of an office building. If you live in the

United States, chances are, the car you drive, the appliances in your kitchen, and the Amazon packages on your doorstep all spent time in a freeport of some kind before making their way to you.

The freeport was conceived hundreds of years ago in Italy, to serve two commercial needs. Merchants on long journeys could use the storage facilities to stow grain and other perishable merchandise at a foreign port for a short time without formally importing it or having to deal with customs authorities. And the governments in charge of their respective locations could use these zones—which included warehouses or silos, but also land around them—to relax certain rules and benefit from the influx of certain types of foreign commerce (and people) without committing to more wideranging domestic reforms.

Freeports function thanks to what's essentially a legal hack that creates a new, different set of boundaries for new, different people and things: "economic dualism" is how one academic paper describes it. And like the empires and nations that established them, freeports have come in all shapes, sizes, and configurations. What they have in common is the way they fence off what happens inside.

The early Tuscan freeport of Livorno, for instance, emerged in the late sixteenth century, an era when the notion of a territorial state, with discrete boundaries, laws, and hierarchies, was inching away from the chaotic fiefdoms of the Middle Ages and toward something a little more orderly, with plenty of gray area left to exploit in between. The grand duke of Tuscany used Livorno as a kind of sandbox, inviting in foreign merchants, mariners, and slavers when they might not otherwise have been welcome in his territory proper.

The Dutch Empire deployed freeports, too, beginning in the seventeenth century. Such entrepôts helped the Dutch to undercut their rivals by pulling trade away from the Mediterranean and toward the Nordic states. They also let them maintain commercial outposts farther afield, in places like Curaçao in the Caribbean, and enjoy foreign goods and expertise. "The attitude was 'We can welcome a Jewish community, an Armenian community, we can have them perform consular functions, and we can invite trading houses from England,'" explains Koen Stapelbroek, an economic historian at James Cook University in Queensland, Australia. "'This is how we make sure [trade] isn't a Trojan horse: we can welcome them but also limit their influence.'"

There's evidence that enslaved Africans in the Caribbean were able to use these loopholes on occasion as well. In *The Interesting Narrative of the Life of Olaudah Equiano, or Gustavus Vassa, the African* (1789), Equiano, an enslaved sailor, recounts buying gin at a Dutch freeport in the West Indies and reselling it in British Montserrat until he had enough money to buy his freedom.

In 1766, the British Parliament gave in to pressure from commercial lobbies and passed the Free Port Act, opening up four colonial ports in Jamaica and two in Dominica to allow trade with foreigners. This broke with previous policies severely restricting foreign trade in the Americas, though the goal was still very much to benefit British merchants, sailors, and economic interests. The British later established freeports in Singapore, Shanghai, and Hong Kong, in the first half of the nineteenth century. Again, these weren't peaceful free-trade agreements drawn up between equals in a boardroom: as colonial powers, the British occupied these places by force and managed them to further their interests.

Freeports shared a form and a function—to suspend their contents in time and space—but for whom, at what cost, and for how long varied, confusingly, by jurisdiction. This is still the case. The contents of these entrepôts also depend on the facilities: some have all the sophistication of a Home Depot, while others engineer their environment to the millimeter. Pharmaceutical companies stored COVID-19 vaccine in extra-cold freezers inside U.S. foreign-trade zones as they awaited FDA approval. An oenologist told me that when she worked at a vineyard in Bordeaux, the wine they produced was bottled and immediately shipped off to a tax-free warehouse in London to age. "I don't think the buyers ever drank it," she said.

There used to be a natural limit to how long perishables could be left in this liminal state. After all, wheat rots. Rice goes bad. Steel rusts. Even wine can be stored for only so long without climate control. When the Geneva Freeport opened in the late nineteenth century, its main feature was a large grain silo, but that fell into disuse as new kinds of wealth slithered into the city: gold bars in times of crisis, humanitarian supplies in times of war, and, in our more recent decades of growing economic inequality, the surplus lucre of the 1 percent. Sophisticated cooling and humidification systems were developed to help time stand even stiller yet the fundamental bylaws of the freeport governing time did not change. The goods in these zones remained in a suspended state: physically sedentary yet legally in transit.

Like Konrad Witz's painting of Christ on Lac Léman, an object in the Geneva Freeport appears before us but casts no shadow. The facility is a lot like the Hotel California: objects check in, but they never need to leave.

Yves Bouvier, once known to the world as the "freeport king," is a thin man with graying blond hair, blue eyes, a wicked smile, and the tweaky anxiety of a mosquito. He is a chain-smoker, a tea drinker, and a self-professed workaholic accustomed to putting in eighteen-hour days. The multivitamins on his office shelf and the toothbrush in his office bathroom seem to confirm this; Bouvier also has at least two and as many as five cell phones deployed at any given time, which syncopate their demands for his attention.

In his expressions and body language, Bouvier exudes a surprising self-awareness. At least, it's surprising in someone who's used to traveling by private jet. The effect can be disarming. He pokes fun at his profligate spending habits, his lack of motivation in school, and a former client's assault, via the courts, on his business and his reputation, which, he freely admits, has seen better days. He also reads as distinctly Genevan to a fellow citizen. It shows in the knowing discretion, the cosmopolitan provincialism, the rationalized ease with dirty, far-flung fortunes.

It's fitting, then, that Bouvier's business is entirely endogenous: he buys, sells, and handles fine art for wealthy foreigners, and stores it in a network of tax-free warehouses. In the two decades he's worked in this business, Bouvier has transformed the eerie liminality of the *port franc* into a glamorous, sought-after social and commercial hub where art collectors can hide their most valued pieces: from the taxman, the public, their spouse, and themselves. Bouvier's job, in other words, has been to lock up some of the most beautiful paintings known to man in a place where virtually no one goes.

Jean Ziegler was onto something when he talked about Ali Baba's cave being in his backyard. But in the legend, the forty thieves at least made visits to admire their treasure. At the freeport, artworks are lonely, trapped in bespoke crates under lock and key.

Yves Bouvier did not exactly reinvent the freeport, but he did rebrand it. He knew, from living in Geneva, what the rich want: technology, exclusivity, walls, doors. The rich come to Geneva for a certain discretion. The rich especially like special places where normal people can't go.

Another thing about the rich: a little darkness never hurts. They like it when the law is on their side. It usually is. But the rich are just like the rest of us: they like to feel they are getting a deal, getting away with something. Bouvier's genius was to recast the *port franc* into a warehouse not just for their things, but for their hopes, their dreams, their desires. This landed him in lawsuits spanning five jurisdictions, with the Geneva Freeport at the center of it all.

Like the Medici scandal that preceded it, Bouvier's legal battle, fought by a phalanx of lawyers, communications specialists, informants, and spies, offers a rare window into the fortunes that come and go through the freeport's doors. It may be decades before we catch another glimpse.

Yves Charles Edgar Bouvier was born in 1963 in a small Swiss municipality called Chancy, just across the Rhône River from Jean Ziegler. He was only a passable student but a passionate outdoorsman, and after a stint studying economics, he dropped out of college to pursue his real passion: downhill skiing. Through his twenties, he supported himself by doing odd jobs for his father, the then-president of a local moving and storage company. Bouvier was a glorified man with a van, and really only in the summer. It wasn't a career; it was pocket money. But having failed to achieve athletic stardom by his thirties, he decided to join the family business in earnest in 1997. He quickly threw himself into the work, taking over the head position from his father a year later.

The family's shipping firm, Natural le Coultre, had been around for even longer than the freeport had. Over the years, it had shipped everything from machinery for industrialists to food parcels for the Red Cross. But those things did not interest Yves. Working with fine art, he realized, was much more lucrative. It was also a window into the lives of the ultrarich—and while Bouvier was by no means poor, it allowed him to inhabit a more rarefied world than the one he knew. The high-end logistics business was "niche." "Like entering a palace or flying first-class—it's a different calling," he said, between drags on a skinny Vogue cigarette in his Geneva office, down the block from a luxury used-car dealership.

Bouvier recalled being dazzled by an eighteenth-century dresser of French royal provenance that he delivered to the *port franc* early in his career. "It was ugly. Today, it's not my style. But when you're a kid and you see something gold-plated and covered with marble that weighs, I don't know, two hundred kilos . . . that was something that impressed me." He got up to boil water. "It's very personal, because when you have an artwork, a painting, you can touch it and look at it from every angle. You establish a personal rapport with the piece."

Bouvier had a hunch about the potential appeal of the freeport to a certain class. He sold off the boring, low-margin branch of the business that specialized in shipping what he describes as "IKEA." To grow Natural le Coultre's art business, he went door-to-door to galleries and museums all over France, making his pitch to curators and collectors. Not only could he ship artworks in secure, climate-controlled conditions, but he also had the perfect place to store them: a tax-free warehouse in a "politically, economically, and socially stable" jurisdiction with "no strikes, few thefts, and good Swiss discretion," as he would put it. He was a convincing salesman, well spoken and increasingly well connected, and before long, he had become a self-professed "octopus," with a tentacle in every part of the art world. The job gave him unique insight into who had what, and where. "To do their work, shippers must know many things," wrote Sam Knight in a 2016 *New Yorker* profile of Bouvier. "They are given records of private sales and the names of collectors, in order to navigate customs. In the course of a typical day, stopping by the homes of dealers and the back rooms of galleries, they learn who answers the door and the phone number of the assistant, and see the other pictures on the walls."

In 1997, Natural le Coultre had rented just two hundred square meters at the Geneva Freeport. By 2013, despite stricter controls regulating the storage of archaeological goods at the facility, and some regulatory requirements on tenants intended to curb money laundering, that number had grown more than a hundredfold, to twenty thousand square meters. The freeport's management liked Bouvier. "He's a person who never cheated with customs, which is important," the facility's former director, Alain Decrausaz, told Alexandra Bregman for her 2019 book, *The Bouvier Affair*.

Natural le Coultre served gallerists, curators, and museums, which often have more artworks than they can exhibit. The firm also worked with art collectors, who were growing keen on the benefits of these nowhere lands: by 2014, almost a third of collectors surveyed by consultants at the consulting firm Deloitte said they'd used a freeport. The tax benefits of the freeport did not do much for institutions rotating a collection (exhibited art does not typically accrue tax, as it is considered a public good). But they could be interesting for clients looking to buy or sell their works without paying the EU's value-added tax, or storing them near home without racking up import duties.

Like the dollars multiplying in Geneva's banks and the coffee percolating in Geneva's commodity-trading terminals, the freeport's contents were not homegrown. These foreign luxuries had ended up in this warehouse because the warehouse, like so much of the city, was placeless, clean, and secure. As an additional incentive, the Swiss authorities allowed freeport tenants to buy and sell their wares within the freeport's walls without paying local sales taxes either.

To further entice his clients, Bouvier created showrooms with white walls and perfect lighting, where art could be assessed, examined, and sold, to outsiders or inside the warehouse itself. He aspired to turn the semi-industrial zone in a nondescript neighborhood into a high-end art "knowledge cluster" packed with industry experts. "Rather than moving a piece of art between the different players, I want them all to come to the artwork, to avoid the associated risks and fees," Bouvier explained, ticking off an endless list of complications and costs. "At the freeport, I wanted to have on hand a guy who did framing, a guy who did restoring, a guy who was an art expert, and a guy who was an analyst. In short, I wanted to bring together all the professionals who worked around the piece."

Bouvier's ascent in the world of art shipping, handling, and storage coincided with three other trends: the ever-increasing accumulation of funds in Switzerland; the gradual crackdown on Swiss bank secrecy; and the seemingly exponential growth in the sales, and prices, of fine art at the top end of the market. According to one report, between 2005 and 2015, the size of the art market doubled, to reach $63.3 billion. Most of the gains were in the top 1 percent of sales: the rich were getting richer and paying more dearly for works by a smaller number of artists. These numbers are more meaningful in relative than discrete terms, because so much art changes hands in undeclared private sales (often owing to the opacity of the freeport).

As the veteran art journalist Georgina Adam writes in *Dark Side of the Boom*, however, "Transactions at the top level are a tiny portion of the volume of the market but represent a disproportionate part of its value." That meant that getting in on these transactions—as a seller, a dealer, an auction house, or another intermediary—could mean reaping gigantic profits. Bouvier positioned himself to do just that.

It's considered gauche for a collector to flip a painting the way you would a condo on a home improvement show; the supposed pricelessness of a work is in constant tension with its dollar value. Still, by Bouvier's time, there was no more dancing around the fact that art was an asset class. It was an illiquid one—the wheeling and dealing required to trade major pieces is as much an art as it is a business—but whether it was a *good* investment or not, it was one that could do all the things other types of investments could.

After the 2008 financial crisis, when more ordinary assets were generating anemic returns for investors at best, art seemed like a better place to put money than stocks, bonds, or real estate. It became more commonplace to speculate on the works of a contemporary artist as though they were so many stock shares: buy low, sell high. Wealthy people, as well as institutional investors like family offices or funds, could put up a Monet as collateral when borrowing to buy a mansion, a yacht, or a Picasso. And the transactions could be as discreet as they pleased. A clever accountant could easily obscure the real owner of a sculpture behind a labyrinth of shell companies and private trusts, to ensure against its eventual seizure by a reviled ex-spouse or estranged relative.

More unscrupulous types might use art to move, hide, or launder money: given how fungible and subjective the price of a painting can be, it is inevitable that criminals take advantage. A mob boss or drug dealer might transfer a large amount of money to a collaborator by "selling" a piece of art at a significant markup, then presenting an invoice to legitimize the sale. Putting mounds of cash into a high-value painting, then hiding it, is also a way to move money *out* of a dirty industry like illicit mining and into an anonymously held asset that can be paid for in cash and holds value.

For any of these financial transactions to be sustainable, though, the art itself has to be kept safe, sound, insured, and shielded from prying eyes: in a freeport, say. "Works bought by art funds and traders, even by collectors, could sit quietly in the vaults, hopefully accumulating value until the right time to sell came along," writes Georgina Adam. The freeport operators and the speculators thus feed off one another: the more art in a freeport, the murkier the market; the wilder the speculation, the more art in the freeport.

And there was another advantage, at least in Geneva. At a time when it was growing more and more complicated (or at least expensive) to seek fiscal shelter through numbered Swiss accounts, the freeport served as a back door into the city of refuge: international transparency rules compelling banks, funds, and other financial institutions to share client information automatically did not apply to warehouses.

The economic anthropologist Oddný Helgadóttir surmises that the Geneva Freeport evolved as a way for the Swiss to accommodate shape-shifting capital. As the European Parliament noted in a 2018 report, because of increased bank regulation, "high net worth individuals have started looking for alternatives and many have substituted their 'bank account money' with replacement goods such as art, diamonds, antiques, wine or bank notes." To curb abuse, many countries, including Switzerland, now require art dealers—whether they're operating out of the freeport or not—to abide by "know your customer" rules and conduct due diligence on the people they are dealing with. But Helgadóttir suggests that the government's preoccupation with narrowly defining what is strictly illegal ends up sanitizing what is only technically legal. Freeports, she notes, "have emerged as new players in a complex, integrated and ever-evolving global ecosystem of tax evasion taking place in specially designed regulatory spaces."

When the rules benefit the wealthy, the wealthy need not break the rules.

. . .

Bouvier took stock of these changes in the market from the service entrance. It didn't take him long to decide to get in on the game. He already had the access and the contacts, and he was in the process of acquiring a sophisticated understanding of paintings, pricing, and people. "I'm no dumber than the next guy," he told me. "I saw art dealers. I realized that in one transaction, they earned more than I did all year with my shipping firm of a hundred employees."

But that business got a lot more interesting when Bouvier fell in with the man whom he would later dub his "adversary": Dmitry Yevgenyevich Rybolovlev.

Rybolovlev was, and remains, one of the richest men in the world. He purchased (then resold) a Florida estate once owned by Donald Trump, and owns a majority stake in Monaco's premier soccer club and the entire Greek island of Skorpios. In 2020, *Forbes* put his net worth at $6.7 billion. In 2011, he left Geneva for Monaco, which has nicer weather and better taxes—that is to say, none.

Rybolovlev didn't come from much. Born in 1966, he grew up in the Soviet region of Perm, near the Ural Mountains. He trained to be a doctor, but instead he struck it rich investing in potash fertilizer and wound up with a controlling stake in a company called Uralkali. It was a dirty, ugly, and violent time to be in the minerals business. Uralkali was essentially stripping its homeland for parts and selling them off on the international commodities exchanges. In 1995, Rybolovlev moved his wife and daughter and at least some of his assets to Geneva, joining a long line of Russians in the city they might call Calvingrad.

Mikhail Bakunin, the famous Russian anarchist leader, lived in Geneva in the 1860s, and spent much of his time radicalizing artisan watchmakers in an anarchist enclave of the Jura Mountains. At the turn of the twentieth century, Vladimir Lenin came to Geneva too. It was there that he plotted the October Revolution, wrote books in the public library's reading room, and dined at a local brasserie, the Landolt, where exiled Bolsheviks and Mensheviks once got into a messy brawl.

Contemporary Russian arrivals cut a different figure. The influence of the *nouveaux Russes* is inescapable: in shop windows, where Gucci and Prada display styles to appeal to a more extravagant taste; in the caviar and vodka rooms that have popped up in the Old Town; in snatches of conversation caught over the bells of St. Peter's; and in Cologny, a posh municipality a couple of miles from the city center, where luxury homes appear to sit empty for much of the year.

Rybolovlev was very much part of this class. Within a few years of his arrival, he bought a property and made grandiose plans to build it up into a sprawling compound modeled on the Petit Trianon, Marie Antoinette's beloved palace. The house already had special alcoves for hanging paintings; the previous owners had displayed a Chagall, and that seemed like a nice thing to have hang there again. The Rybolovlevs, Alexandra Bregman notes, had developed a taste for fine art and culture back home in Perm, and were eager to ingratiate themselves into Genevan society. An enviable art collection was an obvious, and classy, way in.

And that, Rybolovlev's lawyers claim, is how the oligarch ended up outside the Geneva *port franc* one August afternoon in 2002, pacing back and forth in apparent distress.

According to Bouvier, that is when and where he encountered his future client, screaming into his cell phone, furious that he had not received a certificate that proved the authenticity of Chagall's *Le Grand Cirque*, the painting apparently destined for his living room. Sensing an opportunity, the Genevan introduced himself and told the Russian he would be able to help him track down the document.

Rybolovlev, however, has claimed his meeting with Bouvier took place on a different day, and was not a chance encounter but prearranged by an intermediary who was helping him source his painting. At the meeting, Rybolovlev claims, Bouvier offered to find him the certificate through his network. He did—and that impressed the Russian.

A subsequent lawsuit confirmed that the initial meeting hadn't been a serendipitous meet-cute. In fact, Bouvier was the beneficial owner of the company from which Rybolovlev had bought the Chagall. As a middleman, he knew all about how it was bought and sold—and he'd had access to the certificate all along. Rybolovlev, unaware of this, was impressed by his interlocutor's resourcefulness and began calling upon him to help identify, negotiate, buy, and store artworks. Rybolovlev later said that he thought Bouvier had been acting as a simple agent, doing his bidding in the murky market for art. Bouvier conceived of his role differently; in his view, he was not precluded from buying and selling art to get it into his client's possession. Between their initial encounter and 2014, Bouvier tapped into his deep network of shippers, dealers, buyers, and sellers to find Dimitry Rybolovlev thirty-eight major artworks as well as antiques and furniture, the lot worth a total of $2 billion. The collection included a Modigliani nude formerly owned by the financier Steven Cohen ($93.5 million), a Klimt that the Nazis had seized during the Second World War ($183.8 million), and a "lost" da Vinci painting titled *Salvator Mundi*, or "Savior of the World," that cost Rybolovlev $127.5 million.

All the works officially "belonged" to a web of firms linked to Rybolovlev but registered in Cyprus and the British Virgin Islands under the kinds of inane, innocuous names favored by accountants grasping at words: Treehouse, Jolly Times.

It's not entirely clear how much Rybolovlev got to admire his paintings, at least on his living room walls. Many of his treasures, including Rothko's *No. 6* and Picasso's *Musketeer with Pipe*, "lived" in Bouvier's leased space in the Geneva Freeport and, later, in a sister facility in Singapore, before making their way to Cyprus. Bouvier, for his part, conducted his sales through his own tangle of zero-tax jurisdictions, including Singapore, the British Virgin Islands, and Hong Kong.

With Rybolovlev, as with his other clients, it was natural for Bouvier to charge a fee, though the men didn't always draw up formal contracts and would later disagree loudly and publicly on how much Bouvier's cut should have been. Until that day came, the arrangement suited them both. Rybolovlev got his collection, and with it an expedited ticket to the highest echelons of Swiss society. Bouvier got to join his clients in first class—or even better, fly private. He built up his own collection, focusing on contemporary works by industrial and furniture designers and architects like the British Israeli Ron Arad, the Brazilian Campana Brothers, Italy's Ettore Sottsass, and France's Charlotte Perriand, who collaborated with Le Corbusier on his famous serpentine lounge chair. Alongside these favorites, he acquired pricier, trendier pieces, "which I didn't keep for myself," he recalls.

As his star rose, Bouvier dropped the Genevan discretion that had served him so well as a shipper. He threw money at business ventures perhaps best described as experimental: Angolan agriculture, high-tech helicopters, energy drinks. He got big into sailing and horses. And, bankrolled by the money he was making buying and selling art, Bouvier set out to expand his empire of white cubes and black boxes. A freeport at every port!

The city-state of Singapore was Bouvier's first target. He told me he'd been living there since 2009 for the taxes, and right away he loved how efficient everything was. "You can open a bank account and have a checkbook the same day, I'm not even kidding," he remarked. No wonder finance types routinely refer to it as "the new Switzerland." (Bouvier's precise whereabouts were in fact the subject of debate: the Swiss tax authority claimed in a 2017 lawsuit that his Asian domicile was fictitious, putting him on the hook for $360 million in unpaid Swiss taxes.)

To a layperson, to be "the Switzerland of Asia" might signal a locality that boasts a stable government, a tradition (Confucian if not Calvinist) of hard work, compulsory military service, and a zealous passion for following—and writing—rules. But read between the lines and you'll identify a different thread: Singapore, like Switzerland, has made its fortune, from close to nothing, by making itself indispensable to global capital. For Bouvier, there might have been an added element of intrigue: Singapore had originally made its mark on the world not as an independent nation but as a British freeport.

First established by Sir Stamford Raffles in 1819 as a trading outpost of the British East India Company, the joint-stock enterprise that did the British Empire's bidding on the subcontinent, Singapore had been a shabby town with a largely illiterate population on the Strait of Malacca. The British had posted up in Singapore to undercut the Dutch, whose control over Indonesian ports gave them an outsize influence in Southeast Asian trading networks.

At this point, the freeport was a well-known concept—the British, French, Spanish, Dutch, and Danish empires all had and used them—so it was a natural move for Raffles to follow suit as the British moved into East Asia.

"Free trade, following the dictum of Adam Smith, would become a signature for Singapore, highly unusual at the time in any maritime tradition," writes historian John Curtis Perry in his appreciation of the city-state. "The colony would prove a potent example of what private enterprise could do without crippling restrictions and with minimal investment of public resource."

Historically, freeports like Singapore and its counterparts in Asia and the Caribbean let imperial powers like Britain have it both ways. It was all part of an awkward dance that made pluralism and free exchange more palatable in an essentially mercantilist economic environment. In contemporary terms, we might characterize it as an attempt to reconcile nationalism and globalism.

Raffles's appeal to the altar of free trade paid off: just a few years after his first visit to the island, he remarked on the surge in large ships docked in

Singapore's deep harbor, flying flags from all over the world. Their numbers would only grow in the decades after the Suez Canal cleared the way for more transcontinental commerce.

In 1867, the British designated Singapore a Crown Colony, together with Malacca and Penang. In 1938, they opened a naval base there, which was operational until the Japanese army seized the island during the Second World War. After two decades under British, then Malaysian, rule, Singapore gained full independence and UN membership in 1965. Led by a Cambridge-educated lawyer named Lee Kuan Yew and armed with little but the flag on its back and a valuable location, the country redrew the lines between commerce and nationhood in the span of a generation and, the story goes, transformed it from a humble "fishing village" to a glittering metropolis.

Visitors remark that Singapore feels like a country run by management consultants (a somewhat kinder take than the science fiction author William Gibson's "Disneyland with the death penalty"). That's deliberate. Lee's innovation was to deploy the sovereign privilege of passing laws and building infrastructure—what we think of as public projects, with civics and the common good in mind—into economic development schemes to attract the wealthiest companies, people, and industries from abroad. Lee did not harbor rosy visions of individual freedom and direct democracy. He wanted to win, and he didn't have much to work with.

Lee began by giving tax and labor incentives to foreign industrial and manufacturing firms looking for cheap, competent labor. He welcomed to Singapore's deep, sheltered harbor shipping firms riding high on containerization, and oil companies looking for a place to refine petroleum. His People's Action Party (which has yet to lose an election) opened a stock exchange and established the Monetary Authority of Singapore, which acted as both the state's central bank and its financial regulator.

The city made a massive push to turn itself into an international finance center through liberalization and deregulation—euphemisms, in the 1980s, for low taxes, streamlined paperwork, and a culture (or indeed, cult) of putting business first. Asset managers, currency traders, insurance companies, and financial tech start-ups streamed in. So did millionaires and billionaires.

Territorially speaking, Singapore was (and is) smaller than Fiji. But landmass is not destiny. To accommodate the new arrivals, the city expanded its puny territorial footprint by 22 percent since the 1960s, by taking back acres of land from the sea. It has also recently leased agricultural land amounting to twice its size in other countries, including Australia, China, and Indonesia, proving that borderlines between "here" and "there" are blurry.

Singapore hardly typifies free-market orthodoxy, however. Four fifths of its population live in government-built apartments, and the government plays an active role in funding students to study abroad, encouraging larger families, and discouraging homegrown "Singlish" patois in favor of the King's English. These controls help people get by amid gaping economic inequality. They shape national identity—though Singlish, to the state's chagrin, is there to stay. This careful planning has also helped make the country, its people, and its industry more globally "competitive," with stunning results: Singapore's sovereign entrepreneurship has raised its people's standard of living by orders of magnitude, and it has outpaced Tokyo, London, and Hong Kong in GDP per capita since 2015.

Lee Kuan Yew was frank about the dog-eat-dog nature of his battle. "When I started, the question was how Singapore can make a living against neighbors who have more natural resources, human resources, and bigger space," he once said. "How did we differentiate ourselves from them? They are not clean systems; we run clean systems. Their rule of law is wonky; we stick to the law. Once we come to an agreement or make a decision, we stick to it. We become reliable and credible to investors. World-class infrastructure, world-class supporting staff, all educated in English. Good communications by air, by sea, by cable, by satellite, and now, over the Internet."

This opportunistic philosophy helped the city-state top international rankings like the World Bank's Ease of Doing Business Index, which reward countries with little corruption, relaxed regulation, low taxes, and adherence to "rule of law." It was also great for one-upping other states when their regulations became more onerous.

When Switzerland began tightening some of its banking rules at the turn of the millennium, Singapore swooped in to accommodate international banks looking for a friendlier, more secretive (but still respectable!) jurisdiction in which to operate. In this century's first decade, the number of private banks in the city-state more than doubled. The Monetary Authority of Singapore estimated that the total amount of assets managed from the city hit US$900 billion in 2009—the highest in Asia.

To quote Lee once more: "In a world where the big fish eat small fish, and the small fish eat shrimps, Singapore must become a poisonous shrimp."

Singapore was hungry, and Yves Bouvier's warehouse—and the art "hub" he promised would come with it—was live bait. With cash to invest and an expanding client list, Bouvier met with Singapore's Economic Development Board, which, Bouvier recalls, made getting approvals for his facility (again) "very, very efficient." Together with some fellow European transplants, he made plans to build a little Switzerland: the architect, engineer, and security experts they hired to work on the freeport were all from home.

By then, there were things they could no longer get away with in actual Switzerland. After the antiquities scandals of the 1990s, the country had overhauled its customs laws to avoid future embarrassments (the rules did not apply retroactively). Previously, its freeport had been formally extraterritorial, legally suspended in place and time between the city, the country, and the world. As of 2007, it was stripped of its extraterritoriality and staffed with on-site Swiss customs agents, who did not inspect every single item but in theory had the power to do so.

In 2005, Switzerland had also signed on to UNESCO's 1970 Convention legislation banning the trade in unlawfully obtained cultural artifacts. That made it illegal to trade these goods on Swiss land, whether inside the freeport or outside it. Archaeological objects could no longer be stored in the freeport without paperwork attesting to their origins, and law enforcement had the right to inspect them at any point. Singapore, however, had conveniently opted not to sign the UNESCO treaty.

"When you go to a bank and rent a safe, nobody knows what goes in. It's the same thing here," said Alain Vandenborre, one of Bouvier's Singaporean business partners, in a 2010 interview with *The Wall Street Journal* about the Singapore facility. "They only need to give a code that indicates the broad nature of the item—gold, wine or a painting. There's no value, no ownership, no inventory list—all details are confidential. We offer more confidentiality than Geneva."

Another perk was subsidies from government agencies. The National Arts Council and the National Heritage Board of Singapore each held a 5 percent stake in the corporation when the facility opened. This supplemented Bouvier's efforts to finance the construction of the facility with his own money, outside investors, and loans.

By 2010, a fortresslike structure shot up directly adjacent to the city's international airport, with hopes of serving the growing Chinese art market, "but also Indian, Malaysian, Indonesian, Japanese, Korean, everybody," Bouvier told Reuters at the time. It cost US$100 million.

The freeport opened its doors boasting a commitment from the auction house Christie's to lease an initial 64,500 square feet, with more to follow. Dimitry Rybolovlev, who with Bouvier's help had acquired one of the most significant collections in the world, moved much of it over from Geneva "in an attempt to insulate [it] from possible seizure or division orders," a legal filing explained. Rybolovlev had found himself on the wrong side of Russian law after a gigantic sinkhole opened up in a Uralkali mine, giving the government an opportunity to seize control of the company. (They ultimately settled.) What's more, he had separated from his wife, Elena, and might have preferred that she not know what he kept hidden, or where. It was safer to put his paintings in a place with biometric controls on the door.

Bouvier was involved in planning everything in the new freeport, from the doorknobs to the HVAC system, he said. He particularly liked displaying artists he loved and collected in the freeport's common areas (if you could call them that). He went as far as to commission a sculpture from Ron Arad for that purpose. A gigantic piece composed of gleaming steel bars bent into elliptical shapes, it was meant to represent an ark, but it looked more like the entrance to a hedge fund on Saturn. The artist entitled it *Cage sans Frontières*: a cage without borders.

Bouvier set his sights on Luxembourg next. The tiny state—the world's last remaining grand duchy—was, of all the EU nations, the most appealing for his sort of business. Since the 1930s, Luxembourg had made a name for itself as the go-to spot for investment funds, as well as for small-time tax-averse clients known colloquially as "Belgian dentists." As with Switzerland and Singapore, Luxembourg's lawmaking capacities are geared toward making life easier for large companies and the ultrarich. (As we'll see later in this book, Luxembourg even sent this business model into outer space.)

One knock against Le Freeport's Luxembourg outpost was that it had to adhere to European Union transparency rules; the real (or "beneficial") owner of any asset worth more than $10,000 had to be disclosed. But with Singapore in the mix, it didn't much matter. There were options for every sort of client.

In Luxembourg, Bouvier worked with Deloitte, the management consultancy. As one of the country's biggest private employers, Deloitte had been advising the government on how to capitalize on the boom in art investment since the early 2000s, so it made sense for Bouvier to hire them. "I didn't need them in Singapore, but it's a rite of passage in Luxembourg," he explained to me in his office. "I could explain what I want [to the government], but if it's someone from one of the Big Five [accountancies], it reassures people."

For at least a century, intermediaries like Deloitte have helped countries divert their lawmaking and governing capabilities—the power to regulate industry, naturalize citizens, and protect their borders—to benefit private interests. This is how the hidden globe gets made: piece by piece, hole by hole. When Puerto Rico adopted its tax-dodging industrialization regime in the 1950s, it was at the urging of the U.S. consulting firm Arthur D. Little, which we'll encounter in the next chapter. When the nations of St. Kitts and Nevis and, later, Malta decided to sell their citizenship to wealthy foreigners, a firm called Henley & Partners marketed their passport to the world. And when Liberia started selling flags of convenience to ships seeking lax controls on the high seas, their maritime code was written by an American lawyer, not a local elected official.

Carving out a piece of national territory where rich people can hide their art is not so fundamentally different from these kinds of ventures. As a result of Deloitte's lobbying, in 2011 Bouvier's European branch of Le Freeport got a bespoke concession inscribed into Luxembourg's customs law, allowing commerce within its bounds. The venture also scored real estate located mere feet from the international airport and a commitment from the country's central bank to move its gold reserves from the Bank of England to the facility.

In 2014, the neobrutalist fortress opened to much fanfare. The opening night was worthy of a museum exhibition—which it was, save for the absence of, well, art. Waiters in red uniforms passed around trays of champagne. An orchestra played an overture entitled *Freeport*, commissioned especially for the occasion, for an audience that included the grand duke of Luxembourg. White lilies decorated the cavernous lobby, lit by a halogen installation by the American artist Johanna Grawunder, with portraits on the wall by the Portuguese graffiti artist who goes by Vhils.

"The atrium of the Luxembourg Freeport has become yet another mise en scène for the world's hyper-rich, whose wealth has continued to accumulate apace even amid global economic stagnation and crisis," observes Samuel Weeks, an anthropologist at Thomas Jefferson University who has spent years studying Luxembourgian business customs. "It is not that the art world suddenly showed up in this tiny Grand Duchy," he goes on, "but rather that global 'art culture' has come to resemble some of the more questionable activities long found in Luxembourg's offshore financial center."

At the peak of his career in the art world, Yves Bouvier had positioned himself at the dead center of this glitzy new offshore world: between Geneva, Singapore, and Luxembourg, he'd created a network of states within states, microjurisdictions marketing themselves as secret spaces for the ultra-rich, at once benefiting and hiding from the statutes of any one nation. And he was already planning more.

By Bouvier's account, he and Rybolovlev had discussed collaborating on a freeport facility in Monaco but stopped when the local government decided to build its own. They'd also talked about setting up an outpost in Vladivostok. In 2014, Vladimir Putin declared his intentions to turn that city into a trading hub with East Asia. In the wake of Western sanctions on Russia over its annexation of Crimea, an ultrasecure tax-free warehouse, Singapore style, could be an ideal place where in-kind trade of gold, gems, and other commodities could avoid crossing Western banks and the U.S. dollar entirely. At the very least, the warehouse could compete with the European and Singaporean facilities for Asian and Russian clients, who were growing keener on the prospect of collecting art. The discussions culminated in a planned meeting at the Singapore Freeport in May 2016, facilitated by a Luxembourgian diplomat and the then CEO of Le Freeport Luxembourg, David Arendt, which never came to fruition.

Before Bouvier's arrival on the scene, there had of course been many ways for the wealthy to avoid taxes, and plenty of places for them to store their paintings safely as well. Bouvier's special sauce was to make people feel safe, swaddled in multiple layers of assurances. "You can't take any risks when you're dealing with cultural heritage," he said. "Clients need to be able to eat off the floor, as we say in Switzerland.

"I told myself that in these places, you have to feel like you are not in a warehouse, but someplace else," he went on.

In this rarefied world, nobody need touch the ground.

It's fitting that the initial rumblings of betrayal began deep in the Geneva Freeport's vaults, when Rybolovlev quietly removed some of his paintings from Bouvier's leased facilities in early 2015 and transported them to Cyprus. Bouvier assumed it was because of the divorce; by 2014, Rybolovlev's relationship with Elena, now his ex-wife, had soured to the point that the oligarch falsely accused her of stealing a diamond ring, leading to her arrest in Cyprus. (Bouvier did his part by inducing her to visit: he told her he'd uncovered a cache of artworks in storage that she could add to the tab in her settlement.) The charges didn't stick; Elena came up with the receipt for the ring, and the ex-couple ultimately smoothed over their differences to settle "amicably."

It was Bouvier who now found himself on the receiving end of the Russian's wrath.

On a trip to the island of St. Barts, Rybolovlev had found out from a New York art consultant that a Modigliani nude Bouvier had sold back to him for $118 million had in fact cost only $93.5 million. That put Bouvier's cut at $24.5 million, many times what Rybolovlev claimed he'd agreed to. This revelation led Rybolovlev to examine all thirty-eight of the works he'd bought from Bouvier over the span of a dozen years, and to conclude that he had been ripped off by a full billion dollars, or half the art's total cost to him.

The Russian sued, of course: for alleged fraud, money laundering, and breach of trust. His lawsuits claimed that Bouvier had been hired to act as an agent to help Rybolovlev build a collection, but that Bouvier improperly and secretly acted as a dealer, buying art and selling it to Rybolovlev at a higher price. And he sought his revenge many times over: by filing charges against Bouvier that got him arrested in Monaco the following year; by convincing a Singapore court to briefly freeze Bouvier's worldwide assets with a Mareva injunction, the "nuclear weapon" of civil litigation; by putting him on the defensive in a fraud lawsuit in New York, in a Geneva case over his fiduciary duties, and in Hong Kong, where some of Bouvier's hundreds of companies were registered. The auction house Sotheby's was sued in a related case in 2018 for its alleged role in helping Bouvier buy and sell paintings at an inflated price (Bouvier worked with Sotheby's on some eight hundred transactions between 2005 and 2015). A jury decided in the auction house's favor in early 2024. A Rybolovlev spokesperson said that the case nevertheless "achieved our goal of shining a light on the lack of transparency that plagues the art market" and "highlights the need for reforms, which must be made outside the courtroom."

Bouvier never disputed taking large markups. He claimed it was within his mandate, and the reasonable thing to do; no one else had his access, his contacts, his wiles. Before reaching a global settlement with Rybolovlev, Bouvier liked to remind the world, over and over, that none of these suits had yielded an indictment; that in Monaco, in fact, it was Rybolovlev who was investigated, for influence peddling and corruption. (The Monaco authorities have not said whether the case against Rybolovlev will proceed, though Bouvier, personally, has withdrawn his complaint. Through a spokesperson, Mr. Rybolovlev maintained his innocence.)

There's even evidence that Bouvier played the art market's murkiness in his client's favor. Bouvier initially acquired *Salvator Mundi* for $83 million before selling it to Rybolovlev for $127.5 million; in 2017, it went for $450 million, the highest auction price for a painting on record.

In the end, none of the charges stuck. One by one, the criminal cases against him were abandoned or settled around the world, until in November

2023, the last of Rybolovlev's suits was dropped, and Geneva's public prosecutor announced that the saga was finally over. The men were done fighting. No further details were made public. "The parties have reached a confidential settlement concerning all their disputes that involved proceedings in various jurisdictions. They have no claims against each other and will refrain from commenting on their past disputes," said a spokesperson for Rybolovlev.

Still, Bouvier didn't exactly win. In 2017, he sold off his stake in the Geneva Freeport for an undisclosed sum, though he continued to do business with clients there. In 2022, Bouvier sold the Singapore freeport to a Chinese cryptocurrency billionaire for $28 million—less than half its initial worth. He also handed off control of the Luxembourg facility, renamed the Luxembourg High Security Hub, in 2023.

As the men moved on, it was hard not to read the affair as a kind of drama of competing national characters. Rybolovlev, who made his fortune in textbook post-Soviet fashion, had moved his family to Geneva in pursuit of the stability, secrecy, and status for which it was known. To Rybolovlev, Bouvier must have represented more than just a guy who knew about art. He *was* Geneva.

Bouvier helped the Russian spin the wealth he'd extracted from the earth into a more abstract kind of fortune: artworks of imagined value held by a spiderweb of names, numbers, and addresses around the world. Once he'd made the Russian's lucre priceless, Bouvier made it placeless.

Perhaps Bouvier's mistake was not greed, but a lack of discretion. In all of his peregrinations, he had forgotten where he came from.

I had never felt as drawn to Geneva as when it was basically impossible to go there: with an infant, in the middle of a global pandemic, months away from the first vaccine, and with a layover on the way. It was then, I think, that Geneva started to feel like home, like a real place. Against pandemic recommendations, in October 2020 I flew from New York to Geneva to see my mother.

There were only a few travelers milling around the terminal on the evening we left Newark, and the air felt flat without the undercurrent of rushing and anticipation. Duty-free shops were shuttered; even the convenience store was closed. When we arrived the next afternoon, we were ordered by a customs agent to quarantine for ten days. But a week in, I could not resist making one exception: to attend a reading at a Geneva bookstore by a Swiss journalist named Antoine Harari, who had been reporting on Yves Bouvier's feud since 2019. It was there that I first encountered Bouvier in the flesh.

Practically dizzy from the novelty of an outing, I took a seat in a row of folding plastic chairs.

"Good evening, and thanks to all of you for coming," said Harari's editor and coauthor, Serge Michel, in French. "Today, we are relieved, for the statute of limitations for a lawsuit has passed since the book came out three months ago, and we haven't been sued," he continued. "But we're also a little tense."

He paused. "We see that there are interested parties and their lawyers in the audience."

The pressure in the room shot up. Spectators made faces behind their masks. It was then that I noticed that two of the three men sitting in the row before me had laptops open, and that one was typing in a Word document that looked like a legal complaint. To his left sat a rangy, gray-haired man wearing jeans, a blue mock-turtleneck sweater, a blue cashmere scarf, and On Cloud sneakers: the weekday uniform of the moderately but not obscenely rich.

It was Yves Bouvier. And he had comments, not questions.

"I got him four Modiglianis. There are ten in the world. Two are held by foundations and aren't for sale; the rest I physically showed him in person," he interjected the first chance he had, after Harari and Michel had introduced their book and the conflict that inspired it. "Find me one other person in the world who can do that!"

Harari stumbled a little, composed himself, and continued to speak about the markups Bouvier had taken on the paintings in which he had dealt. He referred to Bouvier's "used-car salesman" quality, and the size of the legal team—no fewer than twenty-seven lawyers in a hotel room, working for thousands of Swiss francs per hour—that he'd hired to fend off Rybolovlev's litigation.

"I was attacked in Monaco, Singapore, I was attacked in Hong Kong, I was attacked in London, in New York, in Luxembourg, and I was attacked in Liechtenstein," Bouvier snapped. "Don't reproach me for having twenty-seven lawyers to defend myself. It wasn't my choice!"

It was an awkward scene. It was also funny. While Bouvier sat there twitching, surrounded by lawyers, Harari talked about Bouvier's (still unsettled) conflicts with Rybolovlev, as well as Bouvier's more recent attempts at entrepreneurialism. "It's incredible that someone so nimble, so savvy, would make such a spectacular mess of things," Harari said, referring to Bouvier's investments in energy drinks, helicopters, and real estate.

The Q&A session that followed was also hijacked by Bouvier's entourage. They asked why Harari had used anonymous sources, and why, of the ten chapters in his book, four were exclusively about Bouvier, and none were about Rybolovlev.

"I think one area in which you've succeeded is that both of us are unhappy," Bouvier conceded, though not entirely without humor. He would later tell me that his lawyers had advised him against attending the event, but that he had decided to go because "I'm someone who doesn't hide."

"It's easy [for anyone] to write an article," he said, "but I want to give my version of events—so I told myself, I'll go get him."

The authors had ended the talk by signing books, noting that they would happily sign one for Bouvier. He did not take them up on the offer, but he did sign a handful of books himself.

. . .

On a subsequent visit to Geneva, I walked to the freeport from my mother's house, over a small bridge crossing the Arve River, past the swimming pool and through a bus depot. When I got there, I saw trucks unloading boxes, people entering and leaving, and customs agents watching at the gate. I could see that this was a place in my city, and a rather ordinary-looking one at that. It was not a secret, but part of the scenery; road signs on the highway even pointed in its direction. But by then, I knew too much to walk on by.

In a 1930 essay published in the *Illinois Law Review*, the American jurist Lon Fuller defined a legal fiction as a statement that is neither truthful nor a lie, adopted by its author with full knowledge of its falsity, and useful precisely because it is widely understood to be false.

Under international law, diplomats often operate far from home under the fiction that they are still in their own country—geographically, there is no question that the U.S. embassy in Paris is very far from home indeed. Efforts to grant personhood to chimpanzees and rivers rely on legal fictitiousness as well: by considering these obvious nonhumans as persons, a court can grant them rights that human persons enjoy. Corporate personhood is the most commonplace example of a legal fiction in the United States: we know that corporations are not people, but they enjoy the status of a "person" in political life and in court.

And there's the fiction of the freeport: a space in a place like Geneva, but not of it; a part of a country like Switzerland, but not really; a place where time does not move forward but stands selectively still; a place that is "free" for high-value objects, but certainly not for people. It is a made-up place with made-up rules: a construct that reveals more constructs still.

For Fuller, fictions start to become dangerous when they become regarded as fact: when we take such exceptional notions for granted, forgetting that they are not an inevitability, but a choice. Indeed, a freeport is not just a fiction, but a fiction derived from an even greater fiction of borders and fences and lines. When we say that a warehouse is outside of national boundaries, we lean more heavily on the truthfulness of those boundaries.

Fuller also believed that the legal fiction "represents the pathology of the law. . . . Only in illness does the body reveal its complexity. Only when legal reasoning falters and reaches out clumsily for help do we realize what a complex undertaking the law is."

Walking into a freeport, in Geneva or Luxembourg or Singapore, you are confronted with this spatial malaise firsthand. Your feet are on the ground, and you can see exactly where you are—and yet you can be made to believe that you are not really there at all. Your reasoning falters. You reach out clumsily. You grasp at the complexity of the law, of the world.

4.

In the Zones

The zone is often a place of secrets, hypercontrol, and
segregation. It oscillates constantly between closure and
reciprocity as a fortress of sorts that orchestrates a controlled
form of cheating.

—KELLER EASTERLING, *EXTRASTATECRAFT*

Claude de Baissac's natural habitat has always been the territorial
oddity. Raised on Réunion, an island outpost of the French empire, he went on to build a decades-long career advising countries
on how to carve out free-trade zones within their national borders. He studied the zones in college and graduate school, and as a young man interned at
the UN agency in Geneva that helped to popularize these enclaves in developing nations.

Baissac knew just how to crunch the numbers, conduct the feasibility
studies, and evaluate the costs, benefits, and risks associated with these projects in order to make them appeal to politicians. He estimates having contributed to the creation of dozens, if not hundreds, of such enclaves by selling
governments and institutions like the World Bank on their merits and helping to draw up their boundaries, rules, and regulations.

But these days, he's not so sure if any of that was such a good idea.

. . .

I approached my first conversation with Baissac—on Zoom, midpandemic—expecting the bland, canned accounts one usually extracts from consultants trained in Excel spreadsheets and corporate niceties: allusions to "win-win scenarios" and "incentives" and "scale" floating in an alphabet soup of SMEs, FDI, and GDP. But Baissac was nothing like the buttoned-up McKinseyite I expected. He appeared briefly on my screen in pixelated form from his home in Johannesburg, slumped on a couch under a print by the South African artist William Kentridge, before he turned away to shout at his teenage children to eat their [expletive] dinner. Then he turned his camera off, apologizing for his shambolic appearance, but kept talking for close to two hours about his career, his family, and his political views.

Our next interviews followed much the same pattern, and when we finally met in person, in the lobby of Manhattan's Conrad hotel on a breezy April morning in 2022, he was much as I had imagined him, only taller and punchier. Over hot chocolate, with techno blaring incoherently over the hotel speakers at 11:00 a.m., he recounted his life and times in the zones, from discovery to disillusionment.

Baissac grew up on the island of La Réunion, a French *département* some four hundred miles east of Madagascar that, after centuries of imperial rule, now has the distinction of being the EU's farthest outpost. The image of the Fifth Republic occupying a thousand square miles populated mainly by dark-skinned islanders in the middle of the Indian Ocean may seem like a throwback to the bad old colonial days, but on paper at least, the island is no different from Savoie or Ardennes or any other region in the metropole. Réunion sends delegates to the French Parliament, abides by French laws, requires of its doctors and dentists French professional licenses, and, in spite of its remote location, is a full participant in France's centralized economy.

Baissac's parents, who were second cousins, both came from Mauritius, an island not far from Réunion, with its own patchy history of colonial governance. Starting in 1638, Mauritius was colonized by the Dutch (via their East India Company), then the French, then the British from 1814 onward, finally becoming independent in 1968. Baissac's family spoke French, felt French, seemed French, but for years were technically British subjects.

That made Baissac's great-uncle, with whom he shares a name, and his great-aunt Lise natural-born spies. During the Second World War, they became notorious members of the British anti-Nazi resistance across Europe and pulled off crucial covert missions to sabotage Axis forces in the run-up to D-Day.

Because of their size and distance from world capitals, places like Réunion and Mauritius don't figure into most people's worldview—even people who think of themselves as reasonably cosmopolitan and well informed about geopolitics. But for a local like Baissac, the fact that a place like Réunion could be formally French but culturally, environmentally, and geographically quite foreign—or, like Mauritius, its own island nation, but one dramatically shaped by centuries of outside domination—was always a given. Sovereignty was not fixed, but mutable and contingent. Baissac has always drawn connections between the historical indeterminacy of his native islands and his own muddled identity. "Culturally and by nationality, I'm French," he explained. "But I consider myself a white African."

It's not entirely surprising then that Baissac would go on to make a career in the business of exceptions—or that it was in Mauritius, on a visit to see his grandparents, that he discovered his first special economic zone (SEZ), some forty years ago. "It's the abnormality of them," he says, of what compelled him. "The out-of-pattern-ness, and the idiosyncrasy."

These days, Mauritius is nothing like it was when young Claude visited in the 1970s. It is considered an upper-middle-income country—the result of reforms that, according to one economist at least, amounted to nothing short of a "miracle." But back then it was poor, with high unemployment and a population of Indian, Chinese, and African descent that had, to varying degrees, been subjected to second-class status and struggled to make ends meet. When Mauritius became independent in 1968, the economist and Nobel laureate James Meade predicted a Malthusian trap of overpopulation, underemployment, and poverty. The novelist V. S. Naipaul was no cheerier, describing Mauritius shortly after independence as "an abandoned imperial barracoon, incapable of cultural or economic autonomy."

Baissac's ancestors had been sugar barons who owned hundreds of slaves until the British outlawed the practice, and when he went to visit his grandparents, he still was insulated by his family's wealth and whiteness. Trips beyond the family compound were eye-opening and a little fraught. Baissac remembers the cyclones that devastated the picturesque landscape, the poverty and inequality that persisted since colonial rule, and the precariousness of the island's economy, which was running on volatile sugar exports. He also remembers the scenic drives he'd take with his grandfather along the coastline, from the family's colonial mansion to the nation's capital, Port Louis, and the odd-looking building in an industrial area called Coromandel that they'd pass en route.

"I remember the humidity, the moisture, the green, green vegetation everywhere, and the volcanic red soil. I remember the great poverty and the very primitive dwellings," he says. Then, as though grafted onto the sugarcane fields, was an industrial zone. The zone was unlike other work sites he'd known, with their machinery and men in hard hats; in this one, young Indo-Mauritian women wearing saris always seemed to be milling about. "I'd say to my grandfather, 'What is this place?'" Baissac recalls. "And he'd say, very slowly and deliberately, that it was *la zone franche industrielle d'exportation*": the export-processing zone (EPZ).

"Those words, combined with the different geography and architecture—even though I didn't know what it did, to me it was like, wow, this is something special. So as I grew up and went back and forth to Mauritius, the zone kind of anchored me."

The factory in question was the industrialist's answer to the freeport, one of thousands of such factories now scattered across the world. Like a freeport, an export-processing zone is an inland island (in this case, on an actual island) in which national rules concerning customs and taxation don't fully apply. It distinguishes itself from a storage freeport like Bouvier's by what happens inside.

Materials in an EPZ—or, as they're known more widely, a free zone or special economic zone—aren't just sitting in storage crates; they arrive from abroad to be stitched, hammered, or welded into consumer products by local workers. Then the goods are packed up and shipped off to be sold someplace else. The legislation governing the zone performs a regulatory sleight of hand that makes it as though the raw materials never fully touched the ground.

These zones, too, are legal fictions: on a nation's territory but technically outside its customs and tax borders. Starting in the 1970s, these halfway houses for commerce became regarded, in the halls of the World Bank, the International Monetary Fund (IMF), and other international economics agencies, as a kind of cure for the ills facing closed, underdeveloped, or postcolonial national economies: if a nation was perceived as "unfriendly" to foreign capital because of its politics, its system of taxation, or its rules around opening a business—or if the state was simply having a hard time launching its export market—these zones proffered an island of reprieve.

The timing of this trend was no coincidence: just as dozens of decolonized nations across Africa, Asia, and Latin America were able to exert a modicum of autonomy over their political and economic affairs, experts in Washington and Geneva began advising them to splice off bits and pieces of their territory—and, depending on whom you ask, to compromise their hard-won sovereignty—to serve foreign industry. Mauritius was an early, notable, and relatively successful subscriber to this trend, in part because it had, more or less organically, stumbled upon a new version of it.

The story goes something like this. In the late 1930s, a shopkeeper in the Mauritian town of Curepipe named Alfred Poncini sent his son, José, to Switzerland for college. Poncini, a Swiss with Ticinese origins, had married a

Mauritian woman and emigrated to the islands in 1925 to work for a French company that sold Omega watches. He wanted his son to learn about business before taking over the shop.

At the University of Lausanne, young José fell in with a professor of economics who introduced him to the concept of decentralization—the notion that businesses (and other institutions) can spread their operations around, rather than running everything from one place. The idea stuck with José, but José got stuck in Europe: war had broken out across the continent, and travel to the tropics was close to impossible. Switzerland, at least, was safe, so off José went to work for his uncle as an apprentice watchmaker. Poncini *père* was satisfied with this arrangement: he figured that when his son returned home, he could help him fix the Omegas and Rolexes he sold at his store.

José returned to Mauritius a few years later, armed with technical know-how and new plans to buy out his father's business partner (which he did), and still thinking about his professor's theories. But instead of tinkering with luxury watches, he pitched his father on a different plan, one he believed would contribute not only to the Poncinis' continued success but also to the prosperity of their nation.

Instead of repairing the watches himself, José argued, he could train and hire local women to do it. What's more, if they learned to perform one of the most finicky parts of a watchmaker's work—boring the tiny holes through the center of the jewels around which a luxury watch's hands turn—manufacturers from around the world would contract out this task to them, for a fraction of the cost they would have to pay in Switzerland.

It did not take much in the way of raw material to make watches—José's experience in the watch trade had taught him that much. The components were small, light, and easy to ship, and the skills, while precise, were not hard to learn. And if they could negotiate a break on taxes, or some other economic incentive, in exchange for giving local people jobs, they might make real money.

Before he knew it, José had talked his father, the Mauritian government, the Swiss watchmakers, and local workers into participating in his import–export scheme. He opened a factory, Micro Jewels, in 1967, followed by another in 1972, with more to come. Mauritius was soon successfully exporting watch jewels to other nations. Thanks to a clever ruse enabled by arbitraging taxes and wages, not to mention the resourcefulness of local workers, the country was making money from nothing. It was exporting holes.

The SEZs that came to the country later were not qualitatively different from the Poncinis' setup, although they functioned on a much larger scale. Instead of importing watch parts in a small parcel (or, as legend has it, undeclared in a pilot's coat pocket), spools of yarn or wool would be shipped over from Asia to be woven and knitted into apparel by locals, then exported to the West without incurring duties. By the time Claude de Baissac became conscious of these operations, there were dozens of export-processing factories on the island, producing mostly knitwear and textiles. Many were owned by Chinese firms that had blown through the sales quotas that international trade treaties allocated them and were using Mauritius as a loophole to keep selling to Europeans. They employed mostly women, who were paid significantly lower wages than men working "onshore."

Baissac was a slacker. He had never been a good student; his studies, he says, suffered from his "hyper ADHD." Nor did he have any particular ambitions, other than being drawn to "blowing shit up." But the zones captured his attention and held it, for years. "The zone represented an opening to a more dynamic, mercantile, commercial, and cosmopolitan world than this subprefecture of La Réunion I grew up in," he says. "I was so interested in issues of spatial development, spatial inequalities, and the relationship between space, culture, history, all that stuff."

Having dropped out of college in France, Baissac enrolled at the local university back on Mauritius, with vague plans to further his studies. He ended up reading everything related to free zones that he could get his hands on. He wrote his master's thesis on special economic zones in small island economies, which he completed while working as a substitute teacher, surfing, and smoking pot. He had to get books sent over by a bookstore in Paris that specialized in shipping to the tropics. And in the bibliographies of these books, he kept encountering a certain Flagstaff Institute in Arizona, which was publishing the lion's share of practical literature on the subject.

In 1993, Baissac wrote the organization a letter about himself and his work, not expecting much to come of it. To his surprise, he received a letter in the mail some weeks later: a personal note from the institute's founder, one Richard Bolin.

"He was the guy, *the* guy at the time," Baissac recalled. "Eventually I called him. I remember calling him from Réunion and the phone rings and it answers, '*Bow-linn*.' And I said, 'Ah, Monsieur Bolin, this is Claude Baissac!'"

Richard Bolin may have done more than anyone else to popularize the free zone, particularly in North America. Born in Burlington, Vermont, in 1923, Bolin was the first in his family to attend college. He studied chemical engineering and business, and soon after landed a job at a Boston firm called Arthur D. Little (ADL).

ADL claims to be the world's first management consultancy, a precursor to the McKinseys and Deloittes that dominate today's business landscape. Its cofounder, Arthur Dehon Little, was a trained chemist who fancied himself an intellectual. In 1921, he published a pamphlet entitled *On the Making of Silk Purses from Sows' Ears: A Contribution to Philosophy*. The purse was not a metaphor—in the guide, Little explained how he had actually figured out how to transform an unhappy female pig named Sukie into a thousand-dollar handbag. The treatise is deadpan until the coda, where Little notes that the exercise "was merely a diversion of chemistry at play."

"We have no intention of producing a sow's ear silk for the market," he wrote. "We made this silk purse from a sow's ear . . . because it might serve as an example to clients who come to us with their ambitions or their troubles, and also as a contribution to philosophy."

Little's firm—and to a great extent, the multibillion-dollar management consulting industry that followed—embraced this ethos: of finding novel ways to extract money where there appeared to be none, even if it meant hacking the ears off innocent farm animals to prove a point.

In the early days, ADL was hired to solve a variety of chemical problems, from the mystery of a Massachusetts baker's "tainted cake" (solution: don't bake lemon meringue pie near a gas station) to surveying the market for insecticides for a chemicals company. ADL went on to design Tokyo's and London's stock exchanges, to lead the privatization of the British railway system, and to help deregulate European telecommunications—in each case finding more and more sophisticated ways to squeeze private profits out of public goods.

ADL also won government contracts, and one of its first was part of a massive push on the part of the U.S. government to transform Puerto Rico from a largely agricultural society to a manufacturing hub. This work was done under the auspices of a program called Operation Bootstrap. It was a fitting name for a rehabilitation plan designed by capitalists in Washington terrified that America's most significant Caribbean outpost might turn more decisively to socialism. It also ended up being a "dry run for what was to come with liberal free-trade zone export-led development," writes Ed Morales in *Fantasy Island*.

According to archival documents, ADL was explicitly hired to "aid the government in becoming self-sufficient." Its recommendations for the island weren't so different from those of a standard development scheme you'd encounter today: by attracting investment to a city, state, territory, or nation, the local population would benefit from jobs and better wages, all while helping the outsiders make money. What set Puerto Rico apart from similar initiatives in, say, the American South was the island's unique status, which lay somewhere between a U.S. state and a foreign country.

The United States already had "foreign-trade zones" (FTZs) on the mainland: a 1934 congressional action had let businesses store foreign goods for reexport while avoiding exorbitant, protectionist, Depression-era tariffs. For decades their use was limited, because the law didn't allow manufacturing to take place in these enclaves until the 1950s, and changes to the tax code didn't make them particularly appealing until the 1980s. Today, there are nearly two hundred active FTZs across all fifty states, and they've been used to manufacture everything from Chrysler cars to GE appliances. This was also where COVID-19 vaccines were stored "in" the United States ahead of their emergency approval by the Food and Drug Administration in 2020. Like freeports, FTZs are a bridge between the nation and the world—a place that explodes the binary between nationalist politics and globalist economics. And what better location to experiment on them than Puerto Rico, a place that was similarly hard to place?

As early as 1942, factory managers from the mainland saw that Puerto Rico could let them have it both ways: they could avoid the costs and complications of operating in a foreign country, all while taking advantage of a workforce that spoke English, could be paid piddling wages, and would not be able to exert democratic pressure on the federal government by voting in national elections. The capitalists would pay no tariffs on goods brought to the United States, because Puerto Rico was considered American for domestic purposes. Nor would they pay federal taxes on profits: while nominally American, the island was unincorporated, and therefore foreign enough for this sort of dodge to pass muster. Finally, thanks to an accounting loophole passed in 1947 with an assist from ADL, the tax breaks carried over when the money was brought back to the mainland.

It was the best of both worlds: far from challenging the territorial integrity of the United States, Puerto Rico's in-betweenness was corralled into a business opportunity. A place that was at once American and not turned out to be wildly convenient for U.S. manufacturers looking to save money. Nobody came to understand that better than Richard "Dick" Bolin.

Bolin was thirty-four years old when he moved to San Juan to become ADL's general manager in Puerto Rico. He arrived with his wife, Jeanne-Marie, who had been his Bible camp sweetheart in high school. With three sons in tow, the family was giddy, he recalled, to finally fulfill their dream of living "abroad" (never mind that they did not need passports). "I saw [Puerto Rico] had exploded out of nowhere and changed everything on the island," he told a reporter later in his career. "The Puerto Rican government was smart—they tore up all their socialist plans, and they went back to the private sector, and they started making it work."

Bolin's middle son, Doug, remembers the years they spent on the island well. When we spoke on the phone, he noted his father's enthusiasm for pretty much everything—trivia, pop music, rockets. "He took us to see Sputnik in 1957. We went out to look at it over San Juan," he told me. "I was four, and I couldn't see it, so I started to cry. So the next day when it returned, we went right back."

Bolin was brought in to advance ADL's mandate and, more specifically, to conduct studies about what would convince mainland entrepreneurs to open factories on the island in the final years of the firm's Puerto Rican contract. The studies tended to focus on concessions the island could offer, perks that went above and beyond what a full U.S. state could get away with without running afoul of minimum wage requirements or workplace safety regulations. ADL's archives, housed at the Massachusetts Institute of Technology, show how the firm helped create these incentives (in its capacity as advisor to Puerto Rico's government) and how it promoted them to U.S. businessmen through flyers, pamphlets nestled in magazines, and newspaper advertisements.

Despite Bolin's loudly professed distaste for socialism, much of ADL's advice to the territorial government amounted to promoting welfare, only the corporate kind: improving infrastructure to facilitate opening new businesses, subsidizing companies' rent, investing in worker education, and, most important, guaranteeing that U.S. firms would operate in an environment with low taxes without "running around from agency to agency." But ADL also identified social roadblocks to industrialization, urging officials to quell "fear of 'exploitation by foreign capital'" among locals and "impress upon the Puerto Rican people the importance of working regularly and of striving to produce the maximum amount of first-quality product." Bolin developed a reputation for personally inviting a potential tenant to a factory, opening the door, and saying, "This is your factory, señor." (According to Doug Bolin, his father also flew to Cuba to write an economic development report for Che Guevara and Fidel Castro, because he and his associates were convinced that Che "was an astute businessman.")

The goal of this project, which the United States called "Operation Bootstrap," was, well, bootstraps: to mold Puerto Rico and its people into a territory of workers eager to lift themselves up by serving mainland capitalists. And while the project did industrialize the islands, as well as raise Puerto Ricans' standard of living, the costs of the experiment were high. The corporate profits earned through Bootstrap weren't reinvested in the territory but made an untaxed beeline for the mainland. U.S. companies then took advantage of Puerto Ricans' rising incomes to sell them leftover goods from the continental market. By 1970, more than a quarter of Puerto Rico's residents had left the island for lack of jobs; the small-time agricultural economy that had once sustained them had disappeared. "What this boils down to is that Puerto Rico's economic model was designed to increase production and profits for American corporations," writes Ed Morales.

Like Arthur D. Little, Dick Bolin had a philosophical streak, and his time negotiating business deals between the metropole and the periphery got him thinking. What if this sort of place did not need to rely on a historical accident (or a U.S. invasion, as it were), but was conjured up out of nowhere? What if his sow's ear was not part of a pig, but a place, or a piece of a place just waiting to be made over? Puerto Rico's unique relationship with the United States—and the breaks on tariffs, taxes, wages, and other incentives its special status made possible—were the result of a series of deliberate political decisions, not happenstance. There was no reason why elements of this arrangement could not be replicated elsewhere.

That was the idea Bolin took with him to Mexico, where ADL transferred him in 1961 to run their national office. There, the firm pitched the Mexican government on *maquiladoras*: factories along the border, not unlike those in Puerto Rico, that would allow manufacturing firms to produce goods for export duty-free, primarily to the United States.

Mexico was keen to industrialize its border. Changes to U.S. policy helped their case as well: a recently amended tariff rule let American importers bring back goods that had been assembled abroad but pay duties on only the "value added"—the difference between the cost of a piece of cloth and a T-shirt. This made it profitable for American firms to seek out manufacturing opportunities abroad rather than making products in the United States, where labor cost more. Local industrialists were game; the Mexican government, which had commissioned the initial ADL study, was too. U.S. companies employed Mexican workers at low wages to make goods that could be brought back to be sold to Americans at a steep markup that was still quite cheap.

Bolin was all about free markets, but again, the maquilas were not exactly government-free. They were a state-run, state-supported initiative funded by the United States and hosted by Mexico that depended entirely on nation-states on either side of the border to carve out exceptions and protections for businesses but not people. He conceded as much: "This is Mexico's great secret: it has done the best job in the world as a developing nation because the president said no to direct involvement in the maquiladora industry, but yet the president also protected foreign investors from corruption."

There was a clear ideological allure to this way of thinking—especially to the men in Washington operating under midcentury orthodoxy. If Puerto Rico's semisovereignty had made it an ideal "safe laboratory and . . . training ground for US officials to master the challenges that decolonization posed during the Cold War," as the anthropologist Patrick Neveling put it, then a free zone with the same perks could likewise serve as a Trojan horse in the fight against communism. (Like Baissac, Neveling became interested in the zones while working in Mauritius.) On the surface, an export factory gave ordinary workers jobs; the country might gain trading partners and see increased economic activity around the zone. At the same time, the loopholes that attracted businesses discreetly spread the gospel of no tariffs, low taxes, and free trade. Even a place hostile to free enterprise or dead set on preserving its national territory and identity, Bolin wagered, could be talked into making an exception on its periphery if it stood to make some money.

The first maquila opened on January 1, 1965, and the program grew to encompass thousands of factories along the border. In the mid-1990s, the terms of the North Atlantic Free Trade Agreement, or NAFTA, replaced the maquila regime with continental free trade on steroids. With NAFTA in place, as well as more unified trade tariffs among countries that joined the World Trade Organization, there was no real need for special carveouts; entire countries enjoyed more liberal rules, including Mexico.

This was no tragedy for Bolin and his ilk. All it proved was that their big experiment in deregulation had worked.

Nor did the zones themselves die off, as some economists predicted. They simply found new places to take root: in Africa, Asia, and in particular in China, which would build its economic relationship with the rest of the world on the idea of the exception.

As Bolin's ideas were catching on in the American borderlands, bureaucrats at the United Nations in Geneva observed his work from afar. The political and social upheaval of the 1960s had given rise to an explosion of new ideas at the organization and, with them, competing strains of thought on how the world's economy should be organized, with eighty-nine new independent countries gaining UN membership between 1945 and 1975.

The nonaligned movement, which did not take sides in the Cold War and consisted of poor, small, and formerly colonized states, began advancing a progressive vision of internationalism premised on equity, dignity, self-sufficiency, and cooperation. These peoples had been down for so long; their independence, they argued, was an opportunity to finally shift the global balance of power.

Developed, wealthy, and capitalist countries, led by the United States and former imperial powers, read the room, but in their hearts took a different view. As is the case today, they believed markets were the best way to achieve prosperity around the world, and in political terms would go out of their way to prevent communism from spreading. They did not want to give up these convenient relationships with their poorer dependents—even if those relationships were fundamentally exploitative. They just had to find a more palatable arrangement than full-on imperialism. They would find it in the liminal territory of the zone.

Bolin's dream was really a prophecy: a thousand zones would bloom. This was not part of any master plan or cabal of globalists rubbing their hands together in Davos. In fact, for a moment it seemed that the underdogs might have an advantage. The creation of the United Nations Conference on Trade and Development (UNCTAD)—the same conference that brought Che Guevara to Geneva, and to Jean Ziegler—seemed like an early win for the nonaligned group. UNCTAD was meant to provide a forum for countries to go beyond paying lip service to one another's nominal sovereign equality and forge a more meaningful kind of equity that took into account structural asymmetries of resources and power. To that end, using their majority at the General Assembly, the nonaligned bloc appointed the Argentine economist Raúl Prebisch to be UNCTAD's secretary-general in 1964. Prebisch saw reflected in the world economy the exploitative class relations that Karl Marx had observed in the workplace, with ex-colonies and developing countries assuming the role of workers, and imperial and capitalist powers acting like bosses, profiting off their subordinates' labor. Though he later changed his mind, Prebisch advocated for poor nations to become more self-sufficient by substituting locally grown or made goods for foreign imports, which were sold at a markup. His idea was known as import substitution, and the rich countries hated it. They'd long made a profit buying raw materials from poor countries, manufacturing them into consumer goods at home, and sending them back to sell, pocketing the profits.

Out of these tensions a new UN agency, called the United Nations Industrial Development Organization, or UNIDO, was established in 1966. UNIDO's goal was to democratize industrialization, and it purported to support and complement UNCTAD's progressive goals. It helped countries figure out what kind of industries to promote, based on their location, their natural resources, and their demographics, and ran training seminars for government employees to become fluent in the language of manufacturing and operations. Among UNIDO's projects were initiatives to promote free zones as a development tool. The capitalist countries were happy to support this program, and quickly the agency took a technocratic turn.

In his extensive original research into the organization, Patrick Neveling found that in its first decade, UNIDO produced "workshops, a handbook, and hundreds of technical assistance missions" to countries from Taiwan to the Philippines. In the aggregate, Neveling argues, UNIDO's programs and in particular its advocacy for free zones had the effect of moving jobs from rich countries with high wages to poor countries with low wages. In the process, it created low-tax, customs-free jurisdictions whose larger benefit to their host nation was understudied at best, but that were politically palatable because of their hybrid status, outside the country's national political ecosystem. "UNIDO, an organization intended to strengthen national sovereignty in an era of export-oriented development policies, became the driving force in global EPZ promotion," Neveling concludes.

The irony does not end there. Decades later, offshore manufacturing would come back to bite the rich nations as some of their own citizens saw their wages fall, their jobs disappear, and their incomes dip. They would blame the globalists.

Back in 1969, UNIDO delegates traveled the world compiling reports on industrial activities ranging from petrochemical processing in Yugoslavia to yogurt making in Tunisia. They also visited newly independent Mauritius to study how a free zone might help save the Mauritian economy from the grim downward cycle that James Meade and V. S. Naipaul predicted. But the UN representative noted in a report that his work had been cut short: the government had already decided to go ahead with the scheme by putting Edouard Dommen, an Oxford-educated Frenchman with the plummiest of British accents, in charge of the island's new Economic Planning Unit.

Dommen, now retired in Geneva, moved to Mauritius after marrying James Meade's daughter, Bridget, an accomplished public health expert. He became friends with local hole exporter José Poncini, palled it up with government officials, and got to know the Sino-Mauritian and Indo-Mauritian business communities, which would become instrumental in bringing in manufacturing firms from abroad.

Dommen also got into heated conversations with his father-in-law, often while washing dishes, about what they deemed a fundamental question: "Were the Franco-Mauritians who'd run the island's sugar industry just soused on sugar, or were they capitalists who'd found a good niche?"

The economists concluded that not only were the plantation owners capitalists, but the whole of Mauritian society was capitalist, too, by virtue of its cosmopolitan history. "Even the slaves were capitalists!" Dommen told me, laughing. "Perhaps they were on the wrong end of it, but they understood what capitalism was because they'd been capital!"

What this meant to Dommen and Meade was that there was a future for industry there: that people could be counted on to behave like rational economic actors motivated by profits. All the while, a government-sanctioned study of free zones in Hong Kong, Singapore, Puerto Rico, and Taiwan was under way, to see if the watchmaking model could, in modern parlance, "scale."

In 1970, the parliament passed a law that gave economic concessions to firms that produced exports, including a ten-year tax "holiday," a 15 percent tax on dividends, zero customs duties and controls, and subsidies on rent. Mauritius is very small, so it didn't make sense to carve out a geographical area in which to make exceptions; rather, the whole island could be your oyster if you simply opened the right kind of business and obtained for it a "development certificate." In every little factory-island of industry, recalls Dommen, "you could import anything you need to make your factory work, which means raw materials, machines, and everything you want, duty-free and above all hassle-free. Then you could export it. And that was arranged to be free of hassle, taxes, and duties." One of the projects that grew out of this initiative was Coromandel, the area that left such a strong impression on Claude de Baissac as a child.

Opponents of the scheme worried that this new way of doing things would hurt trade unions, lower the minimum wage, put Mauritius on the losing end of global power relations, and make employees—most of whom would be women, because they were willing to work for lower pay— vulnerable to sexual harassment. All these concerns turned out to be valid, but they were features, not bugs—the very elements that made Mauritian labor "competitive" (that is, inexpensive). And paired with key diplomatic agreements favoring exports to the United States, Europe, and Canada, a weak exchange rate (which makes goods cheaper and more appealing to buyers holding stronger foreign currency), and government investments in roads and electricity, the zones "literally helped transform" the islands into a thriving export economy, the economist Arvind Subramanian later wrote.

According to the International Monetary Fund, in the seven years following the legislation that provided for the export zones, the Mauritian employment market added seventeen thousand jobs, at an average growth rate of 70 percent a year. By 2000, manufacturing made up over one fifth of the island's economy. But Patrick Neveling, who conducted some of his research working as a supervisor at one of these factories, says there was another side to the numbers.

"They blind you with the great stats, but they don't tell you who's paying for this," he told me over the phone. "You have all these workers who are maybe forty, forty-five. And they're not going to die at forty-seven, but they can't go into a factory anymore and sew collars all day, so there's no job for them until retirement. They have a tiny state pension because the state has hardly any social security payments from companies in the zone. That is a massive chunk of [lost] money."

Neveling also pointed out that Mauritius took out millions of dollars in loans from the World Bank in the 1970s in part to build these factories— millions they could repay only by renting out the factories. "There's an ideology to sell this [as an] X factor," Neveling says. "All these mayors or politicians say, 'I will have my statue because I built Shenzhen in Ethiopia.' But so few zones really work. Few come out of the sweatshop phase."

Bolin talked about Mauritius a lot, presenting it as an exemplary case study of how zones helped businesses and local people thrive. He turned into a small-time celebrity, traveling the world and touring international conferences and fairs, where he likened zones to "windows on the world of global manufacture." World leaders rolled out the red carpet for him; the government of Kazakhstan even gave him a traditional robe made of embroidered velvet to thank him for his service. "It was two sizes too small for him, so it sat in a closet until he died," Doug Bolin says. "Now it's two sizes too small for me."

Bolin's advocacy in the 1970s and '80s propelled free zones from a marginal curiosity into a mainstay of development economics. The United States Agency for International Development (USAID), which administers foreign aid on behalf of the American government, took an interest in them, too, and began assisting countries with funding to establish their own free zones. On the back of this initiative, a small cadre of American consultants began crisscrossing the globe, talking world leaders into these new practices. Free-trade enclaves began popping up everywhere: in a port city in the south of Jordan, in remote jungle regions in Costa Rica, and eventually at Subic Bay, once the largest foreign U.S. military base in the Philippines, which in a postcolonial twist now houses duty-free shopping malls, tourism resorts, a yacht club, and gated condo communities.

Ireland, looking to recoup revenues it had suddenly lost when long-haul flights no longer needed to stop in Shannon to refuel, established a free zone adjacent to the airport and convinced businesses to relocate there by offering twenty-five-year tax breaks. Within six years, one third of the country's exports were being manufactured there. Shannon would become another cornerstone of the zone world: UNIDO held a training session that, as industry lore would have it, inspired Chinese delegates to go back to their country and establish Shenzhen, which by some accounts paved the way for China's ascent. (We'll see later how Shenzhen's special dispensations were granted in a last-ditch effort to alleviate poverty after local leaders proposed them as a possible way forward.)

Between labor and capital, there was never any question whose side Bolin was on. He would give talks to UNIDO emphasizing how important it was to keep wages low: "The doubling of the minimum wage . . . has reduced the incentive to establish new maquiladoras in Mexico dramatically and has caused a number of them to leave Mexico," he warned at a 1977 seminar. Doug Bolin recalls that his father was no great fan of unions either, and that his blasé comments about wages to the businesses he worked with—"'You need to not sell so many jobs to American kids who don't appreciate them. I can get you four workers in Mexico and El Salvador for fifty cents,'" as Doug remembers—could sound callous. "It would just irritate people that there was a structure that would make that easy to do," Doug told me.

Even so, by 1974 UNIDO was discussing proposals to create a trade organization for administrators of free zones. That gave Bolin, and his life's work, a boost of visibility. He published a handbook outlining the blueprint for special economic zones, and took charge of the nonprofit Flagstaff Institute, which eventually rebranded as the World Economic Processing Zones Association, or WEPZA. At the time, the trade organization partnered with UNIDO and the World Bank to promote zone projects. Today it mostly plays an educational role, publishing papers and advocating for the industry.

The result of this collective effort is that by the 1980s, free zones—inspired by U.S. imperialism, fueled by decolonization, and spread by a purportedly anticolonial organization—had taken on a life of their own. The IMF prescribed zones to the poor countries it loaned money to, wagering that the presence of foreign industry would help states repay their debts in a more disciplined and timely manner. Jamaica—which just a few years earlier had been leading the charge for more equitable economic systems at the UN—saw the opening of the Kingston Free Zone followed by the Montego Bay Free Zone, the Garmex Free Zone, Hayes Free Zone, and Cazoumar Free Zone, to name just a few of its garment and food-processing plants with low wages, no taxes, and few worker protections. "While the free zones increased the flow of money into Jamaica, little of that has found its way into the hands of the Jamaicans who actually work at the plants, factories and warehouses," Kojo Koram observes in *Uncommon Wealth*, noting that while this might have been good for the country's creditors, it was hardly a sustainable way to support its population. By the late 1990s, there were almost a thousand such zones employing more than twenty-two million people worldwide, and they were quickly gaining a reputation as sweatshops among anti-globalization activists.

Michael Castle-Miller, a longtime consultant currently with the advisory firm the Albright Stonebridge Group, watched this all happen from his position at the World Bank, and then at an independent zone consultancy called Locus Economica, in the early 2000s. "Back then, this was really a tool of the Washington Consensus trying to liberalize the world order and making places friendly to foreign, and especially American, investment, and pulling back government intervention in these countries," he said over Zoom from Vanuatu, the South Pacific island nation where he worked as a consultant during much of the COVID-19 pandemic. "And zones played a crucial tool in that agenda. But I think now, they're no longer really an effective tool even for accomplishing that. They sort of won. It's not just the zones offering benefits. The whole country is."

The fact that free zones dovetailed seamlessly with the economic orthodoxy of the 1980s—Reaganomics, Thatcherism, and the rise of gigantic multinational corporations—obscured a nagging problem: it wasn't entirely clear whether they were the economic Miracle-Gro that their proponents imagined.

The myth of the free zone miracle can, once again, be attributed to Mauritius. In the 1990s, some of the world's most prominent economists descended upon the island to try to explain why, against all odds, this tiny nation, once wholly dependent on sugar prices and highly vulnerable to economic and environmental shocks outside its control, was able to turn itself into an African success story. Between 1977 and 2006, Mauritius enjoyed a streak of 5 percent GDP growth per year, even accounting for slumps during global financial crises; the average Mauritian also saw their income triple and their life expectancy lengthen by twelve years. Inflation was kept in check; even income inequality shrank. Things still weren't peachy—the bar had been pretty low—but all the economists agreed that the country's export zones had done *something*.

But what was it? It turned out that there was an explanation to suit any worldview.

The Harvard economist Jeffrey Sachs, who at the time was a leading proponent of free markets, argued that it was an open trade policy to the rest of the world that lifted Mauritians out of poverty.

Harvard's Dani Rodrik challenged Sachs on the idea that the island was unequivocally "open"; tariffs, he pointed out, had until recently been quite high there, opening a business was rather complicated, and imports were restricted to put local business first, under a policy of import substitution. But inside the zones, Rodrik noted, a different set of rules applied. The special zones gave Mauritius the boost it needed because they provided an exceptional space where trade policy could go off script. They offered the best of both worlds: nationalism and globalism, protectionism and neoliberalism.

Paul Romer, who was teaching at the University of California, Berkeley, took these narratives one step further, arguing that Mauritius had prospered because it made itself open to ideas and strategies imported from elsewhere. The zone allowed the state to keep itself linked to its trading partners, but at the same time to protect itself from the political backlash that might have arisen had it lowered trade tariffs altogether. And "once growth was underway, the government reduced trade barriers, freeing up the rest of the economy," Romer later elaborated.

This openness was crucial because a state can benefit significantly "by using ideas from industrial countries within its borders." In other words: planting foreign ideas on domestic soil made its entire economy more fertile. And in Mauritius, Romer had a perfect case study.

Without the Sino-Mauritian businessmen, there might be no Hong Kong–based factories churning out socks and panties. Ditto its Franco-Mauritian capitalists with connections in Parisian fashion houses. And without the Poncinis' ties to their homeland, the whole idea might never have taken off in the first place.

It's hard to untangle these explanations, and none of the economists chose to focus on the downsides of the zone projects, namely shoddy labor conditions and low pay. What's more, there were other factors at play. Mauritius was uniquely small, diverse, and well organized, and its zone program was run by the local government, which invested in infrastructure. It happened to benefit from two major trade treaties in the late 1970s, the Multi-Fibre Arrangement and the Lomé Convention, both of which drew in foreign investors. And because it was logistically difficult in the 1960s for Mauritian capitalists to move their money offshore, they could be persuaded to invest it closer to home, which kept wealth local. (One man tried, Dommen told me, but the Swiss bank he'd hoped would shelter him refused to convert such a large quantity of Mauritian currency.)

In simpler terms, Mauritius's exceptions were exceptions among exceptions. Elsewhere, it was much more common for free zones to open up, employ a few hundred low-wage workers, save a corporation a bit of money, and have no tangible long-term effect on local quality of life or infrastructure. Many zone projects were of limited value to anyone except the firm obtaining tax breaks and streamlined paperwork. And while it was true that some jobs were better than none, and that limited investment was better than zero, these arguments rested on a defeatist premise: that there was no other way for a nation to flourish.

It might not be surprising to hear, then, that as Mauritius prospered, it began importing cheaper labor from China, India, and Bangladesh to staff its factories. When the treaties that benefited local manufacturers expired, those companies pulled out too. But by then, Mauritius had already leveled up. It was still a tax haven; it was just serving a different bracket.

In 1992, the country began offering foreign companies legal residency, allowing them to benefit from bargain-basement taxes and near-Swiss levels of secrecy. It began building out other midskill offshore industries like accounting and cross-border banking. These perks, paired with an Indo-Mauritian agreement intended to prevent corporations from being taxed twice, created an absurd situation in which the island (population 1.2 million) accounted on paper for almost one third of all foreign direct investment into India (population 1.4 billion) between 2000 and 2016, when the loophole was closed.

Routing money through an island center does not automatically mean the island shares in this diverted wealth, of course. But the cottage industry of bankers, lawyers, accountants, and their support staff that make it all happen add up. Meanwhile, between 2001 and 2005, 112 factories in the free zones shut down, costing the country 25,000 jobs.

What's shocking, in retrospect, is that the institutions pushing for export zones were well aware of their limitations from the start. "EPZ policies are very likely to fail if they are regarded as a substitute for, rather than as a first phase of, a broad-based, outward-looking policy for the economy as a whole," reads an IMF report from 1990. "In essence, therefore, the EPZ concept holds promise of only temporary advantages."

Literature from the World Bank and even UNIDO itself confirms that zones were known to be no magic bullet. Due to inertia or ideology or some combination thereof, however, this did nothing to contain them. Everyone saw what they wanted to see. The zones were just too convenient to give up.

After some short exchanges over long-distance calls, Claude de Baissac met Dick Bolin for the first time at a conference in Malaysia in 1994. Against all odds, they hit it off. Baissac, a free spirit who courts chaos at every corner, had cleaned up as best he could after having spent most of the previous few months at the beach. Bolin, for his part, was every inch the 1950s U.S. businessman, with his crew cut, bow tie, and suspenders. "He was very American and very Republican. He had a rather large belly, he wasn't very tall, and he had blue eyes, a wide face, big jowls, and kind of a hanging bottom lip," Baissac recalls. "He loved ice cream and Richard Nixon."

In Kuala Lumpur, Bolin stayed at a fancy hotel, Baissac recalls, while he went with the budget option. At the conference, he met the people in charge of the zones: civil servants, trade ministers, and third-tier bureaucrats like the head of a midsize Kenyan zone board. "It was a very stately affair, very formal," says Baissac. "EPZs were state-owned and run by civil servants in charge of investor licenses, work permits, and all of that."

He also realized how radically Bolin's idea of a free zone clashed with these more subdued government efforts. "What Dick was advocating for was different. He was pushing privately run zones," Baissac says. He himself wasn't entirely sold on this approach but set his reservations aside. Having grown up in a conservative family, Baissac considered himself on the political right—as a young man, he was a fan of Thatcher and Reagan—so Bolin's radical capitalism didn't exactly shock him.

That year, Baissac moved to Bristol to pursue a doctorate in geography. He hated the city and was put off by his stuffy English classmates. ("The English are okay when they're colonial and decadent and liberated and fun," he told me, "but when you're actually there, you wonder what the fuck is wrong with these people.") So he moved on again and hustled his way into an internship at UNCTAD in Geneva, where, a little starstruck, he spent a few months writing reports for Edouard Dommen. Geneva, as it turned out, was pretty boring too. So on Bolin's invitation, Baissac hopped on a plane to Flagstaff, Arizona, where he would begin a PhD program.

That was where he first began to question Bolin's approach in earnest. "When did I wake up? The first cognitive dissonance for me was when I started at Flagstaff, and I was shocked by the simplicity and the ideological, almost religious, views Dick had," he recalls.

"He was so rabidly pro-American; he believed in the American way of life. He thought everyone wants to be American, and that export-processing zones are the way to educate your labor force, and consumer society emerges. There was no maliciousness, it was a true Doris Day attitude. Jeanne was the same, she was the American dame, from a good family in New England."

Baissac continued, "Hearing them talk about EPZ as a tool of civilization—it was never explicit, but it was implicit. It was like, 'We'll liberate the people with free markets, and they'll be happy because all they want is to be like us.'" His own attraction to the zone—and the appeal of how it played out in Mauritius—had been "as an organic development, not an imposition," he says.

A couple of years after arriving, Baissac left Flagstaff, abandoned his PhD, and took a job at The Services Group (TSG), a Washington, D.C., nonprofit (now called Aecom) that got most of its funding through contracts from USAID. TSG was hired to help create free-trade enclaves in Jordan, Jamaica, Palestine, and the Dominican Republic. The work followed a pattern: consultants like Baissac would show up in a new country, talk to local or national leaders, sketch out a business plan with proposed concessions the government could offer in a free zone, and make projections about how much revenue the zones would bring in, based on success stories in other countries.

By this point, free zones had developed a reputation for exploiting workers, particularly when they were being managed by a private company rather than the state. In the Middle East, the indignities of low wages and long hours were compounded by social relations. "I had a tremendously uneasy feeling of seeing Jordanian and Palestinian women in sweatshops working under the command of aggressive Israelis," Baissac says. "I was also disturbed by the anti-Israeli sentiment among the Jordanian industrialists. I wasn't convinced SEZs would bridge the cultural gap. I thought they were becoming instruments of exploitation. I wondered, when are they agents of good? And I realized you need local entrepreneurs investing and developing their own business . . . or it's a race to the bottom."

There were foundational problems too. Zone bylaws in different places were looking increasingly alike. They were not improving infrastructure, importing new ideas, or allowing specialized clusters of industry to form, as Baissac believed they should. They were mostly just making life easier for businesses, with little regard for the countries where they were located. "Cookie-cutter projects" is how Michael Castle-Miller described them. "They copy and paste what other countries do [to make business] duty-free."

During this period, TSG emerged as a cog in the increasingly professionalized zone-industrial complex. Once they had established themselves as a development tool that could sneakily lower barriers to trade without threatening nationalist politics and rhetoric, even in socialist countries, U.S. government agencies, as well as international institutions, seemed happy to throw money their way, regardless of whether these projects were likely to make a difference. Governments did their part by offering concessions in the form of tax "holidays," reasoning that it wasn't as though they had tax revenues from overseas investors to lose in the first place. And the big development agencies were still pushing zones as part of their economic rehabilitation plans, even though they had been aware of their limitations from the get-go.

Everyone could look like they were doing something—and the consultants had mastered how to make it look like their strategy was working, what with their optimistic projections about job growth and GDP per capita. "The problem with development consulting is that you're constantly looking for new projects and growth, and you cheat the system by always finding positive future returns for your project," Baissac complains. "My bosses would say, 'This project needs a positive rate of return,' and I'd say, 'I can't give you that based on the data we have.' I was asked to put lipstick on pigs, and I refused."

Eventually Baissac was fired. He retreated into stints in the airline industry (on the eve of 9/11) and for security contractors in Africa (just as terrorism was becoming a big concern on the continent), all while working consulting gigs in the zone industry on the side. He briefly chaired WEPZA, the trade group Bolin had started, then handed the reins over to another TSG alum, Jean-Paul Gauthier (not to be confused with the fashion icon Gaultier).

In spite of being an official advocate for the sector, Gauthier is just as critical of it as Baissac.

He started noticing the problems when he worked at the World Bank's International Finance Corporation (IFC), which advises and loans money to private companies operating in developing nations. "When I was at the IFC, there was an argument that [if] nothing else works in these countries, let's try this," he recalled, referring to export zones. "And that was soon proven to be a nonviable idea, because after a few years, the evaluations show that the zones are porous.

"The idea of the zone as an enclave—that there, everything is fixed and better and a haven for international investment—is wrongheaded," he went on. "If it's surrounded by garbage, then it's garbage in, garbage out. You have a problem."

These may sound like shocking admissions, coming from a man who told me he was behind the launch of 134 new zones and 38 new laws or policies enabling them worldwide. But perhaps those numbers are less the markers of an achievement than a reflection of just how ubiquitous free zones have become. According to the Adrianople Group, an upstart free zone consultancy, there are now more than seven thousand of them in the world.

At least several hundred are zombie zones: dormant, operating at low capacity, or outright abandoned. It's impossible to say how many, because "failure is never recognized," Gauthier says. "The institutions in particular, the governments in charge, view themselves as needing to perpetuate their own existence, so they never declare a failure."

Gauthier believes free zones still have potential as long as they don't exist in a vacuum: industry requires things that benefit all citizens, like functional infrastructure, like roads and electricity; a reasonably corruption-free environment; a stable political system that won't change the rules every couple of years. "These things can work, but it's hard, and they can work if you don't make the classic catalog of a hundred mistakes," he says. It's the "put a zone on it" approach to economic development that has produced hundreds of corporate enclaves of marginal economic value, even to the companies working within them.

Not just that, but they can be actively harmful to the communities living around them, who often lack the skills or education to work the promised jobs. "They're very tactile animals, SEZs—whether in the middle of nowhere or on contested land—so you want to get out there and eyeball it: how far is it, who lives there, are there mangroves, what's going on," Gauthier says. In his experience, however, bureaucrats tend to lack the resources or the will to go see for themselves.

Such neglect can end poorly for the communities in these areas. In India, where 231 zones are operational, development projects have displaced entire local populations—farmers, mostly—and left them with no means of supporting themselves, save for perhaps a paltry one-time payout from the state.

Eminent domain is invoked in many contexts—railways, factories, ports, and sports stadiums—everywhere from Southeast Asia to New York City. Displacement is not a problem unique to zone building. But the symbolism of the territorial carve-out adds insult to injury. It says, without ambiguity, to the former inhabitants: this land was not made for you and me.

Baissac had all but left the zone business by the beginning of the 2000s. He was disillusioned; he was also busy working for a new business intelligence company. But one day, at a conference in South Africa, he ran into Paul Romer, the American economist who'd argued that Mauritius had prospered because of its willingness to borrow ideas, people, and technologies from the rest of the world.

Baissac was excited to meet Romer. The economist, a 2018 Nobel laureate, is best known for his theories about the economics of ideas: namely, that ideas are not like other goods, because they do not get depleted each time they're used. On the contrary: ideas have a cumulative effect, and with increasing returns comes more economic growth. They should therefore be treated differently, shared more liberally. This was the case within firms and between states, which could invest in idea-generating enterprise. "If a poor nation invests in education and does not destroy the incentives for its citizens to acquire ideas from the rest of the world, it can rapidly take advantage of the publicly available part of the worldwide stock of knowledge," he wrote in an article on growth. "If, in addition, it offers incentives for privately held ideas to be put to use within its borders (for example, by protecting foreign patents, copyrights, and licenses, and by permitting direct investment by foreign firms), its citizens can soon work in state-of-the-art productive activities."

Romer's writing about "new growth theory" aligned with Baissac's beliefs about what brings about prosperity in an economy: that individuals, when given the chance, will naturally be compelled to pursue profits, creating technological advances and innovation. Romer also broke with tradition when he wrote that economic growth did not just occur thanks to exogenous factors, like natural resources, but also endogenous ones, like ideas—which were possible to create from within, on the level of a company or even an entire country, with the right incentives.

"I thought, I definitely want to work with you," Baissac said of their meeting. He was excited.

"Then one day he called, and he said, 'I'm looking for a government who'll take one of my projects.'"

The projects weren't factories. Romer had decided to take his concept further and to extend the fiscal autonomy of the zone into something more far-reaching and political. His creations would be states within states. He called them charter cities.

5

Hacking the World

The ultimate, hidden truth of the world is that it is something
that we make, and could just as easily make differently.

—DAVID GRAEBER

I hesitated before deciding to include a chapter on charter cities in this
book, in part because the idea is not so new. For one thing, a charter
city, if we use Paul Romer's working definition, is a territory located in
one state that operates under another state's rules, or charter. That describes
pretty much half the world under colonialism. It describes the Vatican, foreign embassies, and Hong Kong under China's "one country, two systems"
policy. It is an expansive, political version of the freeport, and the main reason it sounds so dissonant to our ears is because nation-states put a great
deal of stock in their sovereignty. The idea of charter cities suggests dangerous meddling: a foreign influence in a place it does not belong. Such cities
break up the integrity of the nation. They puncture the whole.

But Romer is not one for orthodoxy. Having already argued that free-trade
zones allowed poorer nations to prosper by opening themselves to imported
ideas, technologies, and, eventually, reforms, Romer would go on to make the
case for transplanting foreign legal systems onto new cities on foreign soil, not

to spread foreign influence so much as to kick-start more comprehensive nationwide change.

In the early 2010s, Romer went on a media spree publicizing these charter cities. He wrote papers, participated in interviews and magazine profiles for *The New York Times* and *The Atlantic*, even gave a popular TED Talk pitching his vision. The moment was right for it. The world was still in an economic recession caused, largely, by the so-called best and brightest, and the clever contrarianism of radio programs like *Freakonomics* and *Planet Money*—which covered Romer effusively—seemed to explain the economy about as well as anyone at the World Bank or the Federal Reserve. In the United States, the postracial promises of the Obama administration had not quite given way to the Trump-era awareness that inequality and bias were structural, not personal. Internationally this was the case as well: the economic press was still in the thrall of seductive fixes like microcredit, which relied on individuals over systemic solutions like a social safety net or functional infrastructure.

It was also a time when big tech firms weren't yet being sued for monopolization and invasions of privacy so much as celebrated for their ability to "hack" everything from personal fitness to political polling.

Charter cities were a hack along these lines, and Romer tried for a while to make them happen. He cast around in Honduras and Madagascar looking for willing host countries with free land that he could give legal structure to, but none of his attempts came to fruition. His quest was the embodiment of that Groucho Marx joke about clubs—that you'd never want to be part of one that would accept you as a member. Only the most desperate, dysfunctional states would agree to entertain such an arrangement. No respectable world leader would willingly enlist in what looked like a neocolonial project.

Eventually, Romer backed away from the project as well, availing himself of a disengagement that is perhaps an occupational perk. "What I do is put messages in bottles, and then I just throw them in the ocean, and I can't really control what happens," he told me. "I'm trying to keep my distance from the idea."

What happened? I asked. Hadn't he gone out of his way to make the cities happen, even as critics loudly derided his attempts as neocolonial?

"Looney libertarian world" was Romer's wry summation.

Buoyed by Romer's (quasi-)endorsement and riding high on booming tech stocks, a new guard, out of Silicon Valley, had taken up the mantle. In their ideal vision, the foreign state administering the charter city from afar was replaced with a private company that enjoyed similar concessions but answered to private interests, not the public. This was a departure from Romer's state-centric vision.

The libertarians started think tanks, launched consultancies, and published journals. They opened investment firms and organized conferences. And in the process, they made "charter cities" rhyme with a brand of outlandish libertarianism inspired by Ayn Rand and Austrian economics. Some of these groups have moved away from these politics and, in the case of the Washington, D.C.–based Charter Cities Institute, begun prioritizing more technical concerns, like zoning and urban planning. They seem to be following in the footsteps of free zone consultants in seeking out contracts from aid and development agencies rather than dabbling in armchair political theory. But it's hard to shake off the whiff of Galt's Gulch: a vision of a market-based society that journalists and academics love to gawk at, but which translates to more talk than action. These people get plenty of attention, and I was— am—reluctant to give them more, the second reason for my wariness.

Two things changed my mind.

On the island of Roatán, a former Spanish, then British, colony off the east coast of Honduras, the beginnings of a semiautonomous enclave are in fact taking shape. Próspera is, for now, a resort town with a handful of buildings, a few housing units, and a convoluted e-residency system wherein individuals can become members of the community and incorporate a business without actually living there. It oversees its own system of taxation, zoning, and governance—a governing board makes these decisions—and hires private security guards instead of relying on local cops. None of the Próspera executives I've spoken to live there full time, though they claim it will become a thriving community of Hondurans enjoying good living conditions and earning a decent wage doing things like telework, all while generating untold returns to its investors through fees and real estate. It enlisted the firm founded by the late British Iraqi architect and designer Zaha Hadid to make futuristic renderings of its dominion, all curved lines and space-age aesthetic.

The origins of the project date back to 2009, when, after a military coup unseated a left-wing Honduran administration, politicians from the country's right-wing National Party, aided by foreign advisers, proposed legislation allowing for largely private jurisdictions on their country's land. Only two have been built: Próspera, and a more industrial zone on the mainland named Ciudad Morazán.

Paul Romer was involved in the early stages of establishing the Honduras law; he quit in 2012 after a falling-out over the government's lack of transparency, but the idea appealed to powerful interests and lived on. In 2013, the Honduran Supreme Court passed what's known as the ZEDE (Zone for Employment and Economic Development) law, essentially allowing approved investors to administer parts of Honduran territory in virtually every respect except criminal matters. "The people there didn't want [meaningful] reform," Romer recalled. "They wanted to create a political jurisdiction where they could consolidate their power."

The law drew American libertarians to Roatán like flies to the farm. Their emissaries include Pronomos Capital, a venture fund specializing in new jurisdictions, founded by economist Milton Friedman's grandson Patri; and NeWay Capital, a D.C.-based firm with a similar remit. Also in the project's orbit are Mark Klugmann, a former speechwriter for Ronald Reagan and George H. W. Bush; Michael Strong, an education-reform activist who cowrote a book with Whole Foods founder John Mackey; Shanker

Singham, a British American trade lawyer who loudly supported Brexit; and the American tech moguls Balaji Srinivasan, Marc Andreessen, and Peter Thiel.

I started following Próspera from the outset, expecting, over and over, that it would fail. Honduras was too volatile. The idea was too wacky. The citizens of Roatán, according to news reports, did not seem wild about the prospect. And the people involved seemed, to me at least, to have their heads in the clouds.

Take Patri Friedman, who was responsible for popularizing charter cities in the Bay Area and has raised money from tech founders and venture capitalists. I first spoke to Friedman in 2012, when he was leading the Seasteading Institute, which promoted the development of artificial, floating nation-states on the high seas. We've had several conversations since. Patri is a lively, engaging interlocutor who feels governments should compete for citizens the way companies compete for customers. He is frustrated by the lack of available land and the inflexibility of national sovereignty. I don't share Friedman's political leanings, but I appreciate his willingness to challenge geopolitical orthodoxy. Seasteading is, if nothing else, a brilliant thought experiment for students of geopolitics. That said, it's not particularly practical.

Próspera's finances aren't guaranteed either. Its backers claim to have raised $100 million, which doesn't seem like very much for a project that was being billed as the next Hong Kong. Próspera's adoption of Bitcoin as a currency, which has taken a beating since the development broke ground, added to my skepticism.

On top of all that, the jurisdiction—which was advertised as sustaining itself through registration fees and taxes—at one point resorted to hosting Zoom info sessions and handing out prospectuses to anyone who'd signed up for its emails, to try to rustle up more investment. In a 2023 PowerPoint presentation, it claimed that the city's real estate could generate returns of up to 5,000 percent. It felt a little desperate.

And yet. As of this writing, Próspera has survived political scandals, pandemic-era lockdowns, a barrage of negative press from around the world, a new presidential administration led by the leftist Xiomara Castro, and a constant churn of publicists who, I can attest, specialize in restricting access to Próspera's CEO, a mercurial Venezuelan American named Erick Brimen. It has also made its long-term ambitions clear.

In 2022, Próspera's Delaware-registered parent company filed a $10.7 billion lawsuit with the International Centre for Settlement of Investment Disputes (ICSID), a tribunal overseen by the World Bank, against the state of Honduras, accusing it of violating investor-state treaty obligations. These treaties (of which there are hundreds) and the tribunals that adjudicate them have always been controversial. The basic argument in their favor is that they help poor countries make money by appealing to outside investors who wouldn't otherwise trust those countries' laws. Advocates think of them as an extra layer of security against, say, expropriation: What foreign entrepreneur would open a factory if they thought it could be taken away at a moment's notice?

The argument against this system is that it puts investors' financial interests before those of the host states' by design, encroaching on national sovereignty and democracy and allowing shell corporations to sue entire countries for absurd sums of money. The data also suggests that the resulting projects don't really move the needle on local prosperity.

In 2023, Elizabeth Warren and thirty other U.S. lawmakers criticized the Próspera lawsuit in a letter, and urged the United States to support Honduras over the American plaintiffs "to ensure that such egregious cases can no longer disrupt democratic policymaking by working to eliminate ISDS [investor-state dispute settlement] liability in preexisting agreements in our hemisphere," Warren wrote. Then, in early 2024, Honduras announced it would pull out of the ICSID convention altogether.

Importantly, this does not retroactively kill Próspera's claim against Honduras. Nor does it give the state free rein to expropriate the Roatán development. Jorge Colindres, Próspera's technical secretary—a governor nominated by the developers but officially appointed by the Honduran state—says the jurisdiction's plans to build and grow have not changed.

In the meantime, the fledgling city hosts wellness retreats, cryptocurrency confabs, and a conference on experimental ways to achieve longevity (having solved the problem of taxes, the only thing left, apparently, is death).

Patri Friedman flew down to receive injections of follistatin, a novel form of gene therapy, yet to be approved by the U.S. Food and Drug Administration, that is purported to help muscles grow and to slow the aging process. He told me he was thrilled with the results. The founders of the company offering it, Minicircle, tested it on themselves before turning to Próspera, where taxes are lower and there is no onerous regulatory process as in the United States. ("I am optimistic that it can create an example of what good governance can look like," one of Minicircle's founders told a documentary filmmaker, "but I worry [the founders] can be a bit historically naïve or historically illiterate, and because of that end up perpetuating the same cycles that impact the Third World.")

If Próspera does succumb, I have no doubt that another attempt will pop up somewhere. The seal's been broken. There's no going back.

Which brings me to the second reason why I chose to write about charter cities: for better or worse, in some form or another, I believe that charter cities will exist—and it's incredibly important we get them right. It's easy to imagine a private jurisdiction becoming what amounts to a company town, governed by corporate charter, full of workers who have no say in their plight. History is full of bleak examples: consider Henry Ford's exploits in the Amazon. It's also not hard to see how Próspera could become something akin to a private members' club—Mar-a-Lago for the Silicon Valley set. But in the best of worlds, such a hybrid jurisdiction could represent a new kind of place, with new rules for all people: a temporary, or even a permanent, city of refuge. To cede this territory to rigidly ideological capitalists alone would be a big mistake.

. . .

When Romer initially proposed his charter city concept, he didn't start with anything terribly radical. Rules, he wrote, were important. Good rules encouraged good outcomes, while bad ones did not. Lots of things contributed to a thriving, growing economy: ideas, trade, technology. But without the right rules, innovations were pointless. You can teach a man to fish, but without regulations preventing overfishing, he wouldn't get very far.

In the context of reducing global poverty, though, the principle of new, better rules borrowed from elsewhere got a little more fraught. Ideas are one thing. Rules—which is really to say, governance—are another. "The people who live in the poorest countries on earth are the ones who suffer most obviously from bad rules," Romer wrote. "The most pressing task is to find ways for them to adopt rules that are already known to work much better."

You can see why readers might be offended. In a few short sentences, Romer—the privileged son of a Colorado governor, with an economics PhD from the University of Chicago—implied not only that poor countries had bad governments making the rules, but that it was crucial to change the way those governments went about their business if their citizens were to become less poor.

Romer didn't mean it that way. He acknowledged his blind spot later, in a conversation on the podcast *Freakonomics*. "As anybody, I guess, besides me will notice, this raises all kinds of alarms about colonialism and the history of colonial exploitation in Africa," he told the host. "It had this guilt by association that meant that everybody was a little bit horrified by the suggestion. But I felt like we just needed to talk about how we could try something else in development, because development assistance, frankly, has been a failure."

That "something else" was to separate laws from lands—only voluntarily this time around. As tone-deaf as he may have sounded, Romer came by his theory honestly, building upon his previous academic work on the economics of ideas. Poor countries borrowed technologies from rich countries all the time to everyone's benefit. And ideas, fundamentally, were for sharing. Why not treat *rules* the same way that we treat other kinds of knowledge? Rules can come from all over. They don't even cost money!

"What types of mechanisms will allow developing countries to copy the rules that work well in the rest of the world?" Romer asked.

Romer's charter cities leaned a lot on the example of China, and the way the country had vastly alleviated poverty thanks, in part at least, to experiments with jurisdiction.

Between 1842 and 1997, Hong Kong was administered by the British as a colony, then a dependent territory. The Crown took control after winning the First Opium War in 1842, expanding its footprint through a series of coercive treaties. In the process, the British installed their own rules and laws—everything from which side of the road people drove on to the courts that adjudicated criminal and civil disputes. This mix of foreign and domestic encouraged Westerners to open shops and businesses, and even move there. It also pushed Chinese people to "opt in" to this new system from over the border. As the city prospered, so did they.

Hong Kong's success inspired the nearby city of Shenzhen, which, under Deng Xiaoping's 1978 Reform and Opening-Up Policy, granted dispensations to let foreign firms and individuals enjoy a more market-based system, with fewer restrictions on trade and immigration than in the rest of the country. There, Romer's narrative repeated itself: new rules, new opportunities, new people, more money.

Nothing's that simple, of course—not least Chinese economic history. The scholar Taomo Zhou has shown that Shenzhen's open system took root somewhat more organically, as residents themselves seized opportunities for cross-border arbitrage and exchange during the Mao era. When Juan Du, an architecture scholar at the University of Toronto, began her own inquiry into the same question, she was so stunned at the discrepancy between the myth of Shenzhen—the old "fishing village" bit—and the city's reality that she ended up writing a whole book about it.

"After more than a decade of scholarly research, architectural projects, and community engagements in the city, I am convinced that this coherent story is less a factual account of the city's evolution than it is a founding myth," she writes in *The Shenzhen Experiment* (2020), noting that her use of Chinese- as well as English-language sources complicated the conventional narrative. "Shenzhen's early developmental history was fraught with political oppositions, policy uncertainties, economic setbacks, and vicious cultural criticism. Its development did not follow the central planning process directed by Beijing; rather, in a struggle to thrive, the city inadvertently challenged top-down policies and drastically altered centralized planning. Much of the city's subsequent unexpected exponential growth was enabled through local initiatives, bottom-up ingenuities, and unanticipated or informal urban processes." (We'll return to the myth of Shenzhen later in the book.)

There are other complexities here too. Hong Kong was a notorious center for sweatshops at the beginning of its ascent, and Shenzhen followed its lead. These freer-market economies did not make people particularly free. To enter Shenzhen, even as a Chinese citizen, you had to produce a passport and a visa until 2006. Finally, China's recent political interventions in Hong Kong show how vulnerable a special zone is when concessions depend entirely on the goodwill of a greater power. In 2020, a new national security law gave Beijing's security services open access to the city. It also tasked Hong Kong's chief executive, Carrie Lam, to personally decide which judges would sit on politically sensitive cases. Then antiestablishment candidates were barred from running in local elections. Journalists were arrested, dissidents were imprisoned, and expatriates began leaving the city, worried about their personal freedoms and their children's education. Two foreign judges who sat on Hong Kong's high court—a relic of the British system that is largely credited with attracting foreign business—even quit their posts in the aftermath of the law's passing. While their official reasons were personal, in statements to the press they obliquely referred to how much power they would have. "The jury is out on how they will be able to operate under the new national security law," Baroness Brenda Hale, the former president of the British Supreme Court, told journalists.

This was hardly the unified, neutral, independent court system that residents—and adjudicators—had been promised. Businesses would likely continue enjoying the same legal treatment as they had for two decades— but the humans of Hong Kong could suddenly find themselves playing by a different set of rules. (We'll return to the question of commercial courts in chapter 6.)

Whether Hong Kong is a good example or not, Paul Romer was right in one important respect when he held up Shenzhen as a model charter city: no gunboats or unequal treaties compelled the People's Republic of China to build it. The pressures were internal: China was, at this point in its history, coming out of the Cultural Revolution unbelievably poor. And any external influences, as we've seen in the previous chapter, seeped in through international organizations and management consultants.

Shenzhen and two other Chinese SEZs ended up becoming part of an initiative for the country to open its economy incrementally, experimentally, and in a controlled setting—another hack to have it both ways. And they delivered. The World Bank economist Douglas Zeng estimated in 2010 that China's special zones were responsible for almost a quarter of China's GDP, almost half of foreign direct investment, 60 percent of exports, and more than thirty million jobs.

For Romer, this (admittedly potted) narrative shows how a new city with good rules for all people could, if designed with broader reforms in mind, raise wages and living standards not just inside but outside the zone.

But Romer has also been thinking about how such a city might help what he sees as the world's most pressing challenge: migration. Indeed, one of the overlooked reasons Shenzhen was able to grow so fast was its ability to welcome millions of migrant laborers from other parts of the country, who, because of internal gatekeeping, would have had a much harder time settling elsewhere. Now, on a global scale, "there's billions of people that

want to leave the jurisdictions they're in," Romer told me. "And our traditional answer—oh, no, stay there, the World Bank will fix it—we haven't
had any success at all." (Romer would know about the organization: he used
to work there.)

"We have democracies that clearly do not want to accept large numbers
of migrants. And if you support democracy, that's kind of the end of that
discussion," he went on. "You can moralize all you want, but that's the deal.
So the thing that a special jurisdiction could do—this is the only mechanism
I can see where you can arguably create a space where people could go."

The logistics of such a zone, per Romer, would look something like this:
A new development, built in a sparsely populated area in country A, would
be governed from afar by democratic country B, and welcome migrants
from countries C, D, E, and so on. It would be a large city—most migrants,
Romer points out, want to move to cities—and it would accommodate, say,
ten million people from around the world who, for whatever reason, could
not remain where they were.

There would be no elections, at least not initially. Democratic control
would kick in only when the city reached its full capacity and no longer
needed to welcome outsiders. Otherwise, Romer believes, the entire mission
would be thwarted by popular demands. "What will happen is the million
people who are already there will . . . through their democratic voice, stop
any further migration," he says.

And that's the rub. "If you're creating a brand-new jurisdiction, there's
probably three things that most of us would support. One is equal treatment
under the law. The second is openness to mass migration, because that's what
we're trying to address here. And the third is local democratic decision-
making," he said. "You can have two out of those three, but you can't have all
three. And I think equal treatment under the law is much more important."

Alexander Betts and Paul Collier, both veteran migration experts, have
proposed that countries deploy special economic zones funded (if not governed) by rich countries, where refugees and migrants can legally work.

The zones would not be in the West, but closer to the areas people are leaving—in the Middle East, Africa, Central America. The objective would be to give refugees a chance to earn a living in a safe place, while avoiding populist backlash spurred by perceptions of newcomers "stealing" jobs or draining resources in host countries, as currently happens.

Existing refugee camps established to accommodate people on the move typically offer few job prospects, and asylum seekers who run the bureaucratic gauntlet in the West often wait months upon months before getting work permits and papers. A third kind of place would split the difference, the reasoning goes, and give people more agency, if not total freedom.

In 2016, a pilot program organized by the World Bank, NGOs, European nations, and the Jordanian government tried to put some of Collier's and Betts's ideas into action. It was a modest attempt: rather than creating a new jurisdiction entirely, European nations offered concessions on imports to Jordanian factories whose workforce was at least 15 percent Syrian. It looked more like Mauritius in the 1970s than Romer's dream metropolis. Overall, the results were mixed: the rules were perceived as murky, the employment options far too limited, and the factories simply too far from where most of the Syrian workers actually lived.

Between this tepid result and the bigger problem of maintaining a separate refugee population, it is easy to denounce these ideas as useless, undemocratic, or worse. I've deliberately chosen to read them generously because I agree with their authors on a key point: that to solve global problems in ways that help ordinary people, not just their governments or multinational corporations, we need to be less hidebound to rigid notions of sovereignty, territoriality, and jurisdiction. The system we have—a "vestige of the postwar international system," as Betts and Collier put it—is outdated. When people come up against borders, the border always wins.

Charter cities or free zones for refugees have their share of problems. Their proponents tend to rely on an essentially capitalist, market-oriented logic of putting people to productive work, rather than a more welfare-based regime of letting them in. The plans elide political and social problems, offering a quick fix when there can be no such thing. And rather than tear down borders, they build new ones. "The landscape of refugeedom," Laura Robson writes in *Human Capital: A History of Putting Refugees to Work*, is "one in which international aid agencies publicly declared their commitment to refugee education, gainful employment, and economic autonomy, while refugees themselves were increasingly hemmed in by camps, border guards, checkpoints, and barbed wire."

At the same time, when you consider the tested options for would-be migrants, the drawbacks of a potential charter city or zone start to look like a somewhat lesser evil. The ferocity with which the United States, the EU, and Australia have resisted newcomers is only growing; as we'll see in later chapters, these countries are already using extraterritorial workarounds to warehouse people offshore. The existing hacks—which include the United States' "remain in Mexico" program, the EU's migrant pushbacks, and Australia's use of offshore island prisons—were conceived not to benefit migrant populations but to keep people out, help nationalists win elections, and preserve the ethnolinguistic status quo.

Charter cities ultimately achieve similar ends: they are not, and never will be, a fast track to more open and cosmopolitan societies. Still, they may offer an alternative to the limited, depressing, dangerous options on offer, and in the longer term could even save lives.

We know this because we've been here before.

In 1944, the *New York Post* published a series of columns entitled "Free Ports for Refugees" by the writer Samuel Grafton. Grafton, a contemporary of I. F. Stone, had been following news about America's first SEZ, Foreign-Trade Zone 1, for some time. He'd observed as crates of goods arrived in the duty-free entrepôt on Staten Island and sat in storage largely undisturbed before making their way back out into the world. Why not apply this same courtesy to safeguard millions of European refugees?

"We do it in commercial ports for cases of beans so that we can make some storage and processing profits," Grafton wrote, deadpan. "It should not be impossible to do it for people."

The context for his column, of course, was the Nazis' mass extermination of European Jews—and the American government's unwillingness to take more of them in. Grafton was conscious of the way xenophobes and anti-Semites had set the terms of the debate, so that human lives were bartered with absurd workarounds normally reserved for merchandise. He lamented this fact. But the time for moralizing was long past. "If we can use a legal fiction to make a dollar, we ought to be able to use a similar legal fiction to save a life," Grafton concluded. He wasn't joking. Though he wasn't *not* joking either.

I learned about Grafton's writings thanks to Dara Orenstein, a professor of American Studies at George Washington University and the author of an excellent history of the warehouse, *Out of Stock*. Orenstein made the discovery while conducting archival research for her dissertation, and she was as surprised as I was to learn that the columns ended up being part of a far-reaching public debate that had made it all the way to Franklin Delano Roosevelt's White House.

Perhaps most surprising—at least, in retrospect—was the fact that the people proposing such human freeports in the press and in the government weren't profit-minded businessmen or bigoted members of Congress. They were Jewish lawyers and activists passionate about social justice and grasping for ways to alleviate a humanitarian emergency. Among them were Felix Cohen, a lawyer at the Department of the Interior who became well known for his advocacy on behalf of Native American tribal sovereignty, and his colleague Nathan Margold, who in the 1930s was a staff attorney for the NAACP when the civil rights organization challenged the segregationist "separate but equal" doctrine.

Samuel Grafton was born Samuel Lipshutz to immigrants of Lithuanian origin. The Popular Front, an anti-fascist group of illustrators, writers, and actors, also took up the cause. The artists even put on a proto–Live Aid "concert and drama dedicated to free ports for refugees" at Manhattan's Town Hall, with appearances by Paul Robeson, Sam Jaffe, and Canada Lee. Xenophobic neoliberal anti-Semites they were not.

On the legal side of things, advocates on President Roosevelt's newly launched War Refugee Board (WRB) had been handed the impossible task of figuring out where to put displaced people whom nobody seemed to want around. It was difficult to change the law, so the agency began to deconstruct it and to think critically about where, to whom, and in what circumstances it might not apply. This way of thinking followed the logic of the modern-day tax attorney, only instead of using loopholes to save money, they sought to save people.

Legal fictions thus became "conceptual tools designed to achieve concrete ends," Orenstein writes in an unpublished paper on the subject. In the suspended nonspace of a special jurisdiction, advocates hoped to forge a brighter path for humanity—or, at the very least, prevent thousands upon thousands of avoidable deaths.

The lawyers first looked to the nation's peripheries: namely Alaska and the U.S. Virgin Islands, which encompassed St. Thomas, one of the original freeports under Danish rule before it was sold to the United States in 1917. The Caribbean islands could be repurposed as a "transit station" and serve humanity the way they had served traders. Jews might not be so unwelcome as homesteaders in the frozen north—"an Arctic substitute for Palestine" is how Orenstein puts it (this is the premise of the Michael Chabon novel *The Yiddish Policemen's Union*). Or, indeed, the U.S naval base on Guantánamo Bay might serve as a temporary haven.

The WRB also looked into ways to bring Jews over not as immigrants but as temporary contract laborers—again, not a permanent solution, but nonetheless a way to wait out Hitler's assaults. In the archives of the 1939

World's Fair—itself a designated foreign-trade zone that could import foreign exhibition materials duty-free—Orenstein found a folder containing "dozens of letters from Europeans, mostly Jews, who had hoped to participate in the fair in order to obtain U.S. visas and thereby flee Nazism."

The Alaska proposal got some attention from Congress, but ultimately it didn't go anywhere. The Virgin Islands plan didn't even get that far. The idea was too weird for politicians, who were trying desperately to appease conservatives. It also drew scorn from left-wing writers, who denounced it for the very reasons Grafton had anticipated: that it treated people like merchandise, or worse. And it's true that "Freeports for Jews" (or anyone, really) don't challenge xenophobic immigration quotas or change the law. They're a Band-Aid for a bullet hole.

The campaign, was, however, a hit with the American public. The War Refugee Board "was inundated with mail about the prospect of 'Free Ports for Human Lives,' ranging from telegrams and handwritten notes, to mimeographed petitions and boilerplate cards," Orenstein writes.

FDR himself was even backed into addressing the proposal at a press conference. He did not like the name, he said, but the idea held water. Roosevelt went as far as to authorize the War Relocation Authority to bring 982 refugees from European refugee camps onto U.S. soil, into a special jurisdiction in upstate New York called Fort Ontario. These were the only recognized refugees (still a relatively new category of person, under international law) to land on U.S. soil.

Fort Ontario was spatially confusing. Were babies born in Fort Ontario U.S. citizens? Were laborers eligible for workers' comp? How would its denizens "emigrate" to the "onshore" United States after the war ended? ("They were laundered through Canada," writes Orenstein.)

Living conditions were pretty ugly too—all barbed-wire fencing and military barracks. Was it a haven, or was it a camp? Residents went with "golden cage."

Meanwhile, ordinary immigration channels during the war gave roughly two hundred thousand people the chance to leave Europe and settle in the United States. This was more than any other country, but nowhere near enough. Of the many hundreds of thousands more who'd applied for American visas, just a tiny fraction received them. Waiting lists for visas were routinely unfilled, and many didn't get the chance to apply in the first place due to embassy closures, a lack of paperwork, and wartime chaos. In a particularly callous moment, U.S. immigration authorities turned away more than nine hundred passengers arriving in Miami on the MS *St. Louis*. A quarter of them would die in the Holocaust.

Fort Ontario was an imperfect solution for a terrible time. Nobody fleeing war or persecution should be treated like a convict and kept behind bars. And yet the greater tragedy in retrospect is that so many more didn't get the chance.

So here we are, nearly a century later, in a world full of war and racism and increasing environmental threats to people's lives and livelihoods: crop failures, soil erosion, drought, and so on. The aftermath of colonialism has displaced millions, and the realities of nationalism make the problem worse. Perhaps it is time to try something new.

Lan Cao is a law professor at Chapman University who has written in support of charter city–style proposals, both as an economic development tool and as an alternative to the refugee camp. As a child, Cao was herself brought to the United States after having to flee Saigon, and she told me that the experience informed her views on the issue. "My migration was very unexpected and traumatic for me. And I would have preferred not to have migrated," she said over the phone in 2021. "But since I've done it, I've grown to be comfortable and welcoming of hybridity. I think of what Salman Rushdie called himself—a mongrel! I welcome mongrelism and hybridity."

Cao extends the same principle to the law. "We are not in the eighteenth century, where the Western powers are carving up the world. This is a post–World War II, human rights universe," she says.

I have written at length in support of open borders. More than anything, I believe people should be allowed to live where they want to live, whether it's in their ancestral village or in a megacity halfway across the world. I think national and international policies should make either option economically feasible. Few people, and fewer policymakers, share my views.

In fact, most politicians would prefer people stay where they are. But they can't, and won't—and to keep people safe, fed, clothed, and healthy, to house people in the event of environmental disasters, and to insulate families from the cruel calculus of nationalistic electoral campaigns, we're going to need more creative, accommodating, and generous rules than those on offer by the 192 nation-states of the world. Nations have failed us, but they also rule the world. Maybe, done right, a charter city could provide a much-needed alternative.

This may mean giving existing cities that want more migrants the leeway to grant foreigners legal residency—a power traditionally reserved for federal governments. It could mean building new cities or towns from the ground up and letting people in until they are full. Some of these places will be temporary by design—a stopgap, like Port Ontario. It is important that these places don't become glorified prisons. It will be crucial to decide this ahead of time, so that people do not languish the way they have in offshore detention camps from Guantánamo to Micronesia (which we will see in chapters 8 and 9).

This world-building endeavor will require acts of imagination from us all. We must begin to understand ourselves as citizens of a nation, of the world, and, increasingly, of the places in between. This means extending humanity, decency, and optimism into places they have not always ventured: places for money, and things, but not people. These are places where any of us might end up. Can we claim them for our own?

6.

The City and the City

All that is solid melts into air.

—KARL MARX

The Dubai International Financial Center (DIFC) contains a universe of its own making.

Geographically, it occupies 110 acres of prime real estate across dozens of buildings in the center of Dubai.

Legally, it is a free zone overseen by a board appointed by the city-state's ruler, with its own bespoke laws drawn up for the benefit of international business. More than 5,500 companies are registered in the DIFC as of this writing: some with tangible connections to the emirate, others mere letterboxes exploiting advantageous regulations. Others still have chosen the DIFC not as their administrative domicile but as their jurisdictional one: the companies are owned and operated abroad, but they prefer to have their day in court here. The court itself doesn't know how many of these "opt-ins" there are—it hears from them only in the event of a dispute.

Their presence gives the DIFC a metaphysical aspect: the center is a portal between a conservative Gulf petrostate and the world beyond. If traditional freeports have for centuries served to store physical commodities, and industrial ones transform these materials from raw to finished, then the

DIFC represents the zone's next mutation: a place where wealth, long removed from its source, goes to defy the laws of time and space.

The DIFC is also a shimmering shopping center with three hotels, luxury apartment towers, high-end restaurants, clothing stores, spas, beauty salons, and art galleries. There's even a house of worship: the markets sleep at night, but the DIFC Grand Mosque is open 24–7.

All that makes the DIFC yet another thing: a microcosm of a world where we will someday all live. This is a world where boundaries are drawn not just around nations but around people and companies and wealth; where cities themselves grow increasingly segregated by income, class, status; and where the lines between the personal, the political, the commercial, and even the spiritual realms blur.

This world will produce new kinds of states, new kinds of laws, new kinds of gods, and new kinds of borders. Dubai is a test case for where they will take us.

The cornerstone of the DIFC is a gigantic rectangular gate inspired by the Arc de Triomphe. It looks much like the Parisian landmark, had the French chosen to commemorate their war dead with millions of gray Legos. Dubai has long distinguished itself by building wacky, tacky, incredible things: a building in the shape of a sailboat, a reclaimed archipelago shaped like a map of the world, a ski slope in a mall in the desert. In comparison, the Dubai Gate is practically muted—business formal to its city's cocktail attire. So when it began to court tenants, in 2002, the DIFC seemed a fitting place from which "to position Dubai as the regional gateway for the flow of capital and investment into and out of the region," to quote its then CEO.

The legal blueprint for the financial center came in 2004. From Abu Dhabi, capital of the United Arab Emirates, then UAE president Sheikh Zayed bin Sultan Al Nahyan changed the national constitution to allow free zones geared toward the exchange not of material goods but of financial assets such as stocks, bonds, and derivatives. Emirati residents had no say in the development, but they don't get a say in much. Citizens constitute barely 12 percent of the autocracy's population; foreigners—from the impoverished migrant workers who likely built the Gate to the billionaires who would trade in it—make up the rest.

What mattered most was that the idea appealed to Sheikh Maktoum bin Rashid Al Maktoum, Dubai's ruler at the time, who, following his father, presided over the city's rise from sun and sand to glass and steel. Dubai's founding myth—that its business-minded rulers transformed it from a mere fishing village to a financial behemoth over a few short decades—is a lot like Shenzhen's and Singapore's. (What is it with capitalists and their fishing villages?) The narrative has been gobbled up and spat out relentlessly by corporate interests, journalists at *The Wall Street Journal* and the *Financial Times*, and the state itself. Never mind that all the cities in question were for centuries outposts for colonial and regional trade, local culture, and political traditions. Free trade was a much more convenient explanation.

In 2004, Sheikh Maktoum signed Law No. 9, and the Dubai International Financial Center was born. In a part of the world that had been hemorrhaging money to wars, civil unrest, and geopolitical shocks, the DIFC promised businesses an oasis of protection and deregulation: a little Switzerland on the Gulf. The center's tenants—who would come to include Bloomberg, Deutsche Bank, JPMorgan, and Goldman Sachs—would benefit from concessions including huge corporate tax breaks, fully foreign ownership of companies, and expedited immigration procedures for expat workers.

But Dubai couldn't stop there. After all, those who wanted Switzerland already had Switzerland—and Luxembourg, and the Caymans, and any number of places that exacted little or nothing in taxes and had long track records in protecting wealth at all costs. So to entice investors further, the DIFC sold them on something else: law.

Law is no static thing. It does not sprout from the soil, like a tree. It doesn't require a particular habitat to thrive, like a bug or a bird. It behaves more like a virus, hopping from place to place, cultivating new hosts and carriers, and mutating along the way.

Nor is the letter of the law preordained. When corporations and people sign contracts, they typically agree whose rules to apply should a dispute arise. To meet demand, plenty of big cities—London, Paris, Singapore, Hong Kong, among others—have arbitration centers staffed with experts where such disputes are settled privately, and largely outside their country's national court systems. In arbitration, the judges are not public employees but private arbitrators typically chosen by the litigants. Records are usually kept private; the location, awards, and other details may vary from case to case. (This is not the case for criminal offenses—murders, assaults, and so on—which are almost always prosecuted in the public courts according to their location. In the United States, jurisdiction also depends on whether the laws deemed to have been violated are federal, state, tribal, or local.)

Dubai already had one of these arbitration centers, so in 2005 it took the idea even further. That year, the DIFC opened a start-up court to oversee civil and commercial matters within the zone. Its laws came from elsewhere. So did its judges. And its plaintiffs. And its defendants. The result was a state within a state within a state, or, to borrow from a DIFC publication, "another example of how globalisation is reconfiguring the relationship between legal institutions and political systems in the twenty-first century."

There was nothing Dubai about it. This made it a quintessentially Dubai thing.

Legal pluralism—the maintenance of multiple systems of law within a given territory—wasn't a new concept to the residents and rulers of Dubai at the beginning of our century. Until 1971, Dubai and its sister emirates had been British protectorates, with one set of rules for non-Muslim subjects and another for natives and believers. After achieving independence, the new nation-state set out to build a devolved judicial system that allowed each emirate to strike out on its own, or to live by federal rules instead.

From a judicial standpoint, the UAE had more in common with the federalism of the United States than with a centralized system. But no matter the emirate, court hearings were in Arabic and rooted in Islamic jurisprudence as well as civil law—a tradition that leans heavily on codes, written rules, and doctrine written by national legislators and scholars, as opposed to common law, which dominates the anglophone world.

This, Sheikh Maktoum and his advisers realized, was a problem: to put it crudely, Westerners did not want to deal with Muslim courts.

They cast around and quickly learned that while a free zone with low taxes and minimal red tape was all very well and good, foreign firms wanted a familiar legal system in which to litigate things like bankruptcy, data protection, intellectual property, and employment. That was an advantage Mauritius had: its highest appeals court remains the Judicial Committee of the Privy Council, a London common law tribunal that issues final rulings for courts in twenty-seven previously or presently British-influenced places.

Grafting on an identically British system would be too close to colonialism for comfort. So Dubai sought another, better way. To stitch together a composite jurisdiction, with regulations borrowed from elsewhere and judges trained in the laws of the world, the DIFC would need its own Victor Frankenstein.

He came to them by chance, in the form of a blue-eyed Englishman named Mark Beer.

I met Beer on a late spring day in 2022 at Sarabeth's, a power-breakfast spot just south of Manhattan's Central Park. I was struck, surprised even, by his geniality. Beer comes off as game and unpretentious, a dad of five who looks like he might be big into rugby and, well, beer. "We went last night to a restaurant called Daniel, the Daniel, around there?" he fairly gushed, sounding more like an eager tourist than an Officer of the British Empire, a title he received from Queen Elizabeth in 2013. "It's absolutely incredible, it's really fantastic. But it isn't cheap!" At Sarabeth's, he ordered an omelet with hot sauce and home fries—not Boulud, but not bad.

These days, Beer is the chairman of a consulting firm called the Metis Institute that advises free zones, governments, judiciaries, and more. He has an eccentric streak: he moonlights as the justice minister of an experimental new nation that has no landmass but rather "lives" on a satellite (more on that later). Beer riffed on law, Plato, outer space, and babies with the same cheerful ease, plowing through his omelet as he deftly dodged questions he'd sooner not answer and barely batting an eye when I nursed my four-week-old infant in his carrier. It was easy for me to picture Beer charming mercurial autocrats and profit-minded executives into starting a court from scratch, only in a custom Ascots & Chapels suit instead of red chinos and a blue rugby shirt. It was hard not to be enthused by his brimming enthusiasm.

Beer began his legal career as a teenager, working as a bag carrier—literally—at a solicitor's office during summers in Birmingham. He went on to read jurisprudence at Oxford, earned a law degree at York, and trained as a mediator in Singapore. In the mid-1990s, Beer worked for a stint in Dubai, but he cut his teeth in Switzerland, at an investment firm in the low-tax canton of Schwyz in the early 2000s. In 2003, Beer returned to the Gulf state to take a job as an in-house lawyer for Mastercard.

As Dubai grew up, up, and out, and began opening specialized business zones—Media City, with nominally freer speech laws than the rest of the country enjoyed; Healthcare City, with technical accommodations for hospitals; and Internet City, where Mastercard is based—Beer began to think more expansively about how laws affect economies. For most of his career, he had operated under the same assumption as his classically trained lawyer peers (and really, most of the people around him): that ever since the world had been organized into a map of discrete decolonized nation-states, laws and lands had become inextricable. "I'd had blinkers on," he told me. But as he spent more and more time in the private sector, he began to think of law—of *justice*—quite differently: of legal systems "not just as a tool for fairness, but as a tool for economic development."

These ideas took on a concreteness for Beer in 2006, when he met Nasser Saidi, the DIFC's then chief economist, and heard him talk about Dubai's free zones. "He spoke about economic zones not as beautiful buildings and the like, which was the sales pitch at the time, but in terms of the reasons they exist and opportunities they offer," Beer recalled. "And as I heard him talk, it made me think about the justice sector within a zone, and what it's for."

Saidi, a former Lebanese policymaker, went as far as to call the DIFC a "Vatican of international finance," comparing the center's authority over its little fiefdom to the pope's in Rome. The analogy can easily be pushed further. What is the DIFC if not a microsovereignty embedded in a global city, insulated from the broader political environment while serving the interests of a group of powerful men who believe they represent a higher power—in this case, the market?

But Beer was in the business of law, not divinity. "What I appreciated was that the role of courts was simply to provide confidence," he says. "I don't think anyone was that fussed about principles of the rule of law. They realized for the zones to be successful, investors needed to have confidence. In order to have confidence, they needed to feel that their promises would be honored. And they wanted to do that in a familiar environment—hence the establishment of that court."

Law, in other words, was not just men in robes codifying the values of a society. It was more like a blueprint for prosperity that could be planted and replanted at will: rootless, cosmopolitan, and highly portable.

During that period, Beer found himself in another chance encounter, with the DIFC court's chief justice, Sir Anthony Evans. Evans was a highly regarded commercial and maritime lawyer who'd had a long career as an appeals judge in the UK before leaving to sit on Bermuda's high court in 2003. Because of their countries' shared legal systems, dating back to colonial times, judges from Commonwealth countries can easily work in many sister courts, and may be offered cushy secondments after retirement. Such women and men make up a small class of elite legal professionals known as traveling judges, hopping from jurisdiction to jurisdiction (each with seemingly better weather than the last) to rule on specialized commercial cases. Most of the time, they are asked to serve because of their expertise, or to pick up the slack in places where there might be few candidates available for the task. They "are sometimes said to enhance the international reputation of the host state" for appearing impartial and unbeholden to the government, writes Fordham law professor Pamela Bookman.

The DIFC saw the value in hiring these tried-and-tested judges—to inspire confidence in their system, mainly—so one of its key bylaws allowed these foreigners to serve. In 2005, Sheikh Maktoum hired Evans as the court's first chief justice alongside Michael Hwang, a Singaporean judge, to serve as his deputy. In 2008, six more colleagues joined from Malaysia, the UK, New Zealand, and the "onshore" UAE.

Only Evans did not move to Dubai, exactly; some of the time, he got "beamed in" from London, as he put it in a speech (all while insisting how important it was that the world understands "the Court sits in Dubai, even if before a 'virtual judge'"). Long before the COVID-19 pandemic forced so many businesses online, a permanent physical presence in Dubai was not a requirement for the philosopher-kings of the DIFC: it was expected that many would live seminomadic lifestyles, jetting between residences, countries, and jurisdictions. Traveling judges didn't need to speak Arabic or have much training in local laws to do their job. They were to behave a bit like mercenaries, only instead of waging war, they would decide the fates of distressed businesses and feuding counterparties.

When Evans and Beer first met, Beer recalls, Evans said he was looking for a competent administrator to deal with the day-to-day work of running the new court. "But I was suggesting if he wanted to be one of the leading commercial courts in the world, it's more than turning up on a Wednesday and doing six hours of work," Beer told me in a video conversation from his residence in Oxford, England, a vintage James Bond poster peering over his shoulder. "And he said, 'If you know so much about it, why don't you do it?'"

Beer had been struggling to split his time between his work and his growing family. After a particularly grueling business trip that took him to Latin America by way of London and New York in the span of a few days, he was ready to jump ship—so long as it didn't actually involve getting on one. "The DIFC then was a domestic play, so not a lot of traveling," he remarked. "I could go home in the evening and not be thinking about my next flight to New York or wherever it might be."

Beyond that, he was eager to finally put some of his bigger ideas about the law into action. Perhaps he could even make his mark on the world. "What I find most fascinating is the broken system and why we allowed it to break," he told me, referring to the generalized state of political dysfunction in the world in May 2022.

"What is likely to create better systems? It's not going to be reforming. It's got to be something else."

Mark Beer took over the post of registrar in 2008. Until then, the court had gone about its work relatively quietly. "They were just trying to figure out who they were and what type of cases they'd hear," says Jayanth Krishnan, a professor of law at Indiana University and the author of a monograph on the court's history. Most were disputes that took place within the compound itself, between tenants.

Beer's mandate was to make the DIFC the go-to place for business in the region. His vision was not confined to the boundaries of the Gate; he pictured the DIFC as a jurisdiction open to the whole world, where anyone could opt in to its familiar and efficient rules and regulations. But just as he was finding his feet, the global financial crisis brought the world to its knees—and took Dubai World, the city-state's equivalent of a sovereign wealth fund, down with it.

Before the crash, Dubai World employed one hundred thousand people working in real estate, shipping, and logistics, spread over some two hundred subsidiary companies. It operated free zones and ports around the world, managing the movement of ships and their cargo at the intersection of land and sea. One of its subsidiaries made headlines when it took over from a British company in 2006 and began servicing twenty-one American ports. The move rankled U.S. politicians, who worried loudly about forfeiting national sovereignty to an Arab state–owned corporation. The company has made a less noisy but arguably bigger splash in taking over a series of ports in East and West Africa during the last decade.

The holding company also had large real estate investments and dabbled in hotels, tourism, and private equity. It was huge—which, in the aftermath of the crisis, translated to almost $60 billion in debts that neither the parent company nor its offspring could repay on time.

The firm's creditors came knocking, of course. To put their minds at ease and save its business-forward reputation, Dubai did something radical: it assembled a team of outside advisers to establish a brand-new insolvency tribunal, to be run by three DIFC judges. In December 2009, the tribunal opened its doors to any of Dubai World's creditors, regardless of where they conducted their business, to figure out how they could be repaid. The idea was to consolidate all the cases under one roof.

Despite the complexities of the individual cases, the court fulfilled its purpose: to show the world it could be counted on to hear them fairly and impartially. In the end, the verdicts were split almost equally, half for Dubai-owned entities and half against, and the company was able to stay afloat thanks to these new agreements (and a rather large bailout from Abu Dhabi). A court located in Dubai could be trusted to rule fairly and heed the advice of foreign experts, even though its unelected ruler had a financial interest in the outcome of the litigation.

In the process, the new court broke the territorial seal. All kinds of parties showed up to file claims, from New York City hedge funds to local contractors. The new court allowed this, on the grounds that a Dubai firm owed the claimants money. "The judges were clearly independent and agnostic as to who owed the money and were quite happy to award damages and costs and all sorts of things against the government," says Beer, who was part of the team that assembled the bankruptcy tribunal. (The tribunal was formally closed in 2022.)

Thus, out of the ashes of the world economy, he got his wish: the DIFC's courts were now open to all. In 2011, the DIFC began letting parties outside its walls choose to have their cases handled by its court. If you and I were to enter into a contract today, we, too, could take a future dispute to the tribunal, even if neither of us ever had any intention of visiting Dubai. All we'd need would be to agree to it in writing and pay a fee—but the sooner we came to an agreement, the less we'd pay. All in the name of speed and efficiency.

The court's YouTube channel offers an intimate look at these proceedings. Around eight hundred videos immortalize hearings on severance payments, bankruptcies, and contractual disputes. Legal jargon and formalities are interspersed with familiar Zoom-era intrigue: who's on mute, whose camera is malfunctioning, what a certain judge has on the walls of her home office. I sat through hours of these archives, waiting for something telling or representative, but was nearly lulled to sleep by lawyers talking. Contracts, as it turns out, are pretty boring.

Then I came across a news item from 2016. The center's triumphal Gate had suffered a breach—but under whose jurisdiction, nobody could quite say.

The year prior, a marble slab had fallen, as though from the heavens, from the Gate's south-facing cladding onto the walkway below. The DIFC sued Brookfield, the Gate's real estate developer, alleging shoddy workmanship that was "common and widespread" and could thus pose further threats to life: the area where the stone had fallen was a popular place for events and ceremonies.

Investigations were conducted. Lawyers got involved. But none of this took place in the new courts. The DIFC itself took its troubles to the "onshore" courts of Dubai.

Whatever the reasoning—incorporation dates were mentioned—this was hardly a show of confidence in the DIFC's new courts. (It also raised a more philosophical question: Are a city's gates inside or outside its limits? To whom does a border—a line—even belong?)

Brookfield sought an order to stop the proceedings, contending that the case ought to be heard where it took place: not in *Dubai* Dubai, but DIFC Dubai, per the original arbitration agreement. The English judge at the DIFC courts, Sir Jeremy Cooke, agreed with this assessment but declined to issue an order preventing the "onshore" lawsuit from carrying on (a separate lawsuit in 2020 went the distance and led to the DIFC judge successfully thwarting an onshore case). The question, the judge wrote, was whether the dispute must be resolved "in DIFC or in non-DIFC Dubai."

The parties ended up in the DIFC after all, but handled their dispute privately, in its arbitration division. The Gate was repaired, the parties appeased. And in the process, legal fiction became legal fact. It was on the record that there was not one but two Dubais.

The episode made me think of China Miéville's *The City & the City*, a science fiction novel whose protagonist, a detective named Tyador Borlú, flits between his hometown of Besźel and its mirror image, Ul Quoman. Each city has a distinct topography and unique customs while occupying the same geographical space. Tyador spends much of the novel investigating a murder before capitulating and joining Breach, the silent, liminal police force that maintains this jurisdictional duality. "My task is changed: not to uphold the law, or another law, but to maintain the skin that keeps law in place," Tyador says. "Two laws in two places, in fact."

The detective explains, "We are all philosophers here where I am, and we debate among many other things the question of where it is that we live. On that issue I am a liberal. I live in the interstice yes, but I live in both the city and the city."

On the surface, such a court might seem like a nice thing for Dubai to have—a little strange, sure, but befitting a city full of migrants and expatriates. There aren't any real losers in these trials, because to be in a position to file a claim in the DIFC in the first place is to be, by definition, in a position of privilege. This is not a venue for the overworked Filipina housekeepers, the trafficked Moldovan escorts, the injured Bangladeshi laborers on whose backs Dubai has been built. Even the court's small claims division is largely white collar.

At the same time, Dubai's newest court reveals something more troubling: that law itself has become a commodity. The stakes here are not about unfair trials or crooked judges; the victims aren't the plaintiffs or the defendants, whether they win or lose. What the DIFC court has done is set a new standard in play: to accommodate the needs of foreign firms, multinationals, and expatriates, countries must offer them a separate system of justice, imported from elsewhere. And when the wealthy turn to offshore courts of law, bringing their fees and lawyers with them, the onshore system takes a hit too.

Beer acknowledges that the court's decoupling of land and law could strike a Western observer as strange, even sacrilegious. In theory, he says, "a foreign-language, foreign-system court in a jurisdiction was [not] a decision any sovereign would take lightly, especially where that system's entirely independent of his or her control." But in this case, the sovereign had invited the court in. In fact, he was very happy to hand off cumbersome commercial cases to outsiders, especially if it meant making more money. "The classic model in an autocracy is that all levels of government know what the [party] line is," Beer continued—but at the DIFC, the benefits of having such a court "was worth more than kowtowing to any decision the ruler wanted to make."

What this also means is that it no longer makes much sense to speak of only a law of the land: the two have, in the modern parlance, consciously uncoupled. The law no longer has a particular connection to the place it happens to govern; it is in Dubai, but not of Dubai. (Demographically speaking, Dubai itself is not exactly of Dubai either.)

Once the court was up and running, the DIFC began exporting its court-in-a-box product to other jurisdictions. In 2008, economist Nasser Saidi proclaimed that "we have been approached by countries as far away as the Caribbean and Latin America and Korea and Africa to establish DIFC clones." Indeed, by 2023, independent commercial courts had popped up all over the place: in Abu Dhabi, Qatar, Benin, Kosovo, Iraq, the Netherlands, France, and Kazakhstan, where Mark Beer would lead the charge once again.

When it comes to seducing capitalists, Kazakhstan's defining features—its enduring autocracy, its dependence on oil exports, its tendency toward graft, that goddamn *Borat* movie—might seem like disadvantages. Who would want to open a company in such a place? Who would go the distance, take the risk, be the butt of *that* old joke?

It turns out that there are perks to doing business in a state with a lousy reputation. Its leaders have delusions of grandeur. Its leaders want to make money. And its leaders can, and will, do what they think they need to do in order to achieve their goals.

Mark Beer first landed in Kazakhstan in 2015 with a mission: to get the DIFC's judgments recognized and enforced by other courts. He needed to ensure that if a company registered in, say, Manhattan lost a suit at the DIFC, the Manhattan court would make the losing party pay, and vice versa. While not legally binding, these agreements, known as Memoranda of Guidance, are generally well respected. For Dubai, they were an important way of legitimizing the upstart tribunal.

Beer had signed these kinds of deals with justice departments in England and Wales, Korea, Singapore, Kenya, Australia, and New York, to name just a few. But on the steppe, Beer would wind up doing more than negotiating reciprocity.

Kazakhstan at the time was governed by Nursultan Nazarbayev, an autocrat who'd clung to power since the end of the Soviet Union. Geopolitically, the nation was caught between an ascendant China—which had in 2013 first announced in the Kazah capital, Astana, that it was launching its One Belt, One Road initiative, a sweeping set of infrastructure projects that would stretch from Europe to East Asia—and Russia, whose currency plummeted in 2014 and took 40 percent of Kazakhstan's oil exports down with it.

Cognizant that hydrocarbons would benefit his nation only in the short term, Nazarbayev took rapid, dramatic steps to integrate it into the global economic and financial system. At a 2015 conference, he called for an "Astana International Financial Center" (AIFC) to cultivate foreign investment. Its legal status would be such a radical departure from the status quo, wrote *The Astana Times*, that it may require "introducing amendments into the nation's Constitution." (The country also joined the World Trade Organization in November 2015, indicating that it would get its trade policies in line with the rest of the world.)

Nazarbayev was, in so many words, grafting Dubai onto the steppe: the AIFC even described itself at one point as "bound to become a unique gateway connecting Europe with Eurasia," just as the DIFC pitched itself as "the financial and business gateway between the Middle East, Africa and Asia." The tax incentives would include a fifty-year exemption from all income tax and corporate tax on revenue earned at the AIFC, and all work visa restrictions would be essentially lifted for investors, foreign employees, and their families. Within the AIFC would be a new court. The AIFC court, like its Gulf counterpart, would be independent from the rest of the Kazakh judicial system and have exclusive jurisdiction over all disputes occurring between AIFC entities.

Nazarbayev's administration also teamed up with their Chinese neighbors to develop a sprawling inland free zone known as the Khorgos-Eastern Gate SEZ, where in 2018, 311 container trains passed through on their way between Europe and China, and where 1.2 million people entered, visa-free, to buy duty-free goods and mingle with their neighbors over lunch.

It was a predictable playbook, written in the idiolect of global finance: the kind of agenda that would boost a country's ranking in the World Bank's Ease of Doing Business index or, at the very least, land a third-tier minister a spot on a Davos panel. Who better to enlist as an advocate than Mark Beer?

If Beer was circumspect about his role in Dubai—he was mostly working behind the scenes, essentially as a fixer—his role in Kazakhstan became more public. In early 2016, he was appointed to an advisory body called the International Council of the Supreme Court of Kazakhstan, whose purpose was to modernize and internationalize the country's domestic courts.

Two years later, the chair of Kazakhstan's supreme court passed a set of judicial reforms called the Seven Pillars of Justice, which aimed to increase confidence in the judiciary. When Beer opened his own firm there in 2020 to advise foreign investors, he called it, in an apparent show of such confidence, Seven Pillars Law.

And in July 2018, the Astana International Financial Center was launched, combining an arbitration tribunal and a DIFC-style court.

Beer was bullish on the AIFC court. He wrote celebratory columns for the local English-language newspaper, and made cameos in AIFC court press releases and videos. In June 2020, Beer wrote a report for the Council of Europe praising the success of Kazakhstan's judicial reforms. "Objectively, no other judiciary has endeavored to achieve so much reform at such an accelerated pace," he wrote. "Our findings are that reforms have been impressive across several measurable factors and that the momentum is robust and positive."

All the while, Kazakhstan was battling a series of high-level corruption cases and experiencing unprecedented popular unrest. While Western news reports emphasized citizens' concern over China's growing influence in the country, the demonstrations were also the result of resentment over deep-rooted graft and profound inequality, and the country's prioritization of foreign economic interests over those of ordinary citizens.

Though, on paper, the country's GDP is said to have doubled in a ten-year period starting in 2006, its share of investment in GDP did not really rise since 2008, and just 162 people held 50 percent of the country's wealth in 2019. The spoils of Kazakhstan's vast extractive resources—billions upon billions of dollars' worth of uranium, titanium, gold, copper, and, of course, oil exports—had been mostly hoarded by politically connected oligarchs who stashed most of their wealth in foreign property holdings and offshore accounts.

In 2016, the Panama Papers leak revealed that Nazarbayev's grandson held assets in the British Virgin Islands during Kazakhstan's mid-2010s economic downturn (a time when Nazarbayev had been calling upon Kazakh billionaires to repatriate their assets). His third wife was later revealed to have received some $30 million for no apparent reason through a series of offshores; and his nephew was forced to hand over $230 million in jewelry.

The Organized Crime and Corruption Reporting Project's most recent investigation into Nazarbayev's billions forensically noted his family's extensive network of nonprofits and charitable foundations, in which at least $8 billion in assets were held or hidden. This is not to mention the numerous high-level officials who have been arrested for corruption since 2015.

A new round of protests was sparked by a deadly house fire in early 2019 in Astana: its victims were five young girls, aged three months to thirteen years, and the cause of the fire was a stove that did not meet safety standards, but which their parents had left on overnight to keep them warm, as the city had yet to install gas pipes in their recently built house in a "new" part of the rapidly urbanizing city. Both parents were away at their respective night jobs at the time of the fire.

As one commentator observed, the case reflected the profound problems fomenting political unrest, namely, the "widening gap between the government and the governed." They noted that "anger about lax oversight—of the country's financial resources, of its rapid urbanization, and of its poor—exposes a lack of public confidence in state structures."

The ensuing protests ultimately pushed Nazarbayev to step down from the presidency, though low-level unrest continued through the next two years before coming back with a vengeance when gas prices rose in early 2022. The new president, Kassym-Jomart Tokayev, tried to distance himself from the old regime (though he was an ally of Nazarbayev's), issuing statements about his desire to address the country's entrenched inequality. He did this all while enlisting Russian troops to violently quell the popular uprisings: 164 people died.

Over the years, Beer has justified much of his work with the AIFC as an effort to increase the low levels of trust that foreigners would (understandably!) have in the country's judicial and political systems. The assumption—expressed by both the Nazarbayev regime and Beer himself—is that any future investment in Kazakhstan is likely to "trickle down" to "the people." But it's not clear that it does. Pamela Bookman, in a 2021 paper, notes the potential negative social and political effects of this commercialization of law. In nondemocratic states, cookie-cutter jurisdictions like the DIFC and AIFC can obscure bigger social problems, offering sound business laws to corporations without civil and human rights reforms to match. These courts may also be lending undue legitimacy to authoritarian regimes. "Especially in non-democratic or not completely democratic states, arbitral courts' outward-facing motives seem to be to inspire investor confidence or attract international commercial disputes, but may not have broader effects of transforming the judiciary or the state," Bookman writes.

I confronted Beer with the objection that he, a white man enjoying the privilege of living in a democratic nation, was helping undemocratic regimes to launder their reputations in an effort to get ahead economically.

Beer invoked the response of Sir Anthony Evans, chief justice of the DIFC courts, when confronted with a controversy about Dubai's treatment of migrant workers and the charge that, in Beer's words, "You're lending your reputation to bolster an undemocratic regime."

Said Beer, "His answer, which I thought was brilliant, was: I must be doing what I do to improve the system. People have access to a system they didn't have access to before. If the court is credible and independent, it must be making a positive contribution."

Beer pointed out that the idea of a female judge was for a long time sacrilegious in the UAE. But after the DIFC appointed one and "the sun continued to rise the next day," the "onshore" system decided to appoint female judges too. There is no jurisdiction where he would not consider working, Beer told me, if he believed he was moving the needle in the right direction.

Even so, Beer's Kazakh editorials eventually started to sound a little strained. "In these bleak times, with the world economy on hold, with many countries locked down physically and metaphorically, it is a relief that leaders such as Kazakhstan's President are pushing for a fairer, more inclusive and just society," read a 2020 column. "I realized that so much has changed [in Kazakhstan]. A refreshed citizen-centric narrative, an edict for officials to listen to the people, and a focus on wealth generation (and, dare I say, redistribution) beyond the hallowed halls of Astana."

Meanwhile, a 2020 USAID report notes that "the AIFC shows that funding for large investment is available when a project aligns with the [government of Kazakhstan's] interests, although investment justice for the rest of the citizens remains inefficient."

Columbia University legal scholar Katharina Pistor offers a more systemic critique of this mode of lawmaking. In *The Code of Capital*, she points to what seems to be a paradox: While national laws create value, capital today "is of the roving kind: it has and needs no (physical) home and instead moves from place to place in search of new opportunities." In order to grow, capital "always needs a state's helping hand," Pistor writes—and any state that is willing to do its bidding, regardless of its respect for humanity, will do.

The Dubai International Financial Center's legal system, and its copycat courts, might be the paradigmatic example of this footloose, piecemeal system of justice: an autonomous, independent court, forged out of thin air by an army of consultants, staffed by both foreign and domestic lawyers and judges, and operating under a charter granted to a corporate entity in a financial free zone carved out by a devolved Gulf dictatorship.

"Capital coded in portable law is footloose," Pistor writes, while "gains can be made and pocketed anywhere and the losses can be left wherever they fall."

In 2017, Mark Beer stepped down from his post at the DIFC, and the center got a new chief registrar: Amna Al Owais, a vivacious young lawyer from Dubai. In this city of expats, migrants, guest workers, and part-timers, Al Owais is a rarity: a native Emirati woman in a position of significant power. Al Owais, who studied in the UAE before continuing her legal education in London, briefly worked at a private firm before joining the court in 2006 as a low-level clerk, just "one step up from the people who'd greet you when you walk in," says Beer. "But you know how if you walk into a house, you know it's the one you want to buy? I knew immediately she had that potential, and we lived the court's journey together."

I met Al Owais in her Dubai offices in November 2021. On my way there, in the main building's lobby, I passed a glass case displaying the right handprint of Dubai's ruler, Sheikh Mohammed bin Rashid Al Maktoum, and those of his six children, all preserved in clay. The artifacts, which belonged to the DIFC Corporate Art Collection, seemed to me a crude (hamhanded, even) attempt at signaling that this cathedral of high finance was still very much a part of Rome.

After going up an escalator to the elevators, then exiting into a marble corridor on the third floor, I waited in a conference room where a secretary apologized for the mess, even though there wasn't a speck of dust on the table. Al Owais showed up fifteen minutes later, a little breathless, her mind clearly still on her last meeting. She wore a black hijab and an elegant gold watch that wrapped twice around her wrist like a snake. She talked quickly and articulately about the court's short history, anticipating my questions before I had a chance to ask them and recounting her own time at the court. "The exciting part is always working on exciting projects and actually creating history, in a way," Al Owais said. "It's very international, the team is quite diverse, and whatever was there from 2006 I was able to be part of it—everything from the construction to new initiatives."

Day to day, Al Owais had taken over from Beer, serving as a court spokesperson and making sure the trains all ran on time. But just as she was getting started, the politics of the courts underwent a subtle, perhaps dialectical, shift.

The nationalist currents running through global politics over the past decade have, so far, shown no sign of letting up, rhetorically, at least; and as dependent as Dubai is on the rest of the world for people, money, and ideas, it is not immune to these pressures. Setting up a court on borrowed law with rented judges was bound to provoke power struggles at some point.

For Dubai, it started happening about a decade in, when the DIFC began to intervene in "onshore" affairs concerning the (non-DIFC) Dubai court. In theory, almost anyone could opt in to the new court's jurisdiction—which could be perceived as a foreign challenge to Dubai's original local courts. Five years earlier, this might not have caused a stir, but against the backdrop of Brexit, the election of Donald Trump, and the electoral success of right-wing nationalist politicians from Austria to China, the setup was starting to feel uneasy.

"Beginning in 2016, the Dubai government said, 'Hold on a second, we're okay with DIFC courts existing, but what we're feeling is that essentially our court system has questions about whether Arabic-speaking courts are being eclipsed,'" Jayanth Krishnan told me. "The real question was whether or not the domestic local courts should really be the ones leading the charge."

Having Al Owais at the helm certainly flaunted the center's commitment to "Emiratization," a federal initiative aimed at employing more local workers. But to deal with more substantive conflicts over which court should prevail in specific cases, authorities set up yet another tribunal, also staffed with a mix of DIFC and onshore judges, that was put in charge of making these calls. This could be interpreted as a weakening of the DIFC's autonomy or a necessary move to maintain a fragile balance.

To distract from domestic politics, the court has turned its focus away from the UAE and Emiratis. In 2015, it launched a wills registry that governs the estates of non-Muslim expatriates. Before the DIFC court, if a dead person's estate was held in the emirate and they hadn't made a will, the estate was distributed according to Dubai inheritance law, which follows sharia principles that pay out more to sons than to daughters. Opting out was possible, but onerous and expensive.

"There was drama!" Al Owais said. "We realized it was an opportunity to have something from the ground up and save time and hassle for heirs to avoid going through the traditional system." The service is now open to anyone with investments in Dubai, whether or not they are residents, and regardless of whether the bulk of their assets are located in the UAE's jurisdiction. They can likewise pick and choose which parts of their estate these rules apply to: a piece of art in a Dubai high-rise, but not a stock portfolio managed by a fund in London.

Dubai's experiment with succession ended up having a national impact: the UAE changed its federal laws to give non-Muslim residents the option to follow their home country's inheritance rules. It went into effect in 2023. In these cases, what matters is where people are born, not where they die.

Al Owais also oversaw Courts of the Future, a think tank dedicated to pushing the DIFC's boundaries even farther outward, using artificial intelligence and exploring litigation in outer space with a moot court.

Meanwhile, Mark Beer found the time to take his legal interests to the final frontier as well.

After a 2017 encounter at the Davos World Economic Forum with the owner of a satellite company, Beer became the justice minister of Asgardia: the world's first space-based nation, whose "landmass" was briefly a server on a satellite orbiting the Earth, whose "population" communicates predominantly on a blog platform, and whose "laws" are decided by the community—and Mark Beer.

"I was really cross about something, I think it was a minister of justice [on Earth] I was dealing with, who was a complete buffoon, and someone said, 'You have to walk a mile in their shoes,'" Beer says of his decision to "run" for "office." So he declared himself an Asgardian, put forth his candidacy to its parliament, and was appointed by its head of state. (Beer had also mounted a run for Oxford City Council in 2022, as a Conservative, but lost that race somewhat more democratically.)

I had signed up to be a citizen of Asgardia, too, back in 2017, before I knew anything about the DIFC or Mark Beer. But they started charging, and the hundred-euro annual fees started to add up. My tax money (if we can call it that) didn't go very far in space. I also didn't find I had much in common with the community I was opting in to.

Beer, on the other hand, persisted, as one of a small handful of Asgardia officials who were not a libertarian or "a Trekkie," as he put it, and who took their positions halfway seriously, whether as cosplay, performance art, or part of a political project intent on pushing the boundaries of privatized, corporate, and nonterritorial sovereignty into the stratosphere.

In 2022, I sat in on a Zoom seminar Beer participated in, on the future of nationhood and territoriality. Alongside an Asgardian official originally from Greece and the nation's minister of trade and commerce, a South African, Beer postulated that the definition of a nation would migrate from "a commonality of jurisdiction—'we all live in this space'—to a commonality of interest."

"Like in Dubai, I want to do more, and perhaps I'm pushing harder than I ought to," he told me. "But we'll soon launch the formation of companies in Asgardia, and I think that gives a whole new dimension and platform to talk about economic zones outside any territorial jurisdiction."

Beer was either light-years ahead of most political thinkers when it came to predicting the silhouette of state sovereignty in ten, twenty, fifty years from now, or he was on a different planet. Perhaps they weren't mutually exclusive. "Fifty percent of Asgardians are astrophysicists and brain surgeons, and I love interacting with them," he said. "But they have to build connectivity and take observer status in the UN, otherwise it remains an idea.

"I think they'll do it," he added. "It's a bit like the pioneers of the internet— we thought they were crackpots too."

Toward the end of our breakfast at Sarabeth's, Beer and I were joined by his wife, Adi, and his youngest son, then four. They were in the United States to visit Yale University, where his eldest son would matriculate in the fall. The family was planning an excursion to the Central Park Zoo, and they were using walkie-talkies to communicate across town. They seemed to take immense pleasure in how well the devices worked—no satellites needed.

But the cosmos was still clearly on Beer's mind: It was genuinely concerning, he said, "that the last major space law was written in 1967, and only countries can be party to it."

He also had more domestic concerns on his mind.

"If my daughter goes to space with Richard Branson, and there's no criminal law or anything—then what happens?"

7

Ad Astra

Outer space stands today as a fundamental interest for humanity. It is not a matter alien to the life of man. It is no longer a purely scientific spectacle. It is no longer just a possibility of a horizon for science. There is an immediate human interest in that outer space should be left free and not allowed to come under the power of one State, but should be used for international co-operation. This leads us to the conclusion—which I consider to be important—that outer space cannot be appropriated; it cannot be exploited; it cannot be used exclusively by one Power or one group of Powers with the material means to do so, because there is a human interest involving mankind's right to the use of outer space.

—FERNANDO BELAÚNDE TERRY, SPEECH BEFORE THE UN GENERAL ASSEMBLY, DECEMBER 5, 1961

On a drizzly afternoon in April 2017, Prince Guillaume, the hereditary grand duke of Luxembourg, and his wife, Princess Stéphanie, floated through the front doors of an office building on the outskirts of Seattle and into the headquarters of a start-up called Planetary Resources. The company's engineers greeted the royals with hors d'oeuvres, craft beer, and bottles upon bottles of Columbia Valley Rieslings and Syrahs. In the corner of the lounge stood a vintage Asteroids arcade game. On a wall, the grand duchy's own red, white, and blue stripes hung alongside an American flag.

Before Planetary Resources was sold to an obscure blockchain company in 2018, it had been one of a handful of start-ups building the tools to "expand the economy into space." In addition to more predictable Silicon Valley investors, the nation of Luxembourg was one of its first and most vocal benefactors, having pledged about 25 million euro in direct funding and state support for research and development. The country's unlikely investment was one element of a wildly ambitious and ongoing national campaign to become a terrestrial hub for the business of mining minerals, metals, and other resources on celestial bodies.

Much like its close cousin, Switzerland, the tiny nation of Luxembourg has enriched itself significantly over the past century by greasing the wheels of global finance. Now, as billionaires, start-ups, and larger aerospace companies prepare for a cosmic land grab, Luxembourg is using its place on Earth to help send capitalism into deep space.

Space exploration has historically been an arena for grand, nationalistic operations that were too costly and dangerous for civilians to take up without state backing. But spacefaring technology has advanced to the point that civilians can take part, and the fledgling "NewSpace" industry—an umbrella term for commercial spaceflight, asteroid mining, and other private ventures—has found eager supporters in the investor class. Twenty-first-century space entrepreneurs speak of a new "gold rush" and compare their mission with that of the frontiersmen, or the early industrialists. Rocket start-ups are banking on finding water on the moon, which would allow them to build refueling stations for journeys to the cosmos's outer depths.

As natural resources on Earth are rapidly being depleted, asteroid miners see a solution in the trove of untapped water, minerals, and metals in outer space. In 2017, Goldman Sachs sent a note to clients claiming that asteroid mining "could be more realistic than perceived," thanks to the falling cost of launching rockets and the vast quantities of platinum sitting on space rocks, just waiting to be dug up. Venture capitalists and other investors have poured cash into the space industry. By one estimate, a total of 1,832 space companies have received almost $300 billion in funding in the past decade.

Space is also an arena for infinitely expandable egos. Amazon's Jeff Bezos believes that not too long from now, a "fourth industrial revolution" will relocate all heavy industry outside the Earth's orbit. In 2000, Bezos started Blue Origin, which manufactures rockets and other devices to explore space. He has personally launched himself into the Earth's orbit; so has Richard Branson, who started the Virgin record label, now a lifestyle brand. Elon Musk's space company, SpaceX, launched Starlink, a private constellation of internet satellites serving the whole planet, and has multimillion-dollar contracts with NASA (the agency has made a conscious effort to expand its private-sector partnerships).

This surge of interest is turning theoretical questions that were once the domain of sci-fi novels and dorm-room thought experiments into pressing legal, regulatory, and commercial concerns. Who can lay claim to an asteroid and all its extractable wealth? Should space be colonized, privatized, and commercialized? What kind of power do individual states have this far from their own borders? Do trickle-down economics apply in zero-gravity conditions?

Following previous frontiers, from colonial conquests to the high seas, space is the latest testing ground for these thorny ethical and legal questions. It could also wind up being host to a full-on gold rush. So while major powers such as China and India plow increasing sums of money into developing space programs to rival NASA's, and the United States and Russia militarize the stars to prepare for future warfare, wily states like Luxembourg are making a different bet: that they can become home to a multinational cast of entrepreneurs who want to go into space in order to make money. For them, space represents the ultimate offshore location: an arena in which to wield power and get rich. So it makes perfect sense that a veteran of offshore activity on Earth would be among the first in line to exploit this final frontier.

It's a contentious business. For every happy shareholder praising Luxembourg's business-friendly rules and money-saving loopholes, there's a critic condemning its willingness to expedite the regulatory race to the bottom.

But then again, what can a poor boy do? In a global economy that ruthlessly pits nations against one another, a country like Luxembourg is left to exploit the most valuable resource it has: its national sovereignty. By crafting innovative rules, laws, and regulations that only it could (or would) put on offer, Luxembourg attracted banks, telecommunications companies, and consulting firms before any of these industries came to dominate the global economy. And by courting asteroid miners and space cowboys before anyone else took them seriously, it may very well end up doing the same for the commercialization of space.

Mining asteroids "is not a new idea, but what's new is state support of the idea," Chris Voorhees, then the CEO and chief engineer of Planetary Resources, told me at the time of the junket in Washington State. "Everyone thought it was inevitable, but they weren't sure when it would occur. And Luxembourg is making it happen." To that end, the world's only grand duchy—which has all the square footage of an asteroid and, with a population of about a half million, not all that many more inhabitants—has earmarked millions of dollars for companies that join its new space sector. The government reported in 2023 that more than seventy space companies and institutions employed fourteen hundred people in the country, making up between 2 and 4 percent of its annual GDP. It routinely sends officials to Japan, China, and the UAE to talk about space exploration partnerships, and has appointed space industry veterans, including the former head of the European Space Agency, as advisers. In May 2017, the country paid for a glossy supplement in *Scientific American* entitled "Luxembourg's Innovation

Is Out of This World." It included listicles about the country's business-friendly environment, a potted history of satellites, and a glowing appraisal of its banking sector, all paid for by the state, to signal its seriousness about space. It also set up the European Space Resources Innovation Centre, or ESRIC, a research center "for scientific, technical, business and economic aspects related to the use of space resources for human and robotic exploration, as well as for a future in-space economy."

Most substantively, in the summer of 2017, its parliament passed the Space Resources Act—the first of its kind in Europe, and at the time, the most far-reaching in the world—asserting that if a Luxembourgian company launches a spacecraft that obtains materials such as water, silver, gold, or any other valuable substance on a celestial body, the extracted materials will be considered the company's legitimate private property by Luxembourg, a legitimate sovereign nation. Companies come and go, and investors are notoriously fickle, but national laws can live on for years, even generations, and make their mark on human history. The Space Resources Act is an example of what Katharina Pistor describes as the state-led "coding" of new forms of capital: in this case, resources that are literally out of this world.

In the months running up to the passage of the Luxembourg law, the country's young royals were enlisted to dazzle, charm, and lend gravitas to the operation, hence the prince and princess's visit to Planetary Resources headquarters. The greater aim of the mission was to impress upon Silicon Valley executives, the bemused Luxembourgian press, and space scientists from around the world that mining asteroids was no longer science fiction. To that end, the royals were accompanied by about forty of their subjects, all of whom had a role to play in this emerging industry.

Etienne Schneider, then Luxembourg's deputy prime minister, led the delegation. Schneider is about six feet tall, with a shiny bald head, smiling eyes, and an easy, jovial demeanor (he has since left public office to work in the private sector). There were no universities in his country when Schneider came of age, so he studied in the UK, picking up a posh British accent that goes perfectly with his impeccably tailored suits. Schneider is a product of European socialist political parties. But he will willingly play handmaiden to global capitalist interests should the right opportunity arise. Schneider is also a bon vivant in the old European tradition, who nonetheless finds the West Coast lifestyle bewildering and seductive. In his spare time, he collects vintage cars, tends to his garden, and on occasion posts selfies with his handsome younger husband on Instagram.

With Schneider came a delegation of scientists, trade attachés, bankers, lawyers, and local journalists who switched between German, English, French, and Luxembourgeois, with the occasional foreign term thrown in to supplement: *meeting, framework, brunch.* ("We don't have all the words," a member of the delegation confessed sheepishly.) The name of their dialect pretty much says it all: With a GDP per capita of $140,310, the duchy's six hundred thousand citizens are the wealthiest in the world, according to the International Monetary Fund.

The Planetary Resources team took their benefactors on a tour of the labs where its hardware was being built. The company never got to actually mine asteroids, but to benefit from Luxembourg's concessions it had opened an office—a glorified mailbox, really, but who's checking?—in the grand duchy. Up close, its Arkyd-6 spacecraft looked just like satellites look in the movies, only smaller. It had multiple flaps and appendages, including an infrared sensor, a star tracker to orient the craft in space, and a GPS unit.

Once the tour was complete, cocktail hour began. Schneider, who owns a vineyard, bounced from one conversation to another, brimming with childlike joy. The company's engineers milled around in their jeans and hoodies, seeming proud and confused.

Chris Lewicki, the CEO of Planetary Resources, gave a toast praising Luxembourg's contributions "to an abundant future for all of humanity." As a parting gift, he presented Her Royal Highness with a necklace studded with tiny fragments of asteroids.

. . .

It is reasonable to wonder how, exactly, a marginal European monarchy, egged on by a vivacious socialist, ended up convincing American entrepreneurs on the cutting edge of innovation that their hamlet-size state could propel humanity—and capitalism—into deep space. The grand duchy in 2017 had no national space agency, no launching sites, and only modest research capabilities. It opened its first and only university in 2003, and its military consists of 1,128 troops, all of them on Earth. Luxembourg does not fit the image of a spacefaring nation; in fact, some have questioned whether it should even be a nation at all.

Yet Luxembourg's very essence—as a speck in the heart of Europe—allows, even requires, it to partake in such ambitious ventures. The country's national motto is "We want to remain what we are." Over the centuries, this independent spirit has endured occupations by the dukes of Burgundy, the kings of Spain and France, the emperors of Austria, and the king of the Netherlands. Today, the state, which gained full independence in 1867, occupies a curious position in the global imagination: a country with an outsize economic influence that everyone has heard of but no one can quite find on a map.

According to the economist Gabriel Zucman, the country is hard for observers of the financial world to miss. "Luxembourg has private banks like Switzerland, it has a big mutual fund industry like Ireland's, it's used for corporate tax avoidance like Bermuda or the Netherlands, and it also hosts one of the two international central depositories for securities, so it's active in Eurobonds," he explained over the phone. "It's the tax haven of tax havens, present at all stages of the financial industry." Tony Norfield, a former banker in the City of London who now writes on global finance, has described Luxembourg as "a paragon of parasitism."

The story of how a marginal and relatively powerless country has survived world wars, economic crises, and cataclysmic technological advances to become a banking and finance powerhouse echoes Switzerland's. It tells us a lot about how far beyond its weight class a small country can punch if it pledges allegiance to the hidden globe.

Luxembourg was, for the first decades of its independent life, a sleepy little country whose main export was steel. But long before its iron ore mines shut down in the 1980s, the grand duchy came to represent a discreet but powerful regulatory freedom. A homegrown economic model began to take shape: over the next decades, it would make a name for itself by passing legislation "designed to tempt the world's hot money," notes the Tax Justice Network, an anti-tax-evasion advocacy group.

Its first significant attempts at making money from nothing began in the mid-1920s. As radio became a popular medium for entertainment and communication, the grand duchy decided not to create a publicly funded radio service like its neighbors in France and Germany did. Instead, it handed its airwaves to a private broadcasting company and collected revenues from the licenses the firm granted. That company became the first ad-supported commercial station to broadcast music, culture, and entertainment programs across Europe in multiple languages. "By handing the rights to a public good to a private company, the state commercialized, for the first time, its sovereign rights in a media context," notes *The Fruits of National Sovereignty*, a book on Luxembourg's economic history published in 2000 by a Luxembourgian bank.

Then, just three months before the stock market collapsed in 1929, Luxembourg's parliament passed legislation exempting "holding companies"— that is, parent firms that exist solely to own parts of or control other companies—from paying corporate taxes. In the first five years after the law's passing, seven hundred holding companies were established there; by 1960, there were twelve hundred, and at the turn of the twenty-first century, some fifteen thousand "letterbox" firms—one for every eighteen citizens—

were incorporated in Luxembourg. (In 2006, the European Commission found that this exemption violated EU rules, so Luxembourg promptly created a new designation, the "family estate management company," that complied with the country's EU treaty obligations while offering many of the same money-saving advantages.)

Luxembourg was also instrumental in the denationalization of money. The somewhat complicated tale goes like this: By the 1950s, many foreign governments held reserves of U.S. dollars in American banks, which they could use to buy goods, earn interest, take out loans, or exchange for gold. Initially, these dollars were held by banks located in the United States, but some made their way abroad via loans, transfers, or other transactions in the postwar period. American currency living outside American jurisdiction was given a new name: the Eurodollar.

The oxymoron was the point. "The charm of Eurodollars, to bankers, was that they didn't belong anywhere and owed no allegiance to anyone; therefore, nobody regulated them," wrote George J. W. Goodman, under the alias "Adam Smith," in *Paper Money*. "The Federal Reserve can require banks to put up a portion of their deposits as reserves; other agencies govern the character and size of loans. But not in Eurodollars; these dollars could be deposited, lent, and repaid, all while the Federal Reserve looked on from afar." (Confusingly, a U.S. dollar held in a Nigerian or Thai account far away from Europe is still called a Eurodollar.)

It wasn't just the Fed that was confused. Foreign governments had no idea how to regulate these nowhere bucks either. And rather than complaining to the authorities, American banks decided to join in on the fun: there was good money to be made buying, selling, speculating on, and securitizing these placeless bills in the uncertain space between nations.

Eurodollars laid the groundwork for Eurobonds, or debt sold outside its home country that pays interest in that currency—U.S. dollars (called Eurodollar bonds), but also South African rands (Eurorand bonds) or Japanese yen (Euroyen!). The bonds could until recently be owned anonymously and paid interest to whoever held on to them. Naturally, they were a hit, in large part thanks to Luxembourg.

In his book *Moneyland*, Oliver Bullough describes a game of "jurisdictional Twister," whereby an early Eurodollar bond pioneer figured out how to get around a continent of barriers and currency controls. To that end, the first Eurodollar bonds were formally "issued" not in London, where the bank underwriting them was located, but during a layover at the Amsterdam airport—a technicality to bypass British tax. The money raised from the sale of the bonds went "to" the Italian state highway corporation, which was not the intended recipient, but rather was acting as a shell corporation through which still more taxes could be avoided. Then, thanks to the 1929 holding company loophole, the bonds paid out their interest "in" Luxembourg—again, on paper—to avoid another tax, before landing in Switzerland, where they could be stashed in secret indefinitely. (Some 40 to 60 percent of Eurobonds were held in Swiss custodial accounts; half of all Eurobond sales were brokered by a Swiss institution.) This transaction shows the hidden globe operating at full capacity: an archipelago of fake firms and nonplaces working in concert to make something—in this case, money—disappear and reappear in a new, abstract form.

As financial innovations like these hit the marketplace and took advantage of Luxembourg's lax rules, the nation's policymakers began to realize that when it came to regulation, small was beautiful, and less could really be more. On the consumer level, the state's low taxes drew Europe's tax-averse petty bourgeoisie. Starting in the 1960s, "Belgian dentists" and "German butchers"—the prevailing stereotypes cited in the international financial press—began taking jaunts to the grand duchy to deposit money there, thus avoiding tax at home. The Luxembourgian state even lowered the price of fuel to attract the day-trippers.

But the dentists' and butchers' hidden savings were no match for deindustrialization.

In the 1970s, the country's steel industry declined dramatically. Luxembourg needed some new tricks.

In 1981, it introduced legally binding bank secrecy regulations comparable to Switzerland's, to compete for higher-end avoiders and evaders. (The rules were curtailed in 2014, under pressure from the international community.) That same year, the government coaxed Georges Schmit, then a young University of Michigan graduate, away from a consulting gig and into the Ministry of the Economy. Schmit, whom I interviewed in New York a few months after our trip to the West Coast, is an important figure in Luxembourg's economic history. "Luxembourg was in bad shape when I joined the government," he told me. "The last iron ore mine had just closed. We were in the middle of a serious steel crisis. I joined thinking, 'What do you want me to do?' I was asked to design an innovation policy and worked on it for a year. Our industry had gone to sleep because we'd done so well in the past, and we'd set up no capacity to renew ourselves."

Some of the solutions were hiding in plain sight: Luxembourg just had to do more with what it had—which actually meant doing less, with more purpose. According to Schmit, Luxembourg's biggest draw "wasn't our doing; it was the lack of our doing anything." For instance, Luxembourg did not have its own central bank. The country had been in a monetary union with Belgium since 1921, so it used the same currency but didn't impose reserve requirements on financial firms. This meant its banks—whether they were holding people's savings for a rainy day or actively investing client money abroad—could lend or spend the money they would have had to keep on deposit in other jurisdictions: more chances for speculation and moneymaking.

Schmit's mandate was initially to study manufacturing, not financial services or technology. But in 1986, his department set up a trade office in San Francisco to keep tabs on telecoms and tech. "Since independence, we needed to find larger economic spaces, be they regional or continental," he said.

One of these spaces happened to be above Earth. In 1977, Luxembourg got into the business of satellite TV. Much like its foray into the radio business almost fifty years prior, it saw a chance to commercialize this intangible asset by selling access to that space—a public good—to private operators. The time was right for it: the United States was already leading the charge. Clay Whitehead, Richard Nixon's head of telecommunications policy, had successfully pushed for an "open skies" agenda in the United States that brought free markets to the Earth's orbit. His ideas paved the way for the modern cable TV industry by making it possible for networks to broadcast via satellite, rather than by leasing landlines from AT&T, the monopoly provider.

In 1983, Whitehead—who was at this point working for Hughes Aircraft Company (now Boeing)—was approached by the American wife of Luxembourg's ambassador to the United States with a proposal: Could he bring his expertise to Luxembourg and set up a satellite company there? Whitehead agreed, and Schmit flew to Los Angeles to meet him. "I was thirty years old, and I had no idea what was going on," Schmit recalled. Still, he realized his country was in a unique position. "The big innovation is that this was a privatization of space. All the other operators were intergovernmental companies, owned by the governments through international agreements. This was the first commercial company that set out to use space for broadcasting."

Société Européenne des Satellites, or SES, became Europe's first commercial satellite TV business broadcasting directly to viewers' homes. It ended the European state-run broadcasting monopolies and became one of the biggest private satellite companies in the world. When SES grew profitable, Luxembourg's bet on deregulation paid off: the tiny country became home to a telecom giant, and, as an early investor, received a piece of the pie. It gave the nation a firm foothold above Earth—and an idea that the sky was not the limit, but only the beginning.

In the early 2000s, Luxembourg revisited this playbook for another kind of invisible resource: assets bought, sold, and transferred online, like movies and MP3s. As the digital economy grew, the nation pounced at the chance to court retailers such as Amazon and Apple with novel incentives.

There were the perks the state was happy to publicize—the lowest value-added tax in Europe, for instance, which made it cheaper to buy and sell digital goods. And then there were private deals with large companies, known as tax rulings, which it kept rather quieter.

Amazon, Microsoft, and Spotify, to name just a few, all opened outposts there, while Georges Schmit made the same journey in reverse. In 2009, he moved to California to continue his life's work, as his country's general consul and trade envoy to Silicon Valley.

The 2007–2008 financial crisis showed no mercy and knew no borders: virtually every country on earth had to reckon with the cascading effects of the collapsing U.S. housing market on banks, employment, state budgets, and consumer confidence. The trouble did not spare Luxembourg, which had to bail out a few local banks along with suffering a mild rise in unemployment, and sluggish economic growth. Still, the nation fared relatively well, particularly compared with its European neighbors.

Then another sort of crisis turned up at its doorstep. It was a public-relations debacle, and it was coming at the duchy hard.

In 2014, details of Luxembourg's tax rulings were published by the International Consortium of Investigative Journalists. Known as the Lux leaks, the massive trove of leaked data revealed that, from 2002 to 2010, the country's tax agency approved a series of confidential deals that allowed American Insurance Group, IKEA, Deutsche Bank, and more than three hundred other large firms to save billions of dollars they might have owed had they been based in other states. The rulings weren't necessarily illegal, and they certainly weren't unique to Luxembourg—Belgium, Ireland, and the Netherlands had versions of them too—but they did cause a scandal, provoking damning reports in the media, protests around Europe, and promises of tighter regulation from within the EU.

Investigations on both sides of the Atlantic on related matters followed, and lawsuits revealed information on additional Luxembourg-based companies. (One memorable detail: Amazon's twenty-six-step tax-restructuring arrangement in Luxembourg was named Project Goldcrest, after the country's national bird.)

Around this time, Gabriel Zucman, then a recently minted PhD who had studied with Thomas Piketty at the Paris School of Economics, began looking into Luxembourg's role in international tax avoidance and evasion. His focus was not on the multinationals, but rather on Luxembourg's thriving investment fund industry, which through niche regulations and loopholes allowed investors to avoid certain taxes too.

Luxembourg was by this point well known as a financial center, but the statistics Zucman dug up while researching his book *The Hidden Wealth of Nations* took him aback: in 2015, national data showed that $3.5 trillion worth of shares in Luxembourgian mutual funds were domiciled in the grand duchy, while data from other countries accounted for only two of those trillions. The missing $1.5 trillion suggested to him that the money—which, he notes, was probably accumulating interest by the day—had no identifiable owner or home. This meant that the countries to which tax was owed on any of that ungodly sum were unaware of its existence.

Globally, Zucman calculated that almost $8 trillion in financial wealth (which did not include real estate, luxury goods, gold, or other commodities) had been stolen from countries and taxpayers in this manner thanks to secrecy jurisdictions such as Luxembourg, the British Virgin Islands, and Panama working "in symbiosis." In his book, Zucman describes Luxembourg as an "economic colony of the international financial industry" and challenges its right to sell off its greatest asset: its sovereignty.

"Imagine an ocean platform where the inhabitants would meet during the day to produce and trade, free of any law or any tax, before being tele-ported in the evening back home to their families on the mainland," he writes, referring to the country's unusual demographics: 47 percent of Luxembourg's six hundred thousand residents are citizens of other countries, and 44 percent of its workforce commutes across nation-state lines each day for work.

"No one would dream of considering such a place, where 100 percent of its production is sent abroad, as a nation," writes Zucman. "The trade of sover-eignty knows no limits. Everything is bought; everything is negotiable."

Luxembourg is not the only state to commercialize its national sovereignty. It's not even the most shameless.

For example, Luxembourg does not sell citizenship outright, as close to a dozen states, including Malta and Antigua and Barbuda, do. (I investigated the global passport market in my last book, *The Cosmopolites*.) Luxembourg does not offer its territory to multinationals, as Madagascar did when it sold swaths of agricultural land to the Korean firm Daewoo (a domestic coup invalidated the deal in 2009). Nor does it rent out entire islands to a Chinese company, as Tulagi, part of the Solomon Islands, briefly attempted in 2019 (national authorities stopped the deal).

Luxembourg has never auctioned off its area codes or .lu domain names to fly-by-night adult entertainers, as the Pacific islands of Niue and Tuvalu did in the 1990s, thus becoming international hubs for phone sex. "These countries are being courted by marketing companies because their data lines are cheap to lease, they have ample surplus digits available to reroute calls, and most do not impose content restrictions applied by other regula-tors, since the calls terminate elsewhere," explained the *Australian Financial Review* in 1996.

The practice of making money off the mere fact of being a country doesn't have to be seedy. It can be almost quaint. Philatelists might be tempted by offerings including "Elvis Presley [stamps] issued by Burkina Faso, Chad stamps depicting Marilyn Monroe, Chechnya stamps picturing Groucho Marx, Mongolia stamps with the Three Stooges and the X-Men, and Montserrat stamps with Jerry Garcia," according to University of Michigan business school professor Joel Slemrod, himself a collector. (Happily for Slemrod and his ilk, Chechnya, though part of Russia, retains a measure of sovereignty over its postage.)

The core idea behind all these schemes is the same: sovereignty is an asset, albeit an intangible and infinite one, which makes it possible to make theoretically limitless money off the mere fact of being a country. In addition to having what the sociologist Max Weber characterized as a "monopoly on the legitimate use of physical force," or the right to condone physical violence in the form of, say, policing or warfare, nation-states also have a monopoly on what we might call "state products." These can encompass something as sweeping as laws and as petty as stamps, as primeval as land and as functional as a phone number.

Some of these resources, like land, are finite; others, like stamps, can be produced without limit. This isn't an idea that political theorists or economists have fully reckoned with, but it is a powerful force in international commerce that at once challenges nationalistic mythologies and reinforces the nation-state's bargaining power. For small, resource-poor countries at the bottom of the international food chain, the sales of these products can be a lifeline and, more qualitatively, a way to punch above their weight class on the world stage.

Slemrod coined the wonderful euphemism "juridical entrepreneurship" for this kind of practice. (A less even-handed observer might call it bottom-feeding.) Slemrod ran a statistical analysis of countries engaging in these practices and found "considerable overlap among these aspects of commercialization of state sovereignty." A tax haven, per the economists, is 2.5 times more likely to issue limited-run Daffy Duck stamps than a nonhaven—which would make it 1.8 times more likely to be labeled a money launderer, which, in turn, makes it almost 5 times more likely than a nonlaunderer to be a tax haven. The implication is that there "may be common underlying factors driving these decisions," including size (small), population (also small), and flexibility of laws (high).

These countries are also perceived to be well governed—at least by the denizens of Davos and institutions like the World Bank—which makes sense if you are parking cash there. Capitalists want their money to be safe from theft and seizure. Where corruption exists, you want it to work for you. If you were to fall on hard times and needed to use one of your novelty stamps for actual postage, you'd want your letter to get to its destination.

Still, technical legitimacy doesn't erase controversy. Scrutiny of Luxembourg's maneuvers—from the press, the public, and the EU—spread at an awkward time. Prime Minister Xavier Bettel's coalition government of democrats, socialists, and greens, which was in power when the leaks came out, wanted to distance itself from the economic policies of former prime minister Jean-Claude Juncker and play by the EU's rules. "Honestly, I am fed up with being accused of being a defender of a tax haven and a hotbed of sin," Bettel said in a speech to the Luxembourg Bankers' Association shortly after taking office. "We need to work on our image . . . we have much changed in the last years, now it is time to make sure that everybody knows."

Etienne Schneider, then economy minister, was part of this effort too. But instead of being applauded for breaking with the past, from the moment they took power the politicians were constantly being reminded of their country's previous indiscretions.

The new government needed to square the Luxembourgian model of economic development with new political realities. It had to keep looking ahead. It had to find a way to change the conversation.

A curious possibility had emerged in the summer of 2012, when Georges Schmit was back in California visiting NASA's Ames Research Center in

Palo Alto and found himself in conversation with Pete Worden, who had recently left his position as director of the center. As soon as his mandatory "cooling-off period" ended, during which he was not allowed to work for a competitor, Worden took a job advising the Luxembourgian government.

An impish man now in his seventies whose deep nerdiness belies a fierce pro-business streak, Worden describes himself as Schneider's "coconspirator." He became Luxembourg's fixer in Silicon Valley, and their main link to the spacefaring elite. "Pete was our first introduction to Luxembourg," Planetary Resources' Chris Vorhees told me. "He represented them as a tech and science ambassador. He was very entrepreneurial, with good relationships there and in the U.S."

Over coffee, Worden told Schmit about the emerging NewSpace sector and about his dream of finding life on other planets. Schmit sensed Worden would hit it off with Schneider, so he introduced them. At first, asteroid mining struck Schneider as crazy. "I listened to him and wondered what this guy might have smoked this morning; it sounded like complete science fiction," Schneider recalled in a speech. But the more he listened, the more it made sense. Worden convinced Schneider that "it's not if it will happen, it's when it'll happen. And the countries who'll be the pioneers will be the ones that'll get the most out of it later on."

From 2014 to 2016, a series of meetings between the Americans and the Luxembourgeois took place. Schneider hung his hopes—and his political prospects—on the stars. Here was a chance to turn the conversation away from taxes and toward the cosmos; to establish an industry for Luxembourg's deep future; to contribute to science and human knowledge even. Besides, in such trying times, who *didn't* like talking about the wonders of the great unknown? NewSpace companies were certainly eager to work with Luxembourg. They were thirsty for funds and attention, and they felt invisible in the United States. Luxembourg was a place where they could get meetings with high-level politicians in minutes; where everyone spoke great

English; where the bureaucracy was minimal and the promise of low taxes remained. As one NewSpace executive told me: "We just want to work with a government who won't get in the way."

The only catch was the ambiguity of space law: companies wanted assurances that the fruits of their extraterrestrial labor would be recognized here on Earth. This is not a given. Unlike on Earth, where a country can grant a company a mining concession, or a person can sell the right to exploit their land, no one has a clear legal claim to what's outside our atmosphere. In fact, for decades countries have been prohibited under international law from claiming sovereignty over celestial bodies. And if nobody governs the moon and stars, who is to say who gets to own a little piece of them?

Space law is a slippery concept by definition—primarily because space is not a place, but infinite, and composed of mostly untouchable and unreachable matter. There can by definition be no borders in space, because there can be no fixity; and without fixity, no containment. The prospect of ascribing the laws of man to a realm so vast, so unknowable, and so timeless is a futile and egocentric exercise that only humans could attempt. Heaven knows, we've tried.

As early as the thirteenth century, a Roman jurist named Accursius proclaimed, "Cuius est solum, eius est usque ad coelum et ad inferos" (Whoever owned the soil could claim it all the way to Heaven and all the way to Hell). The vertical conception of property rights, which is often abbreviated to *ad coelum*, made its way into English common law when Accursius's son, Franciscus, took a job at Oxford lecturing on jurisprudence. Over the next few centuries, the principle was invoked to settle disputes ranging from who owned a flock of juvenile goshawks to whether a landowner was allowed to build a house up against his neighbor's window, blocking out the sun.

Centuries later, the advent of hot-air balloons, then airplanes, raised the stakes of the doctrine. Could a landowner stop a balloon from flying over his field if nothing touched the ground? Was it trespassing to shoot a migrating duck from your backyard at the moment it crossed into your neighbor's garden? Could a plane or a rocket you could barely see be considered a legal nuisance if it briefly flew over your house? How high *was* the sky?

Over time and around the world, *ad coelum* was weakened by national regulations over airline routes, telegraph cables, and, later, technologies like drones. Nations, rather than private parties or smaller jurisdictional units (states, in the United States), were deemed to have sovereign authority over their skies, and an elaborate system of permits and licenses facilitated the comings and goings of commercial and chartered flights in and out of the spaces above. Meanwhile, international conventions turned much of the airspace between these nations into extensions of the high seas, with pilots enjoying freedoms of navigation. As with ships, the nation to which an aircraft is registered usually determines its jurisdiction when in flight.

These rules have made possible what we now refer to broadly as "globalization," from tourism to next-day shipping, and they're unquestionably more useful to mankind than a policed and cloistered sky. But if the idea of *ad coelum* was always a little silly, theologically or otherwise, then so is the idea of regulating airspace at all. Like the Portuguese and Spanish kings who drew lines down the ocean to mark their territory, nation-states were now applying their made-up rules to thin air—contrails, with teeth.

In a poem commenting on this very human tendency, the literary critic William Empson wrote in 1928 that the law "makes long spokes of the short stakes of men." Empson's poem, entitled "Legal Fiction," was a pithy commentary on mankind's unwavering determination to impose its will and laws beyond its reach. "Your rights reach down where all owners meet, in Hell's / Pointed exclusive conclave, at earth's centre . . . And up, through galaxies, a growing sector," he wrote.

In invoking the "growing sector," Empson anticipated the challenges that would face delegates at the United Nations charged with deciding how, why, and to whose benefit humankind would regulate outer space.

When the Soviet Union launched Sputnik out of Earth's orbit on October 4, 1957, it opened up a vast legal vacuum, twenty thousand leagues (and then some) above the sea. The satellite the size of a beach ball took a little more than an hour and a half to orbit the Earth, repeating its journey every day for ninety-two days, emitting regular beeps for three of those weeks that were broadcast on radios around the world as it crossed over what might, per *ad coelum*, have been considered other nations' turf.

By breaching the gap between heaven and earth, Sputnik gave space a legal geography: while its elliptical path was miles and miles removed from the nation-state system, the presence of a 184-pound Russian machine carried with it the metaphorical weight of the world. Space still looms above us all, but on that day, it became of the Earth: indelibly bound to land by science and technology and war, and subject to the laws and whims of nations.

The question was: Which nation?

After the Russians' successful incursion—in the middle of the Cold War, no less—member states of the United Nations began a series of discussions about how outer space would be used and navigated. The delegates were preoccupied by the prospect of space becoming a military proxy for Earth, so a United Nations working group on the Peaceful Uses of Outer Space was formed. Early talks included the usual suspects—the United States, the UK, France, Russia, Italy—as well as a smattering of smaller states: Poland, Argentina, and Mongolia, along with Chad, Sierra Leone, and Morocco representing the decolonized world. (The Chadian and Sierra Leonean delegates ended up having to miss meetings held in the still-segregated United States, as they had trouble finding and paying for accommodation.)

The parties quickly agreed that territorial sovereignty did not extend into the universe, by *ad coelum* or by other, nonlinear means. Invoking the legal scholar Wilfred Jenks, the committee noted that countries claiming areas of space as their own "would be inconsistent with the basic astronomical facts." The delegates also broadly agreed that the UN Charter should apply to the cosmos. This meant that international relations and international law applied, even in the absence of territorial nations, in outer space.

As on Earth, definitions of "peace" varied from total demilitarization to a mere lack of active military operations, but the delegates made it clear that the moon could not, for instance, serve as a military base for a proxy war between the United States and Russia.

The talks also dealt with questions about nations and appropriation, property rights and pollution, inequality and technology. Nations without any spacefaring capacities expressed concern about being frozen out of space exploration in the future just because other nations had gotten there first. The United States argued for minimal regulatory oversight, while the USSR argued the opposite, in pushing (without avail) for stronger environmental controls.

Meanwhile, the nonaligned countries in the working group—some of whom had agitated for a seat at the postcolonial table at the United Nations Conference on Trade and Development—advanced a more collectivist vision of extraterritorial domains. They hoped that natural resources, scientific knowledge, and intellectual property produced outside the established boundaries of nations would be shared among all countries.

In the context not only of the Cold War and nuclear proliferation, but also of accelerating capitalism and the opening up of new markets in decolonized territories, space thus represented a fresh start: a second chance at fairness and redistribution, and an opportunity to rectify past sins in an entirely new arena. On Earth, nations, aided by consultants, were coming up with more and more creative ways to slice up territory in the service of private capital. Above it, the nonaligned countries helped push through the committee's position that outer space and the resources to be found in it were *res communes*: not subject to occupation or appropriation, and to be freely used by all members of the international community.

In retrospect, this seems like a massive diplomatic achievement, and in a sense, it is—today it is almost impossible to imagine this level of consensus over potentially lucrative resources, wherever they may be. But when these ideas were enshrined in the Outer Space Treaty of 1967—to date, the most important document on space law—the "commons" remained vaguely defined.

That irked Fernando Belaúnde Terry, who represented (and would later lead) Peru. He warned his peers that stronger rules were needed to safeguard against the unrestrained exploitation of the cosmic commons by nations, private actors, or individuals. In a sprawling 1961 speech before the UN General Assembly citing Pascal, Hegel, Shakespeare, and the book of Genesis, Belaúnde worried that since the study of things "infinitely small" (nuclear power) had had quite the opposite effect in promoting peace, the conquest of the "infinitely great" might lead to annihilation. He remarked that power knew no bounds, and that dominium over space would inevitably lead to "domination of the earth itself."

It was not enough to declare space *res communis omnium*, Belaúnde insisted. The sovereign equality of states meant only so much on Earth, thanks to unequal access, resources, and power; it would mean even less across the universe. Here was a one-time chance to ensure that the content of the cosmic commons was used to produce favorable changes on the blue planet.

He exhorted the committee to give the UN more leeway to exercise international jurisdiction over space—to act at once as its groundskeeper, lawmaker, and policeman, rather than as a mere bookkeeper for cosmic activities. Only that would prevent the same patterns of domination and exploitation from reproducing themselves in an endless loop between Earth and sky by empires, nations, and the corporations that would follow.

. . .

As of this writing, space has not ended up enabling Fernando Belaúnde Terry's fears of human annihilation. The seeds of our destruction seem firmly rooted in blood, soil, and, increasingly, carbon. But the diplomat's warnings about the fate of the intergalactic commons feel more prescient than ever.

At the heart of this matter is what counts as a resource and who is entitled to claim it from afar.

A decade after the Outer Space Treaty was signed by 110 member states of the UN, representatives of eight equatorial countries—Brazil, Colombia, Ecuador, Indonesia, Kenya, Uganda, and the nations now known as the Democratic Republic of the Congo and Congo-Brazzaville—met in Bogotá to issue a statement on a "growing sector" in which they had a very keen interest: satellite technology. It was not that these countries were technologically advanced—for many, centuries of colonial exploitation had thwarted their ambitions. They were, however, fortuitously positioned to take advantage of other countries' advances by virtue of their location along the Earth's horizontal axis, some 22,236 miles beneath a section of the universe known as geostationary orbit.

Many of the satellites we rely on every day for communications, meteorology, and data are synchronous with the Earth's orbit, which means they follow the Earth's rotation perfectly.

Their location tracks consistently with the same point on Earth as it spins. This works because the satellites sit in the orchestra seats of the space opera: seats that happen to be located above these eight terrestrial states. But the spaces are limited in number because of rules governing how far apart satellites must be placed to avoid collisions. This scarcity creates value.

Many of the countries that showed up in Bogotá were influenced by the radical demands of the New International Economic Order. They knew too well what was about to happen if capitalism took control of the cosmos: they'd been cheated out of their own riches by colonial powers before. So they decided not only to consider these parking spaces common "resources," but to formally claim them for themselves. They argued that their geography entitled them to do as they pleased with the space above their land, the same way they would with the minerals beneath—"all the way to Heaven and all the way to Hell." In keeping with this logic, they argued that the slots above the high seas ought to be considered *res communes*, with the spoils apportioned equitably among all the nations of the world.

It was, in a way, a throwback to the old *ad coelum* doctrine, only this time wielded by historically marginalized states in an attempt to redistribute resources downward and perhaps even to begin to right the wrongs of colonialism. But the Bogotá declaration, for lack of widespread adoption, went nowhere. Instead, the allocation of these slots has been managed for the past half century by the International Telecommunications Union (ITU), an organization based—where else?—in Geneva. And its own system of splitting the orbital pie was far from impervious to the manipulations of capitalists on Earth.

The way slot allocation works is relatively simple: The ITU allows nations—either as individual petitioners or as members of a specialized trade group—to claim satellite parking spaces through a branch of the organization called the International Frequency Registration Board. Companies must make requests through their home state. But in the beginning, for lack of demand, the ITU imposed few requirements on the states making these requests beyond sending over a form with the relevant information.

Early adopters included the United States and Russia, which were the only countries with spacefaring abilities; Luxembourg, which leased its slots to SES; and the kingdom of Tonga, the Polynesian island nation located between New Zealand and Papua New Guinea.

The process by which Tonga entered outer space was a kind of prelude to Luxembourg's twenty-first-century ambitions: the story of a small but determined monarchy, an American entrepreneur, and the encoding of a new kind of property, to be bought, sold, and speculated upon far, far away. It is also about the capacity of the human imagination to transcend the limitations of land in ways surprisingly informed by the past: yet another example of how national sovereignty can be commercialized far from its terrestrial borders, in exceptional zones and liminal jurisdictions.

Tonga's diminutive size is often its hallmark in the eyes of development economists. But unlike the landlocked Luxembourgeois, who lived for centuries in the shadow of powerful territorial neighbors, the Tongan people have never identified as "small." To characterize them by landmass alone is to overlook a more essential element of their spiritual, social, and economic life: the Pacific Ocean.

First settled some 3,000 years ago by the Lapita people and spread over 169 mostly uninhabited islands, Tonga (as well as other island countries in Oceania) has a long tradition of seafaring. Instead of drawing a strong binary between land and sea, they view their domain as a rich and ever-expanding continuum unconstrained by modern economic and political borders. "If we look at the myths, legends and oral traditions, and the cosmologies of the peoples of Oceania, it will become evident that they did not conceive of their world in such microscopic proportions," writes the Tongan Fijian intellectual Epeli Hau'ofa in his essay "Our Sea of Islands." "Their universe comprised not only land surfaces, but the surrounding ocean as far as they could traverse and exploit it, the underworld with its fire-controlling and earth-shaking denizens, and the heavens above with their hierarchies of powerful gods and named stars and constellations that people could count on to guide their ways across the seas. Their world was anything but tiny. They thought big and recounted their deeds in epic proportions."

It is unlikely—or at the very least, unclear—that it was with this legacy in mind that an American entrepreneur talked Tonga into speculating on the stars.

Mats Nilson, a Stanford-trained engineer, was part of an early cadre of experts who built the modern telecoms industry that Georges Schmit spent the 1970s and '80s courting. After a stint at the U.S. office of COMSAT

(Communications Satellite Corporation), a satellite network provider that established the first phone connections across the Atlantic, Nilson was transferred by the firm to Geneva, where he lived for five years before returning to the United States in 1975. After working for another satellite firm, Nilson tried branching out on his own and competing with COMSAT, but he was unsuccessful and made some industry enemies in the process.

After Nilson's wife died in 1987, he traveled to Tonga with plans of perhaps retiring there someday. Amid the grief and dislocation, Nilson could not shake an idea he'd come up with while observing his industry and, in Geneva, the rules set by the ITU: that there could be real money to be made by claiming, then leasing out, orbital slots in partnership with a sovereign nation. It didn't matter how small it was. What mattered was that it was a state.

Thus, Nilson "identified aspects of international laws that give disproportionate powers to sovereign microstates," writes Anthony van Fossen, a senior lecturer at Griffith University in Australia. "The number of satellite slots is limited by international law to prevent interference between satellites, but the slots can be reserved at no cost by nearly any sovereign nation on an essentially first-come, first-served or squatter basis."

In Tonga, Nilson teamed up with the king, Taufa'ahau Tupou IV, to apply to the ITU for sixteen precious unclaimed orbital slots; they were granted a total of nine. He set up a company known as Tongasat to be Tonga's agent in all matters concerning the satellites, and over the next few years helped the country become the world's sixth-largest slot-owning nation. "Mats was a bit of a pirate. His reputation was as a bit of a pirate. But he was very entrepreneurial: he'd try just about anything," recalls James Simon, a former business associate. "And so he met with the crown prince of Tonga, got talking with the princess of Tonga, and formed a corporation where Tonga applied to ITU for satellite positions."

The move shook the world of telecoms, which, somehow discounting the wiles of both small states and Stanford-trained entrepreneurs, had relied on gentlemen's agreements to go about their business. "At that time [there were] a lot of positions available over the Pacific in Southeast Asia that were empty, and Tonga applied for all of them, which wasn't against the rules," Simon explained. "At the end of the day, Tonga ended up with seven or so prime satellite positions; their footprint went from Denver to Europe. It was pretty massive: the little mouse that roared." The United States and Tongan parties leased out the slots to foreign satellite companies and split the proceeds of the multimillion-dollar business.

The endeavor illustrates the unintended results of giving each nation an equal say at the international table, even—or especially—without rectifying the balance of political and economic power between them in the first place. "Sovereign equality" creates a Monopoly board out of the world map. On the one hand, marginalized or relatively powerless nation-states will, as is their right, do what they can to collect rents. But the pressures to do so— from their people, but also from international agencies like the World Bank and the IMF—run the risk of turning them into playthings that capitalists can exploit for their personal gain.

The agency of each state depends a lot on the context in which they operate; these days, Switzerland has a lot more leverage than, say, Palau. But each finds its place in the world market in its own way. In rich nations like Luxembourg, it happens via tax arbitrage; in impoverished ones like Chad, by hawking postage stamps for peanuts; it happens on land, at sea, and even in space. "With a staff of six people and little capital, Tongasat is in effect proposing a flag of convenience for satellites," wrote Anthony van Fossen, at the time of the affair. "This allows capitalists to escape or minimize heavy regulation and the direct and indirect taxation by the core governments that have hitherto controlled outer space."

Nilson's scheme ultimately unraveled into a decades-long legal battle involving members of the Tongan royal family, Russian and Chinese satellite companies, a tangle of shell corporations around the world, and bankruptcy proceedings stretching from Nevis to Indiana. Nevertheless, his incursion showed that the failure to provide for an equal, fair distribution of resources in space—be it through access to spaceflight, a common pool of funding for exploration, or some other way of sharing the wealth internationally—will inevitably lead to speculation, competition, and capitalist accumulation. As Fernando Belaúnde Terry predicted in 1967, it is power, not consensus, that ends up making the rules. Belaúnde hoped for better guardrails to prevent this from happening, more solid assurances that space would not become the domain of entrepreneurs hoping to making a buck. He wanted a lunar Eleanor Roosevelt. Instead, we got Elon Musk.

The Commercial Space Launch Competitiveness Act, passed by the U.S. Congress in 2015, was the world's first "finders keepers" law, recognizing ownership of space resources. It might seem odd that one country can permit something this radical without other states' input, but the letter of international law did not prevent it from doing so. Nor was there any way for another state to stop the United States from extending its property-rights regime extraterritorially. After all, it was not laying claim to the oceans; it was merely catching fish. (An analogous question is being asked by environmentalists about the deep sea: Nauru is selling licenses to a Canadian mining company hoping to trawl the seabed in its territorial waters for nickel and manganese—a practice some international lawyers have condemned for its far-reaching consequences, but that, much like asteroid mining, seems to be technically permissible, at least for now.)

One state really is all it takes for space resources to enter the terrestrial market. Five years after the Space Act, in 2020, NASA selected four companies to deploy robots to collect lunar regolith (aka moondust), which it would buy for a token price. "Right now, we're trying to prove the concept that resources can be extracted, and they can be traded," said NASA administrator Jim Bridenstine at the time. "And not just traded among companies or private individuals, but also among countries and across borders—private individuals in other countries." A Colorado company called Lunar Outpost plans to deliver on its promise by the end of 2024. It has (naturally) received funding from Luxembourg.

When push came to shove, it would not matter if Costa Rica or Guinea objected to the law. Our hypothetical asteroid miner could sell their moondust in the United States, or to a U.S. company, obtain dollars in exchange, and spend them freely wherever she pleased.

Supporters of the Space Act claimed that the prospect of private property in space would encourage hard work and innovation. In a *Wall Street Journal* op-ed, Paul Stimers, then an attorney at the corporate law firm K&L Gates and an adviser to Planetary Resources, celebrated the law's passage with a reference to John Locke's theory of property, which is based in natural law. "The U.S. recognizes that the cosmos belongs to everyone. But under the new law, resources can be retrieved from their location in space and subsequently developed," he wrote. "Property rights spur hard work and innovation—in Locke's day, in ours and in the age of commercial spaceflight to come."

But there was a key limitation of the American legislation: it recognized the rights of companies owned only by U.S. citizens. Aware of this limitation, Luxembourg immediately commissioned a study from the management consulting firm Deloitte on whether it could fill that legal void for multinational corporations. The report, which has since been taken offline, noted that "while legal uncertainty remains, under the current legal and regulatory framework, space mining activities are (at least) not prohibited," and concluded that Luxembourg should pass legislation giving miners the right to keep any extraterrestrial bounty they might extract.

Such a law was drafted, and on August 1, 2017, it went into effect. Luxembourg's bill does not discriminate by nationality, or even by the location of a company's headquarters. In fact, the law indicates the country's willingness to serve as a sort of flag of convenience for spacecraft, allowing them to play by one country's idea of the rules in the absence of universal, binding agreements.

Rick Tumlinson, a venture capitalist who invests in NewSpace companies and hosts a space-themed radio show, told me he liked Luxembourg's law because it saw no citizens and no borders: just one blue planet from high above. He was invoking what's known as the overview effect—the feeling of wholeness and transcendence that astronauts have reported at their first glimpse of Earth. By this logic, Luxembourg wasn't making dispensations for the most privileged citizens. It was leveling the playing field—in space.

Six weeks after I reported on the grand duchy's trade mission to Washington, I boarded a flight from Geneva to Luxembourg City. It's a shuttle service of just more than an hour that's popular with bankers. Everyone on board looked comfortable and a little bored, as though they were riding a commuter train to the suburbs.

Disembarking from the tiny plane into a melee of gray suits and black carry-on bags, I made my way to the parking lot past advertisements for wealth management firms and equity funds. There I caught the bus to the city center, passing dozens of huge new building projects, a tramline under construction, and two enormous yellow towers that, in the afternoon light, resembled twin gold bars reaching for the sky.

I must have passed the Luxembourg freeport, then still under Yves Bouvier's management, as well, but it was largely hidden from view. This was by design. The anthropologist Samuel Weeks recalls being met with a "blank stare" from a taxi driver he asked to take him to the warehouse. "The driver left to consult some of his colleagues. The verdict: one of them had heard of something, sometime of a 'port franc'—but he was not certain what it was or where it was located."

Within the hour, I was sitting at a table outside a dive bar opposite the old city's bathhouse with Lars Schmitz and Gabrielle Taillefert, members of a local theater-and-art collective called Richtung22 (Direction22). Over the previous few years, the group had staged a series of performances lampooning their country's mercenary modus operandi. Instead of writing scripts from scratch, the collective fashioned dramatic collages almost entirely out of primary documents: laws, press releases, speeches, transcripts from par-liament, promotional videos, and so on.

One of Richtung22's early works satirized the Luxembourg freeport. In that play, an actor playing its director, David Arendt, asserted that "Money laundering is cultural heritage here!"—to which Yves Bouvier's character answered, "That is clear, as a Swiss I know my colleagues," before demand-ing changes to the country's tax laws. The collective's next production was a send-up of Luxembourg's nation-branding committee, which aimed to pro-mote the country abroad. The play, which was financed in part by the cul-ture ministry, was entitled *Lëtzebuerg, du hannerhältegt Stéck Schäiss* (that would be *Luxembourg, You Sneaky Piece of Shit*). Schmitz told me that after that one, the group's state funding mysteriously dried up.

In his spare time, Schmitz, who is slight of build with cropped blond hair, works on anti-fascist and anti-capitalist organizing. He has the droll resignation of a left-wing activist operating in a country whose politics are, to him, so tragic that grassroots resistance must necessarily come in the form of farce. Richtung22's next play savaged the country's efforts to attract the NewSpace industry. Its title was *Luxembourg's Private Space Explorevolu-tionary Superfancy Asteroid Tailoring*.

Schmitz sees space mining as a high-tech spin on an age-old scam: sell-ing sovereignty. "The country's business model is hidden," he said. "It's making laws that companies want, and taking a risk on those companies. But the government uses it to say, 'This is how modern we are! This is some-thing new!'"

Gabriel Zucman, the economist, shares Schmitz's view. "Adapting this strategy to the business of space conquest is what being an offshore financial center means," he says. "It's not diversification. It's just extending the logic of being a tax haven to a new area."

Onstage, the entire space enterprise was portrayed as a cynical, money-grubbing, reputation-washing debacle dictated by private-sector interests.

"We feel bad that our country does this to the world, and no one else here talks about this stuff," Schmitz told me. He ticked off a dozen or so Luxembourgian transgressions, including but not limited to aiding and abetting tax evasion and weaseling its way out of EU banking regulations. In such a small country, it was hard to be so outspoken against the national interest. "People think we're traitors," he said.

Was there anything good about his country? I asked. "It's beautiful," Schmitz conceded. He was right: Luxembourg is beautiful, and it was particularly charming on that balmy May evening. The city rests on two levels: the smaller "low" city's quaint little streets and sidewalk cafés skim the river, while the "high" city center is home to a lively main drag with pricey boutiques, fancy chocolate shops, and chains such as H&M. Cafés advertise *crémant*—a local sparkling wine—and local dishes that borrow their richness from the French and their stodginess from the Germans.

The next day, I went to meet Marc Baum, an MP from the democratic socialist party, Déi Lénk (the Left). He handed me a policy paper his party published criticizing Schneider's space-mining proposal: they believe his law is inconsistent with Luxembourg's 1967 treaty obligations, that it creates opportunities for billionaires to further enrich themselves, and that it could be harmful to the environment. Even worse, it enshrines the notion of "competition instead of cooperation" between states. "It's infinite capitalism!" Baum exclaimed over a cold beer on a cobblestoned terrace.

Baum, as it happens, is an actor too. When we met, he was preparing to perform in Eugène Ionesco's *Rhinoceros*, an absurdist play about a town whose protagonists speak exclusively in clichés, and whose unquestioning conformity ends up turning them into rhinos. Over the course of the drama, the townspeople justify their decision to "go rhino" by declaring that "humanism is dead, those who follow it are just old sentimentalists." The play's sole hero, Bérenger, resists succumbing to "rhinoceritis," but he fails to save anyone else in the town.

The analogy between the play and Baum's own predicament seems a little on the nose. He had been one of just two politicians who voted against the space law.

In June, about a month before his signature legislation was passed by the parliament, Schneider and some of his associates flew to New York for yet another sales pitch—this time, for the benefit of venture capitalists on the East Coast. His speech focused on the financial aspects of Luxembourg's space race, and the country's intention to get in on the ground floor of commercial space exploration. "Under the U.S. Space Act, your capital has to be majority U.S. capital," he said, referring to U.S. willingness to recognize property rights in space for its citizens. "We don't really care where the money comes from in our country, as long as the money is clean."

On Schneider's telling, Luxembourg would do for the space-resource trade what it had done for the Eurodollar market, international holding companies, and tech giants: provide a safe, reliable base where they could operate in tandem with a keen and cooperative—or, by his detractors' assessment, pliable and sycophantic—state. Schneider announced that after passing its law, Luxembourg would create its own space agency, which it did, in 2018. They weren't sending astronauts to Mars—at least, not yet—but they would be promoting space education, sending delegates to other space agencies, and solidifying Luxembourg's role in this nascent economy. If asteroid mining does, in fact, take off, Luxembourg will be what Schneider's friends in Silicon Valley might call an early adopter.

It's a gamble, of course, particularly when the future of the Earth, let alone the cosmos, feels more precarious than ever. But it's difficult to imagine where Luxembourg would be had it not deployed its ingenious development strategy continually over the past century. After all, this is a country that has defied all odds and made virtues of its apparent weaknesses. Its small size did not prevent it from becoming the largest center for investment funds in the world, after the United States. Its tiny population did not deter massive multinationals from basing their headquarters there. It has parlayed its status as a neutral country and founding member of many European organizations into sending three of its politicians—more than any other country—to preside over the European Commission since the EU's executive body was founded. It even has a freeport, probably filled with world-class art. Never mind that no one can see it.

The global economy offers few options other than to serve it, and it rewards its enablers richly. Perhaps a mercenary spirit is just what a small country needs to succeed in the world. And maybe "We want to remain what we are" is just Luxembourgeois for the old French saying: *Plus ça change . . .*

8.

Titanic

There was a flag, of course, flying above the stern. The flag, however, was so pale, so flimsy, so shredded, that it might have represented any flag of any country in the world. It looked as if it had been flown from the battle-ships of all the fleets that had partaken in sea-battles for the last five thousand years.

—B. TRAVEN, *THE DEATH SHIP*

In April 2022, a pale white cruise ship heaved onto the coast at Gadani, Pakistan, twenty-five miles northwest of Karachi along the Arabian Sea. A plume of exhaust streamed out from her funnel; her anchor, visible from the beach, dangled portside above the turquoise water. The ship was in good shape: her hull was free of dents and scuffs, and her coat still looked pretty decent, with a bright stripe of blue paint some fifty feet above the water. Near the top deck, between the gym level and the nightclub level, life rafts hung—waiting, perhaps, to once again save somebody's life.

Only it was the ship herself that needed saving, and it was much too late for that. She was on the last mile of her final journey. She had come to Pakistan to die.

Dying isn't easy when you have a sixteen-thousand-ton steel body that has been afloat for forty-seven years. You cannot return to dust. You must die slowly, deliberately, piece by rusting piece. Lawfully, too—there are so many rules governing what happens to a ship's decomposing corpse. But the vessel knew how to get around those, and the myriad other laws that get muddled in the world's waters. Until quite recently, the ship had been known as the *Salamis Filoxenia* and sailed under Cypriot colors. Now she was the *Titan*, and she flew the funeral flag of Palau, a fictitious identity tailor-made to evade environmental regulation.

Nobody cared that the *Titan* had been around the world, but never once to the Pacific island republic of Palau. Her allegiance to that nation was paper thin by design. Besides, she'd never played favorites. She'd hosted Soviet and American vacationers during the Cold War and employed British dancers, Egyptian cooks, and Romanian engineers at the turn of the millennium. She'd delighted enthusiasts from Turkey, Greece, and Cyprus, who circulated snapshots of her comings and goings at Mediterranean ports of call. She'd charmed an Indian manager and a Ukrainian actor, who went online during the pandemic to find footage of their old friend. "I was with her from 2009–2013, love her, every corner of her I still remember," commented Mahi Maji, a member of the crew, on a Facebook post.

Oleksander Babii first boarded the ship in his hometown of Odessa in 1983, as a tourist, then returned to perform as a mime in 2011. When he learned of her demise, days after Vladimir Putin pledged to escalate his war against Ukraine in the fall of 2022, Babii was gutted. "This is real? I did not know," he wrote. "Now I do not follow the news in the world because we are at war here. But if it's true, of course it hurts. I'm so sorry."

Sharing the sentiment were 3,700 members of a Facebook page created in the ship's honor, in which former passengers mourned the summers aboard they had known and loved. They remembered lavish spreads of carved watermelon and shrimp cocktail, crepes with ice cream, the hot buffet, the cold buffet, magic shows, belly dancing, the piano bar, the disco ball, and an exuberant rendition of "YMCA" after dark. Two full years of COVID restrictions meant that these reminiscences were the closest many of them could get to recapturing the feeling of being truly carefree—let alone carefree on a budget cruise catering to a thousand-odd middle-class Europeans.

I'd never met the *Titan*, and now I never will. But I know how she smelled: like wet hair, well rum, and Club Med.

The party's over now, the summer long gone. In her final resting place, in a shipbreaking facility far from home, the *Titan* is dismembered, her entrails left to dry in the baking sun. The tables where diners overate spaghetti carbonara are auctioned off in bulk; the light fixtures that illuminated drunken conga lines are pulled off the walls. Mattresses are removed from cabins, which are torn from decks, which are pried from the hull, which is broken into chunks, melted down, and recycled into another ship.

The *Titan* is dead.

Long live the *Titan*!

The *Titan* began her life in a shipyard in Turku, Finland, in 1975 as *Gruziya*, the second of five sister vessels commissioned by the Soviet Black Sea Shipping Company. Her given name—the first of many—was the Russian term for the then Soviet Republic of Georgia. By her side were the *Belorussia*, the *Kareliya*, the *Kazakhstan*, and the *Azerbaijan*. In true Soviet fashion, each ship was created equal: 512 feet long, 54 feet deep, and painted white with a handsome dash of red. In true Soviet style, the vessels flew the hammer and sickle at sea.

Over the next five decades, this flag would be replaced time after time as the tides of history swept the *Gruziya* and her sisters away from their home port of Odessa and across the world. She would survive regime changes and economic catastrophes, only to serve new gods and new masters. She would weather storm after economic storm until she met her end in a watery grave.

Gruziya's first assignment was as a passenger ferry. In her early days, she earned her keep shuttling Soviet citizens, functionaries, and their cars between the Caucasus and Crimea. Then, in the 1980s, she was kitted out with small luxuries—nicer cabins, a movie theater, a bar—and began working cruises on the Black Sea. Her clientele was made up mostly of domestic tourists, but the trips were also open to Westerners looking for an affordable holiday that was "not Las Vegas," as one travel agent put it to *The New York Times*. That's when Babii first boarded for a seven-day cruise. It stopped at the Soviet ports of Yalta, Sochi, Sukhumi, Batumi, Sebastopol, and Novorossiysk.

When the USSR collapsed in 1991, the Black Sea Shipping Company became Ukrainian, and the *Gruziya* and her sisters were managed by the state-owned company known as Blasco. The firm, once among the biggest in the world, was caught between socialism and the market, with the new Ukrainian leader, Leonid Kravchuk, angling for it to be privatized without delay while the old communists in the Ukrainian parliament sought to slow the process down. The standoff escalated into a political battle, with the parliament investigating Blasco's management and finding significant misappropriation of state funds (the company denied any wrongdoing). That, in turn, spooked potential investors in the firm; after struggling for years, the company declared bankruptcy and sold off its fleet.

Boardroom drama did not stop the *Gruziya* from taking advantage of her newfound freedom. That first summer, she sailed the Mediterranean; the next, she set off for Canada's St. Lawrence River. In Montreal in August 1992, her hammer and sickle were replaced with a large trident; the ceremony, which marked Ukraine's first anniversary as a sovereign nation, was attended by officials and dignitaries, including the first Canadian ambassador to Ukraine, three high-ranking members of the clergy, and a Ukrainian youth orchestra.

Later that fall, the ship made her way down the Atlantic coast to St. Petersburg, Florida. A civilian flotilla sailed out to greet her; she was the first ex-Soviet ship to sail out of a U.S. port in a decade, and she took passengers to Bermuda, Mexico, and the Honduran island of Roatán, and on a "party cruise to nowhere" that lasted two drunken days. On a Caribbean hardship assignment in 1993, a reporter for the South Florida *Sun Sentinel* looked on as an American bartender explained to a young Russian crew member how to mix cranberry, orange, vodka, and peach schnapps into a Sex on the Beach. "It is one thing to hear that the Cold War is over," wrote the reporter. "It is another thing altogether to sit on a former Soviet ship in the middle of the Gulf of Mexico and watch a foodie from Tampa presiding over the making of prurient cocktails."

But ships are creatures of circumstance, and cocktail hour would be over before the dinner bell rang. In May 1994, the U.S. Department of Defense put out a tender: it was seeking vessels, complete with crew and staff, for a lucrative gig in the Caribbean. There was trouble in Haiti—a military coup, compounded by crushing poverty, tangled up in two decades of repression, corruption, and foreign meddling—and the Military Sealift Command needed all the help it could get corralling thousands of frightened Haitians trying to leave their country. The ships would not be guiding the migrants to safety, or helping smaller vessels navigate to shore. They would be housing military personnel, fishing people out of the ocean, and carrying out asylum screening procedures on board, with the intention of sending the migrants home as soon as possible.

The *Gruziya* met all the requirements: she could be free to start work by the end of May and would accommodate up to seven hundred passengers. A ship broker representing the Pentagon contacted a second broker, who tapped the *Gruziya*'s management, and their bid to charge $34,000 per day won out against the competition.

That was how, practically overnight, the vessel transformed from booze cruise to a facility aiding in the "interdiction, reception, transportation, detention, security, control, and processing of Haitian migrants."

The *Gruziya* wasn't the first vessel enlisted for this kind of work, known in legal and policy circles as interdiction. The United States had for decades gone to extraordinary lengths to keep immigrants in general, and Haitians in particular, as far away from its territory as it could—a move designed to prevent them from claiming and asserting U.S. constitutional rights. Its strategy relied on creative and callous use of offshore space. If the migrants would not stay away from the border, then the United States would move its border.

The story of interdiction began in the late 1960s, when ordinary Haitians, fed up with the corrupt and violent Duvalier regime, began leaving their country—first in relatively small numbers, then in much larger ones, aboard vessels that ranged from rickety dinghies to expertly crafted sailboats. Earlier on, a smattering of migrants made it to the United States without attracting too much attention, but when the unauthorized migrations didn't let up, the newly elected president, Ronald Reagan, stepped in to pass an executive order in 1981 authorizing Coast Guard cutters to systematically intercept Haitian migrants at sea, beyond U.S. territorial waters. His administration even struck an agreement with the Haitian government, allowing U.S. troops to pull migrants off Haitian-flagged boats, in waters belonging to Haiti. The reasoning behind these policies was cynical from the start: if the migrants did not technically arrive on U.S. territory, the United States could act as though they did not exist.

Aboard these ships, law enforcement agents were supposed to interview Haitians to establish whether they had a credible fear of persecution at home, because it is against international law to send an asylum seeker back to danger. The agents would then either return them to Haiti or admit them to the United States. But if the interviews appeared at first to give migrants a chance to plead their case, they were soon revealed to be a farce. Of the 24,600 people who were captured in this fashion between 1981 and 1991, only 11 were allowed to pursue an asylum claim to the United States. The rest were labeled "economic" migrants and sent away, sometimes to dangerous, even life-threatening, situations.

In September 1991, things took an even darker turn. Haiti's first democratically elected president, Jean-Bertrand Aristide, had come to power after promising to end corruption and empower the poor, but seven months after his election, a military coup led by Raoul Cédras kicked off a new surge of violence. For six weeks, President George H. W. Bush suspended interdictions and allowed Haitians to enter the United States, but his administration quickly reversed course and resumed the shipboard interviews. When the ships became too crowded, the United States began to corral the Haitians into yet another offshore jurisdiction: Guantánamo Bay.

Before it became a maximum-security prison for alleged terrorists following 9/11, Guantánamo had been a relatively unknown naval base that the United States leased from Cuba: consensually between 1903 and 1959, then unilaterally since the Cuban Revolution (as of this writing, Cuba is sitting on millions of dollars' worth of uncashed U.S. rent payments). Gitmo's physical location was strategically useful to the Americans, but its legal geography could not be beat. Being neither "domestic" nor strictly "foreign" territory, it let the U.S. government argue that it was a place where the Constitution did not apply.

What this liminality meant for the Haitians being held there was that they could not enjoy protections such as habeas corpus or the right to legal counsel. Nor could they apply directly for political asylum in the United States, because Guantánamo was a mere rental unit and not part of the country where asylum claims must take place. Rather, the Haitians would need to be "screened in" before being given the chance to make asylum claims.

Between shipboard interdiction and extraterritorial detention, the United States in the 1990s pulled off a veritable hat trick of offshore acrobatics. The land was not its land; the laws were not its laws; and the people did not even count as real people. Such interpretations meant that it could indefinitely hold people without consent in a place it was indefinitely holding without consent.

By the spring of 1992, the humanitarian situation at Guantánamo was becoming untenable. Lodgings at the base were getting crowded, with more than 12,500 people interned in makeshift camps surrounded by barbed wire. Most controversially, a group of 300 HIV-positive refugees remained confined in an encampment named Camp Bulkeley. In spite of having been found largely eligible to begin asylum proceedings, part of the group, which included pregnant women and small children, was detained for twenty months because of a U.S. ban on HIV-positive immigrants. "The conditions under which they are living, if you can call it that, are out of Dante's *Inferno*— the ninth circle of Hell," wrote Michael Ratner, one of their lawyers, when he visited his clients. "For fourteen months they have used portable toilets that are rarely cleaned, that are filled with feces and urine. The camp is bleak— no grass, hardscrabble ground and temporary wooden barracks on concrete slabs. Within those 'homes' 15 to 20 Haitians are huddled with only sheets hanging from the rafters. Rain, vermin and rats are the other occupants."

Stateside, legal challenges to the administration's treatment of migrants on land, sea, and the spaces in between started piling up. Detainees in Gitmo staged hunger strikes for better living conditions, lawyers, and free- dom; activists in the United States wrote letters, held rallies, and protested in front of courthouses. It was becoming clear that Gitmo was not serving its main purpose, of keeping Haitians out of sight and out of mind.

But the goal was, and still is, to keep asylum seekers as far away from the United States as humanly possible. In an executive order passed on May 24, 1992, Bush Sr. announced that Haitians intercepted at sea would be summar- ily sent back, no questions asked. When the Federal Court of Appeals ordered a halt to these summary interdictions, the Bush administration kicked the case up to the Supreme Court, which ruled in its favor. This precedent would be- come the most meaningful rollback of refugee rights in modern U.S. history.

According to the 1993 *Sale v. Haitian Centers Council, Inc.* decision, no rules prohibiting *refoulement*, or returning people to dangerous places, applied to Coast Guard agents pulling people from the sea, because such rules did not apply extraterritorially. In the ruling, the justices "effectively created a black hole in international refugee law with regard to refugees seized on the high seas," wrote Yale Law School professor Harold Koh, who was part of the team representing the HIV-positive Haitians. Although Bill Clinton had campaigned on stopping summary interdictions, they continued well into his first term. The difference was that this time, they were carried out with the Supreme Court's blessing.

That wasn't the end of Gitmo either.

The Bulkeley detainees languished until a judge ordered their release in the summer of 1993. The Clinton administration, which had taken office that January, responded to the order with a deal. They would free the remaining Haitians at Gitmo without appealing the court's decision, but only if the court would strike it from precedent. Ratner and Koh's legal team agreed, and the result was that by mid-1994 Guantánamo once again had a population of fourteen thousand people, and the naval base's exceptional regime of indefinite detention would stand.

In the meantime, Clinton had found a way to have his political cake and eat it too, and this is when the *Gruziya*'s new contract entered the picture. The president finally resumed shipboard asylum screenings for Haitians, as he'd promised on the campaign trail; after all, he was a humanitarian. To aid in his mission to protect Americans from foreign intruders, he would use the Ukrainian ferry staffed with American cops to interdict Haitian migrants in Jamaican territorial waters. Overall, interdiction between January 1993 and November 1994 was the Coast Guard's biggest peacetime job ever.

As soon as she won her charter from the Military Sealift Command on May 14, 1994, the *Gruziya* canceled vacation plans in order to participate in what became known as Operation Sea Signal. The decision surprised the cruising community. "The last time I remember hearing anything similar to this type of situation was when the *Queen Elizabeth II* was taken over by the British government during the Falkland Island War," one travel agent told the *Tampa Bay Times*. "It's very unusual."

Alexander Bout, the executive vice president of the *Gruziya*'s cruise company, was unapologetic. "We are not running a charity," the Odessa executive told a Ukrainian American community newspaper. "Never before has the U.S. State Department used any vessel from the Soviet Union in performing its duties."

After a short delay to repair the onboard ventilation system and install migrant processing teams, the *Gruziya* began her journey. According to U.S. Navy archives and press reports, the ship sailed from Florida to Jamaica, whose government had agreed to let U.S. ships anchor in its territorial waters from June 10. The order of operations was reported as follows: Migrants leaving Haiti would be picked up by the navy's own cutters patrolling the Windward Passage. The cutters would take the asylum seekers to the USS *Comfort*, a thousand-bed hospital ship anchored near Kingston, where asylum interviews, newly resumed under Clinton, would take place. Migrants who did not fit on the *Comfort* would be transferred to the *Gruziya*, where they would sleep on cots or mats on the ship's garage deck. Then they would either be sent back to Haiti or continue their journey on to Guantánamo.

Bout remembers the arrangement differently. The *Gruziya* "was for military personnel—for eating, sleeping, laundry, cabins. This ship was too luxury for the refugees."

Indeed, the *Gruziya* did not end up housing any asylum seekers—just some four hundred American customs, immigration, medical, and military staffers preparing for their mission, and the original crew. "When we withdrew the ship from its charter and moved it back to Florida, [the crew] were keeping relations with the American personnel," Bout recalled in a phone interview from his home in Florida. "Some of them fell in love! We have beautiful girls in the Soviet Union."

The *Gruziya*'s contract with the navy ended the day before shipboard processing began, a result of bureaucratic and operational delays. She was a stopgap vessel, largely unprepared for this kind of work, but a Marine Corps officer would remember her fondly in an official report as "a well-run ship, accustomed to meeting the demands of European and American passengers." On June 15, she was replaced by another Blasco vessel, the *Ivan Franko* (a "dirty, substandard option," the same report recalled), which took custody of the passengers and equipment.

Even so, the *Gruziya* made history by becoming a small part of a growing constellation of offshore spaces that rewrote how wealthy Western countries would come to process migrants for decades to come (a topic further explored in the next chapter). "With interdiction, new policing interventions—crafted to evade judicial review—erupted into these spaces as punctuated expressions of sovereign power beyond territory and its fixed, earthbound core," writes Jeffrey Kahn, a legal anthropologist, in *Islands of Sovereignty*. "This renewed search for sovereign control and liberated bureaucracy drove the asylum-screening apparatus outward into a space-time of relative oceanic freedom, a laboratory of sorts in which new forms of border governance could be tested, contested, and routinized over the years to come."

There is a dark symmetry to the American origins of interdiction. If new arrivals to the United States had historically been intercepted at way stations like Ellis Island for registration and quarantine, the use of ships cruising in the open ocean served an opposite purpose: to keep them out. And if the borders of the territorial United States had been inspired by Manifest Destiny, or the idea that settlers were ordained by God to grow their dominion, then expanding the reach of the immigration authorities off land, out into the ocean and into the jurisdiction of other sovereign states, made a certain metaphysical sense in a period of escalating globalization.

. . .

After the Haitian debacle, it was time for the *Gruziya* to reinvent herself. So she sailed back north to the port of Montreal and began shuttling passengers up the St. Lawrence River, along the Saguenay Fjord. Their destination was St.-Pierre and Miquelon, a vestigial French overseas territory that Al Capone once employed to smuggle alcohol into the United States during Prohibition. Miquelon is a blustery, frigid island, but like its tropical counterpart, Réunion, remains an unlikely part of contemporary France: the road signs are built to French specifications, and the lone hotel accepts euros. On board, though, the *Gruziya* never fully left the USSR behind. "Below decks, the entertainment highlights Ukrainian and Russian folkloric groups, in dazzling costumes, who sing and dance their way into passengers' hearts," reported *The Hamilton Spectator*, praising the ship's onboard Black Sea Band for its renditions of French Canadian classics. "The *Gruziya* also offers classes in making Borscht, trap shooting, poolside games—even a sampling of vodkas from various regions of the former Soviet Union."

On one such trip, the *Gruziya* came home with a new name: the *Odessa Sky*. Monsigneur Igino Incantalupo, a Catholic priest working on board as a chaplain, spent the cruise giving counsel and Communion to vacationers who, between watching whales and getting wasted, wanted something more. In an email, the priest recalled being tickled by the ship's (re)christening: it was almost as though the cold air and bracing water had cleansed her of her brush with darkness.

But to be a ship is to exist in permanent limbo, and sin can be kept only so long at bay. In the summer of 1995, *Odessa Sky* was arrested by the Canadian Coast Guard at the port of Montreal. Blasco, which was in the process of going bankrupt, had fallen gravely behind on its bills, and the only way for its German creditors to recoup the money was to take legal action. Vacationers saw their trips cut short as the *Odessa Sky* was anchored at the port.

After the vessel was emptied of passengers, 212 Russian and Ukrainian crew members remained on board.

The crew's visas did not grant them the right to disembark and take up residence in Canada while their ship's legal woes were resolved. Most did not have the funds to pay their way home. Complicating matters further was the fact that the *Odessa Sky* was no longer technically Ukraine's problem. It was owned by a Blasco subsidiary based in the UK; operated by a cruise line based in Mineola, New York; and newly reregistered under the flag of Liberia. That meant that no matter where it sailed, the ship was a little island of Liberian sovereignty, with that country's rules, laws, and regulations.

In popular culture, the ocean is often portrayed as an unruly, anarchic medium—the only free space left in our orderly, bordered world. But the *Gruziya*'s journey from Baltic cradle to subcontinental grave paints a more complex and interesting picture. Under the floating jurisdiction of a half-dozen flags, party to countless international treaties, and in the hands of a rotating cast of owners, creditors, captains, and managers, the ship did not suffer from a lack of laws. If anything, there were too many to make sense of.

The laws were, of course, twice or thrice removed from their origins. Enforcement was arbitrary, even meaningless (in that respect, a ship on the high seas is a lot like a bear in the woods). But there are no true vacuums in our world—and if there were, a ship could not sail in one. Sovereignty at sea moves like a current, contingent on political gravity, ideological winds, and social friction, which makes freedom of the seas a lot like all other freedoms: more free for some than it is for others.

The United Nations Convention on the Law of the Sea, or UNCLOS, is a sprawling, complex set of treaties whose environmental, regulatory, and legal guidelines took more than a decade to negotiate. The convention was signed in 1982 and went into force in 1994; 169 countries have joined, though the United States has yet to sign on. It would be absurd to distill a convention

208 • THE HIDDEN GLOBE

that governs uses of two thirds of the world's oceans and their resources into a mere sentence, but the essence of the treaty is that the world's largest bodies of water can be categorized into different maritime zones. The area within twelve miles of shore is considered to be the closest nation's territory, where ordinary national rules apply. Within two hundred miles of a coast is the country's Exclusive Economic Zone, meaning that fishing and prospecting for natural resources are under the control of the state, but that navigation in these areas is open to all. This arrangement encompasses 35 percent of all seas, contains 90 percent of the world's fish, and "neatly conveys a capitalist logic where the sea is functionally exploited as a resource, rather than politically occupied as a territory," write Alejandro Colás and Liam Campling in *Capitalism and the Sea*.

Beyond those boundaries, the sea is technically "free" for exploitation and navigation, but subject to reams of environmental and commercial restrictions. The responsibility of ships to follow these rules falls on the flag state, which also determines labor, tort, and contract law on board, regardless of where the ship is located.

This system of governance had been followed more or less informally: for centuries, ships were identified by their flags. But over the course of the twentieth century, the links between a vessel, its flag, its owner, its crew, and its country of origin were coming apart. Right before UNCLOS was signed, as many as 42 percent of the world's fleet by gross tonnage was flagged to one of a dozen "flags of convenience" (FOCs); by 2019, the proportion was nearing three quarters.

Vessels are supposed to maintain a "genuine link" to their flag state under international law, but this concept is vague too. For countries like Liberia, but also the Marshall Islands, Cyprus, St. Vincent, Comoros, and Palau, the relationship is financial: anyone willing to pay tonnage fees and to purchase an insurance policy can find a flag for their vessel.

FOC countries have taken a page or two from Switzerland's playbook: in exchange for their jurisdiction, they enforce few rules, tax their fleets a pittance (if at all), and cloak their owners in anonymity, making it hard to sue for back pay, accidents, or abuse. Large cruise firms enjoy particular perks. If Carnival, the biggest U.S. cruise line, wanted to flag its fleet in the United States, its boats would have to be built in America, staffed by Americans, pay federal taxes and minimum wage, and adhere to myriad regulations, like making cabins wheelchair accessible. Instead, it rents Panamanian or Bahamian laws, stuffs its crew cabins with foreign workers, and saves itself millions upon millions of dollars a year.

To limit the inevitable "race to the bottom" and make sure basic safety rules are being followed, a few dozen countries have signed a series of memoranda allowing local port agents to search and enter ships docked at their harbors if they suspect they are mistreating workers, polluting the environment, or committing one of a laundry list of other transgressions. But inspections happen less than workers would like, and accountability is hard to come by. Often, the flag state purposefully helps obscure the ship's beneficial owner. This means that if something goes wrong on board, there is no clear recourse in the courts.

The International Transport Workers' Federation (ITF), an alliance of trade unions that advocates for seafarers, has been attacking the flag system publicly for more than seventy-five years for this very reason. "Ship owners are forced to look for the cheapest and least regulated ways of running their vessels in order to compete, and FOCs provide the solution," states the organization. "In an increasingly fierce competitive shipping market, each new FOC is forced to promote itself by offering the lowest possible fees and the minimum of regulation."

When the *Odessa Sky* was arrested in Montreal, port inspectors did in fact board the vessel. They found conditions to be adequate, despite one sailor's claims that the food was inedible and the cabins lousy with asbestos. Indisputably the crew was unhappy, broke, and out of options. The ship's owners were spiraling into bankruptcy; the captain had reportedly resorted to threats and violence to keep his meager staff from deserting; and with no money to travel home, they found themselves, absurdly, in a bizarro slice of Liberia, which meant absolutely nothing at all. This was not because the system was broken, but because it worked. The flag was not a meaningful guarantor of rights, but a legal fiction behind which businesses from one country could claim to be from someplace else.

Perhaps fittingly, the origins of this fiction were not even Liberian, but as American as apple pie.

To understand Liberia's decision to start selling its flag to unscrupulous shipowners, it's necessary to rewind the clock and sail to Panama, a country that in the early 1900s made the fateful decision to open its maritime registry not just to Panamanian citizens, but to shipowners from around the world. The country's initial objective was to grow its merchant fleet—if only on paper—once the (U.S.-built) Panama Canal opened in 1914. But in the 1920s and '30s, it found an eager clientele in the highest ranks of American industrial and state power.

During Prohibition, the Panamanian flag attracted American shipowners—among them New York governor W. Averell Harriman—who insisted on selling alcohol on board their vessels to satisfy sailors, in spite of a ruling by the U.S. attorney general banning the practice. Booze turned out to be a convenient foil. American labor laws were growing stronger, forcing fleets to raise their pay and improve sailor accommodations. "Reflagging" let ships switch from a U.S. registration to a Panamanian one with fewer rules and restrictions.

Harriman ended up saving millions when his new flag allowed him to hire foreign workers and avoid certain tariffs. By his side was John Foster Dulles, the former U.S. legal counsel at Versailles who later became Panama's top lawyer in the United States.

Lawyers for Standard Oil also turned to Panama, particularly when war broke out and American neutrality laws restricted the movement of U.S.-flagged ships. In parallel, U.S. diplomats advised Panama on how to sell its upstart flag business out of a network of embassies and consulates around the world—a business that would earn the country tens of millions of dollars per year. And when there were no Panamanian ambassadors to be found, the Americans sent their own men instead. "Panamanian ship registration became an adjunct of American officialdom," writes historian Rodney Carlisle in *Sovereignty for Sale*, arguing that rather than undermining U.S. geopolitical interests, Panama's flag bolstered them. "Americans could have their social justice legislation for American flag ships," he goes on, "but Americans could also compete internationally with cheaply operated vessels under foreign registry."

The flag hack was ingenious. It was also perfectly legal, according to both recent U.S. regulations and an international tribunal dating back decades. In 1905, the Permanent Court of Arbitration in The Hague had heard *Muscat Dhows*, a case in which England challenged the French practice of leasing its flag to alleged slave traders (the United States had used FOCs to transport slaves from Africa too). The court decided that "generally speaking it belongs to every Sovereign to decide to whom he will accord the right to fly his flag and to prescribe the rules governing such grants."

In other words: it was a country's prerogative to decide which ships were theirs, and no other country could do anything about it. The decision has helped justify "flagging out" to this day, whether shipowners are doing it to protect themselves from unions, trade embargoes, taxes, immigration laws, or environmental regulations.

(Curiously, an arbiter who wrote the decision was U.S. Supreme Court chief justice Melville Fuller. In the United States, Fuller is best remembered for his "separate but equal" ruling codifying racial segregation in *Plessy v. Ferguson*. Fuller also struck down early attempts at establishing a federal income tax, dissented against anti-monopoly rulings, voted to limit labor protections, and prized individual property rights above much else. Although the contexts for his decisions on shipping and segregation aren't morally or ethically comparable, both rest on expedient legal fictions: in one case, the equality of citizens, and in the other, the equality of states. Just as

African Americans could not enjoy the advantages of their white compatriots, Panama could not compete with the United States on the international stage—but to claim that they were equal was, and is, awfully convenient.)

This isn't to say that FOCs are all bad, all the time. In the 1930s, ships cloaked in Panamanian neutrality spirited Jewish refugees away from ports on the Black Sea and the Adriatic and on to Palestine, though at a certain point, British immigration quotas interfered. Greek shipowners registered vessels to Panama to get around their country's nonintervention agreements and deliver supplies to Loyalist forces fighting fascism during the Spanish Civil War. One Alexander Davaris renamed his ship after every trip to avoid getting caught and, deadpan, told an American diplomat that he was not funding anti-fascist fighters but merely avoiding Greek taxes. Today, the ocean remains a site of idealistic desperation—or desperate ideals. Floating clinics have provided abortions and birth control to women in countries that prohibit them. With the overturning of *Roe v. Wade* in 2022, a U.S. nonprofit now hopes to do the same in the Gulf of Mexico.

Nevertheless, the flags have always been incredibly unpopular with organized labor. The unions' objections concern workers' rights, of course, which are flouted at sea, if not more often then certainly more easily, thanks to shoddy oversight, laborers recruited from poor countries, and the travails of life aboard ship. But more fundamentally unsettling is the way that FOCs can, from one day to the next, defy the dictates of space and time to meet the demands of capital.

In 1926, a German writing under the name B. Traven published a novel called *The Death Ship*. The novel's protagonist is Gerard Gales, a sailor from New Orleans who misses his boat in Antwerp and finds himself functionally stateless after losing his sailor's ID card. Like the hundreds of thousands of stateless people drifting around Europe after the war, Gales is caught in the in-between, battling petty bureaucrats until his eyes fall out. He ends up with so little faith in the system of nations and states and borders that he gives up explaining where he came from. "No, sir. No nationality. Without a country. League of Nations, Geneva," he proclaims.

Because of his predicament, Gales is reduced to working on the *Yorikke*, a decrepit gunrunner with a flag "so pale, so flimsy, so shredded, that it might have represented any flag of any country in the world." His descriptions of the *Yorikke* make the *Odessa Sky* look like a five-star hotel; still, the ship provided meager wages and desperate companionship for men who didn't belong. Gales comes to love the *Yorikke* like a mother, even though she is—literally and figuratively—a vessel for humanity's worst impulses.

The ocean is no haven for Gales: not from nationalism, and certainly not from capitalism.

"All nations have their death ships," Gales bemoans. "Proud companies with fine names and beautiful flags are not ashamed to sail death ships. There have never been so many of them as since the war for liberty and democracy that gave the world passports and immigration restrictions, and that manufactured men without nationalities and without papers by the ten thousand."

The *Yorikke*'s crew members decide their own fates, but they are still slaves to the nations and markets that bind the world. Any freedom they experience is a function of having nothing left to lose. For Gales, there is no escaping these prisons of our own making—and certainly not at sea, where the hierarchies and tragedies of land are reduced to a potent brew.

"A good capitalist system does not know waste. This system cannot allow these tens of thousands of men without papers to roam about the world. . . . Why passports? Why immigration restriction? Why not let human beings go where they wish to go, North Pole or South Pole, Russia or Turkey, the States or Bolivia? . . . The walls all nations have built up since the war for democracy will have the same effect. Expanding markets and making large profits are a religion. It is the oldest religion perhaps, for it has the best-trained priests, and it has the most beautiful churches; yes, sir."

214 · THE HIDDEN GLOBE

. . .

As the titans of the shipping industry became more and more reliant on Panamanian sea power, its administrators put their sovereign advantage to use. The registry charged increasingly high fees, the consuls running it engaged in petty corruption, and international labor groups were angry at the ease with which shipowners could skirt the rules. Ultimately, a contested presidential election in 1948 and the unrest that followed shook American confidence that the Panamanian flag could indefinitely remain a precious but subservient pet. Shipowners wanted options. It was time for capitalism to do its work and create competition.

The man for the job materialized in the form of Edward Stettinius, a handsome Staten Islander with silver hair and a smile that could sell toothpaste. Stettinius knew business about as well as he knew his flags: born into a wealthy business family, he worked as an executive for General Motors and U.S. Steel before serving as Secretary of State in the Roosevelt and Truman administrations. As U.S. representative to the San Francisco Conference in 1945, he was instrumental in composing the United Nations Charter.

In 1945, Stettinius accompanied the American delegation at Yalta, where he was photographed alongside Joseph Stalin, both with great hair. On his journey back to the United States, Stettinius stopped in Monrovia, Liberia, for a ceremony to open its port—and to do some reconnaissance. Liberia had been founded in 1822 by an American organization seeking to deport freed slaves from the United States—an early, global attempt at "separate but equal." Now that it was established and recognized on the world stage, it was time to mine its sovereignty for parts, using a well-worn strategy. "Like Panama, Liberia had a small maritime tradition, but possessed no modern merchant fleet of its own," writes Rodney Carlisle. "Both countries were tropical states of about one million population, each governed by a small, factionalized oligarchy with a long tradition of rule. . . . Like Panama, Liberia originally had been formed with American assistance; yet, both in fact had their own heritage of jealously defended independence, and each was fiercely proud of its sovereignty and national heritage in ways that Americans usually failed to recognize."

In keeping with the "benevolent hegemony" ideal of the American Century, Stettinius had big plans for public–private partnerships involving exports, mining concessions, and new infrastructure. But his first and most successful move was to establish an open shipping registry to rival Panama's. What Richard Bolin was plotting at that very moment for Puerto Rico, Edward Stettinius would dream of bringing to Liberia—but instead of carving out free zones for factories inland, it would rent out little pieces of Liberian laissez-faire in the form of its flag.

Stettinius, who became close friends with Liberian president William Tubman, had invested in shipping in a personal capacity, so he knew all about flag arbitrage: some of his investments were flagged to Panama, and he was bullish enough on Liberia's competitive prospects to put $200,000 of his own money into the venture through his firm, Stettinius Associates. He also played up his staff's connections to the CIA, the navy, and the State Department. His men had no official connection to the U.S. government and were in Monrovia as private actors, but could easily pass themselves off as U.S. officials (they had also impressed upon CIA operatives that they would be happy to provide the agency with intel). Crucially, Stettinius knew what the shipping industry wanted.

In 1948, Stettinius's group began drafting Liberia's maritime and corporation codes, and entered into agreements with the Liberian government. Their firm was structured to take 65 percent of any profits, while the Liberian government would get a quarter, leaving the remaining 10 percent to a charity. Thanks to a formidable public relations campaign, more than five hundred news articles were written about their plans. Many of these stories talked up this profit-sharing scheme and humanitarianism; few delved into the shameless conflicts of interest that went into the creation of the Liberian flag law.

E. Stanley Klein, a staff attorney with Stettinius's firm, and James G. Mackey, the company's treasurer, were tasked with drafting the new maritime code. Both men were invested in shipping firms that stood to profit nicely once the registry's lax rules came into effect. By their side was Bushrod B. Howard, a member of the board of directors of Standard Oil, which became Esso (and later ExxonMobil). Howard had dabbled in legal fictions before: in the 1930s, he'd overseen part of a labyrinthine shell game through which twenty-five German tankers were flagged by the short-lived Free City of Danzig to avoid being requisitioned by the Allies, then transferred to Panama once Danzig was absorbed into Germany.

Before presenting the document to the Liberian government, Stettinius Associates cleared every word and provision with the oil shippers on whom they would rely for business. Esso was an investor in the joint venture, too, which meant that it owned part of the Liberian registry and stood to make money from fees it would itself pay. The Liberians would play down these uncomfortable alliances by boasting that they had consulted with the best and brightest. And to this day, a revolving cast of registry employees represent the nation in international forums, blurring the line between the private and public sectors.

In 1948, the Liberian legislature passed the law. The following year, the Greek shipping magnate Stavros Niarchos was the first to reflag his tanker, the *World Peace*, to Liberia. Shortly thereafter, Stettinius died of heart failure at the age of forty-nine. By the mid-1950s, Liberia surpassed Panama in registered tonnage.

In a sense, Stettinius achieved his goal. Today, Liberia counts around four thousand ships in its fleet—almost 15 percent of all the ships in the world, which makes it the biggest registry in the world, by UNCTAD's estimate. The maritime business is the country's biggest source of revenue. In the world of business and trade, it put Liberia on the map; in theory, it could have contributed to Liberians' prosperity.

But there's a dark side to the flag—one that the peace-loving Stettinius should have anticipated but could not have condoned.

For starters, the flag was never managed by Liberians, but by concession-aires in the United States: even in the early days, Stettinius's International Trust Company was registered in the tax haven of Delaware and operated from an office in northern Virginia. In the late 1990s, the flag registry was taken over by a second Virginia firm, founded by Yoram Cohen, a public re-lations adviser to the Liberian president and convicted war criminal Charles Taylor. During the Liberian civil war, Taylor's cabinet used money from the ship registrations to buy weapons, in violation of an international arms em-bargo. And while Western countries cracked down on imports of "blood" diamonds from Liberia in a show of humanitarianism and solidarity, the multimillion-dollar flag business continued registering ships as usual.

Even in peacetime, Liberia's gain is often the planet's loss. The Liberian flag flew above some of the greatest environmental catastrophes of the twentieth century: the *Torrey Canyon*, which sank in 1967 west of Cornwall, spilling 850,000 barrels of crude into the sea; the *Argo Merchant*, which ran aground near Nantucket in 1976 and spilled 183,000 barrels off the coast of Massachusetts; and the *Amoco Cadiz*, which in 1978 spilled 1.6 million bar-rels of light crude near Brittany, to name just a few. The Liberian merchant flag is crucial to the transport of fossil fuels across the globe—a process that creates its own carbon emissions before the oil is even used.

More recently, Liberian-flagged ships have been convicted of intention-ally dumping oil and accused of enabling illegal fishing and abusing sailors. And because of the deterritorialized nature of their sector, not to mention the ongoing race to the bottom among flag states to attract clients, the ship-ping industry has lobbied aggressively against environmental interventions and taxes: even a recent proposal from the Organisation for Economic Co-operation and Development (OECD) for a global minimum corporate tax of 15 percent left out shipping firms completely.

Liberia is just one of many such flags, each as fictitious as the next. This was the ground on which the old crew of the *Odessa Sky* stood. They lived for years in Liberia without so much as setting foot in the country.

If you've noticed a handsome white ferryboat that hasn't budged from the Old Port for a week, it isn't there because its passengers love Montreal too much to leave," quipped a French-language newspaper in September 1995 about the *Odessa Sky*'s seizure. In fact, the ship was still stuck in the middle of a dispute between its owner, Blasco, and a German charter company called Transocean, to whom it owed millions of dollars. Blasco's mounting financial woes were following its fleet around the world, and the German creditor had obtained a warrant for the authorities to seize the *Odessa Sky* in the hopes that selling it would help them recoup some of the lost funds (they made the same move to arrest Blasco-owned ships in other ports of call, including India and Italy).

The warrant went out on August 4, and upon the arrest, 212 crew members remained stuck on board. Not unlike the Haitians they'd picked up the year prior, the seafarers were caught between national rules and international agreements, unsure of how or where to seek justice. Only instead of being forcefully repatriated from the Canadian port to their hometowns in Ukraine and Russia, they were left to their own devices: to stay on board and hope to be paid once management worked things out, or to move on, find their own way home, and pursue the company for the money later.

Most cut their losses: the sailors and cooks and waiters and dancers filtered out over the course of the year, until only forty-six people were left the following July. Seven more deserted in the summer of 1996. A barmaid fell in love with a Canadian she met onshore and got married; seven of her colleagues applied for political asylum in Canada after two of them alleged that the captain had threatened their families back home.

The last of the sailors remained in Montreal for the greater part of a year, biding their time until a court released the ship from custody. An observer saw her at the port, later remarking on a message board that "she looked absolutely terrible—huge sheets of paint had fallen off where the hull and superstructure were rusting."

On August 31, 1996, the vessel set sail for the port of Wilhelmshaven, Germany, with a skeleton crew running shipboard operations. The *Odessa Sky* was to be fitted with a new starboard engine, then take up a charter with a German cruise company, which would in theory allow Blasco to start repaying some of its debts. But the deal fell through, and as soon as she arrived on September 11, the *Odessa Sky* was chained up again.

The crew left the ship and was replaced in July 1997 by another team, also from Ukraine, who did not get paid either. Before long, the sailors had used up all the ship's provisions, and Blasco had gone MIA. "There was no contact with the owner," recalls Juergen Maly, a labor lawyer who worked on the seafarers' case. "The ship was left behind. Abandoned." The one time that Blasco did get in touch was to threaten to put the seafarers on other ships' blacklists if they made a scene, recalls former sailor Michael Kolesnichenko. In his late forties, he had left his wife and daughter in Ukraine, thinking he'd work in passenger service on board the *Odessa Sky*, see the world, and come home with some extra money in his pocket. He ended up stranded in Germany for more than a year, playing interpreter in an increasingly nasty labor dispute. "An agent of the company who worked in Germany told the more active members of the crew, 'Do you understand that the door will be closed to future employment?'" Kolesnichenko recalled on a video call from his kitchen. "We felt hopeless, like we would never be paid and be stuck there forever. It felt like a dream that we would ever get a salary."

In situations like this, sailors have little recourse until the company comes up with funds to pay them. So the *Odessa Sky*'s crew sought help from the ITF and the local nonprofit seafarers' mission, which supports sailors with ship visits, advocacy, and financial assistance.

Otto Bohme and Dieter Wagener, the nonprofit's two local volunteers, boarded the ship in 1996. They were taken aback by what they saw in their orderly German port town. "There was only a little fuel for the engines and therefore no heating for the ship," Wagener wrote in an article from that time, noting that the temperature in the cabins didn't go above 10 degrees Celsius. Supplies like laundry detergent "came only irregularly" from the company, until they stopped arriving at all.

Wagener, a retired sergeant in the German military, asked his old army colleagues for their menu plans and, by soliciting local businesses for discounts and donations, managed to feed the crew on five deutsche marks (just under three dollars) per person per day. "Overnight, I gained an extended family of thirty-one people," he wrote. "With careful planning, all while taking advantage of all the special offers—free bread deliveries from the Wilhelms-haven town bakery, plus yesterday's vegetables and fruit once a week provided free of charge from the [supermarket], and an insane discount on potatoes, eggs and poultry at the weekly market—we managed to get by."

The organization delivered newspapers, ran errands, organized birth-day celebrations, and threw a Christmas party (with a Ukrainian menu) to maintain morale. They stayed in touch with Maly, the lawyer, who took the case to the local court and obtained a ruling for the ship to be auctioned off.

All the men relied on Kolesnichenko to translate from German to Ukrai-nian and back again. Before training to be a lawyer, working as a cop, and taking to the sea, Kolesnichenko had fallen in love with German literature, reading Erich Maria Remarque as a student, so to find himself immersed in the language felt like fate. The crew passed the winter as best they could: doing odd jobs around town, heating the cabins with bricks they warmed on electric stoves, and abandoning the hierarchies of the sea for the camara-derie of the in-between over vodka shots when they could afford the ex-pense. On deck, the engineers and sailors serviced the ship; the captain's mates stood watch around the clock.

The *Odessa Sky* may have been abandoned by her country—whatever, or wherever, it was. But at the port, she was anything but alone. "Almost every-body from the ship found friends in the town," Kolesnichenko recalled. "The citizens of Wilhelmshaven brought us everything they could."

More than twenty years later, when Russia invaded Ukraine, Kolesni-chenko's old friends even arranged for him to move back to Wilhelmshaven. The kitchen he was calling me from was in the rental they'd helped him find. He was hoping his daughter could join him there too.

"It's a beautiful town. It looks like a very big park. And there is a sea. For me it's very important," he said. Still, he felt—he *was*—displaced. Wilhelms-haven was not home, but a familiar exile.

"The citizens of Odessa live every day as their last day," he said. "I can live only in Odessa."

The summer of 1998 was a jubilant one in central Europe: France beat Brazil in the World Cup, the European Union was on the verge of adopting a continent-wide currency, and Celine Dion's "My Heart Will Go On" played on, and on, and on as the James Cameron film *Titanic* began its migration from theaters to VHS.

Amid all the excitement, the *Odessa Sky* was put up for sale at auction on the orders of a German court. The crew's ordeal was finally coming to an end.

Juergen Maly had tried repeatedly over the course of the year to get hold of the ship's ostensible owners in Ukraine, but Blasco never responded. Li-beria wasn't much help either. In fact, it was not even part of the conversa-tion. "Liberia is fake," Maly said. "The registry is located in the U.S., there are no real authorities in Liberia, and many companies take this flag be-cause there's no responsibility for anything."

In a way, this simplified the proceedings. Once the auction was sched-uled, nobody cared to get in the way.

The district court ruled that the auction proceeds should first compen-

222 • THE HIDDEN GLOBE

sate the crew before repaying Blasco's creditors, so in August 1998, when the *Odessa Sky* was sold to a Dutch company for around 17 million deutsche marks (about $16 million today, with inflation), the sailors received the equivalent of $2,500 for each month they had spent on board—a huge sum at the time and by their standards. Maly recalls that the money was deposited into accounts at a German bank with branches in Kiev and Odessa. The crew, the lawyers, and the volunteers from the seamen's mission celebrated their victory in a local restaurant. They raised the first glass to Kolesnichenko, whose knowledge of German had made it all possible.

Happy, exhausted, and a little sad, the crew members prepared themselves to finally go home. The days before their departure were bittersweet—"the ship was a sister, a mother for us," Kolesnichenko recalls—and the former Soviet Union was changing so fast that they weren't sure what would await them. Ukraine's economy was still adjusting to the whims of the free market, and consumer goods were hard to come by, so the sailors spent some of the cash in Germany. They rented an old bus, loaded it up with electronics, household appliances, and other items they'd have trouble finding at home, and hired two armed guards to make sure they did not get robbed on the way back through Poland. Kolesnichenko drove with a colleague who'd bought a car. Kolesnichenko hadn't seen his wife and his teenage daughter for more than a year, and when he arrived at their apartment, "I was the happiest man in the world." He pledged then and there that he would find work closer to home. "I decided no ships, no sea anymore," he said.

Still, the first thing he did was buy tickets for the three of them to take a cruise—aboard a Blasco ship, no less. Her name was the *Lev Tolstoy*, and she took them across Europe to Istanbul, Rome, Naples, and Marseille. "As a passenger on board, it was the opposite of when I was at work," he says. "You enjoy every day, every minute. It was a happy ship." The *Lev Tolstoy* was sold for scrap in 2014.

The *Odessa Sky* hit the waves again too. She crossed the Wadden Sea to Bremerhaven to be fitted with new cabins, a fresh new hull, and an in-house casino. Her new owner, a Dutchman named Gerard van Leest, gave her a new name, the *Club 1*, and his firm, an upstart in the cruising world, would buy four other ships with the hopes of popularizing drunken jaunts out of the port of Rotterdam. Financially, though, the short trips were a flop, so the ship was renamed the *Van Gogh*, flagged to St. Vincent and the Grenadines, another absentee registry, and leased out to other companies.

As the *Van Gogh,* the ship could not seem to stay out of trouble. In 2004, she crashed into an eighty-thousand-ton oil tanker near the port of Gibraltar, narrowly avoiding complete disaster. "It was very foggy. We were in the prow of the boat when a large tanker loomed across our bows," recalled Pam Sykes and Rene Williams, elderly British sisters who watched the wreck from the deck over lunch. Nobody was hurt, but the ship came out of the accident with a gigantic gash along its front that reminded the sisters of a shark. They didn't hold a grudge. "We have already booked another holiday on the *Van Gogh* because we love our time on board so much," they told their local paper. "We certainly will remember our stay in Gibraltar that we can tell our family and friends about."

In 2006, the ship was struck by repeated outbreaks of the norovirus. One killed an elderly passenger; another led to the cancellation of a cruise to Norway. Overall, hundreds of passengers were sickened.

Then, in 2007, at the age of thirty-three, the former *Gruziya* took her maiden around-the-world voyage. The trip began in Falmouth, UK, crossed the Atlantic Ocean by way of the Portuguese Azores, then sailed to several islands in the Caribbean before heading south to the Pacific, with stops in Tonga, New Zealand, and Australia. The Indian Ocean was next: the *Van Gogh*'s ports of call there included stops in Mauritius and Réunion. She continued her journey south around the African continent, visiting Cape Town and Durban before the South Atlantic island of Saint Helena (a British territory), the North Atlantic island nation of Cape Verde, and finally, Funchal in the Portuguese Madeira archipelago.

The first round-the-world cruise went off without a hitch, but the next year's would be her last. After undertaking a similar itinerary, the ship wound up back in maritime jail. Its charter company, Travelscope, had gone out of business in 2007, and its creditors came knocking. Only this time, it wasn't just the crew who were trapped, but the passengers too. One passenger confessed to *The Guardian* that they didn't exactly mind the extra time in Madeira.

"You couldn't be in a better place to be held ransom."

The ship flourished in her final decade of life. After her Madeiran arrest, she was acquired at auction in the port of Eleusis, near Athens, by a firm called Salamis Lines, reflagged to neighboring Cyprus, and renamed the *Salamis Filoxenia*. Between 2010 and 2019, she was deployed to the Greek islands and Israel, with Russian and European vacationers on board. *Filoxenia* is a Greek word that means "love of strangers," and the name suited her well. At the age of thirty-five, she had traveled—and contained—the entire world.

But although her planks, her engines, her cabins, and even her hull had been replaced many times over, the ex-*Gruziya* was still recognizably herself—a maritime palimpsest of the late twentieth century. The Soviet Union fell, and still she sailed on. Blasco went under, and still she sailed on. She had been arrested in Canada, marooned in Germany, freed, arrested, refitted, repainted, and still she sailed on—searching, perhaps, for a place to call her home.

She found it in an unlikely location.

Cyprus is considered a flag of convenience for its nonexistent taxes and lax regulation—not the most lenient flag, because it must adhere to European standards, but certainly no stickler. According to the OECD, most of the ships on the books in Cyprus—as with other FOCs—are held by anonymous companies, offshore from even offshore, like little nesting dolls of corporate dissociation. For the *Salamis*, though, pulling into the sparkling

port of Limassol felt like coming home. For the first time since she left
Odessa as the *Gruziya*, the stars above her aligned: her legal status matched
her place in the world, which corresponded to her owner's location, which,
incredibly, was also where she began and ended every voyage: a rarity in the
maritime world.

The fiction had been made real, her metaphysical problem resolved.
Thus made whole, she tended to some unfinished business.

Early on the morning of September 25, 2014, the *Salamis* was making
her way back to Limassol from the Greek island of Syros, carrying several
hundred Cypriot passengers, when she received an emergency call. A fishing trawler carrying 345 people had put out a distress signal some fifty nautical miles from the Cypriot port. The vessel, which had departed from
Syria, had been at sea for three full days and was on the verge of succumbing to the waves. Its captain had fled the sinking trawler in a speedboat; the
passengers he'd left adrift were asylum seekers—many of them women,
children, and even babies—who had paid between $3,000 and $6,000 apiece
to leave the country wracked by civil war.

That sum was orders of magnitude more than what the vacationers had
paid for their trip, but a ticket to ride is a useless thing without the right
papers. Like the stateless sailors on board the fictional *Yorikke*, the asylum
seekers were limited in where they could go and how they could get there.
They had little choice but to board a ship that might or might not deposit
them at death's door.

Luckily, the *Salamis* sped to their rescue, and over the course of the next
day, delivered all its passengers to safety. Footage taken by a Cypriot TV
crew on board the cruise ship depicted a scene that would recur endlessly on
network TV around the world over the next few years: families huddled
with children on the crowded deck of a barge as it was pummeled by large
waves; mothers clutching babies as they were evacuated through a hatch
on the ship's bottom deck; the cries of sailors shouting "children first"; a

fifteen-year-old explaining to grown men that the reason they risked their lives to leave Syria was because life there "was unbearable."

The original passengers on board the *Salamis* disembarked upon arrival, but the castaways refused to get off the ship. Their crooked captain (who'd reportedly made off with $2 million) had promised to take them to Sicily, and they demanded to complete the journey they had paid for. If they didn't, they would have to begin their asylum proceedings in Cyprus, where few of them had any connections. Not being part of the Schengen Area, the country would not allow them to slip into other European countries unannounced either.

After some negotiating, the new arrivals were coaxed off the ship. A handful were taken to a local hospital to be treated for illness and injuries, while the rest stayed in a temporary shelter until it was shuttered early the following year.

After that, the group dispersed. Dozens never applied for asylum in Cyprus and wound up in legal limbo, some sleeping on the streets, some disappearing completely. Others made their way to Germany and other EU countries to join family members who'd endured their own dangerous journeys across the sea. A few stayed on in Cyprus to start a new life.

Adnan Massri, a stateless Palestinian who was born in Damascus, Syria, was barely eighteen when he was rescued at sea. He remembers planes and helicopters flying above their heads, and taking his first bite of Cypriot halloumi aboard the *Salamis* after having barely eaten for days. "I was so hungry, I will never forget the taste," he recalled in a 2020 article in a Cypriot newspaper. Massri left Damascus during the Syrian civil war with his father, aunt, and cousins. His father was one of the passengers who'd been resistant to leaving the ship—he'd wanted to end up in Germany—but ultimately they decided to remain, and were able to bring over Adnan's mother and siblings to join them. The transition wasn't always easy, but "I have come to love this country," wrote Massri. "I could not imagine my life outside of Cyprus."

. . .

The *Salamis* completed her final cruise in the winter of 2019. It's hard to overstate the COVID-19 pandemic's impact on the cruise industry: the last place anyone wanted to be in early 2020 was in a boat packed with strangers. But national border closures were an even bigger obstacle for the broader maritime economy, which supports more than 80 percent of world trade. One by one, with barely a day's notice, countries closed their doors to foreign citizens and sometimes even goods and vehicles, sowing chaos at ports of entry and making it virtually impossible for sailors to get home. At the height of the pandemic, some four hundred thousand seafarers were stranded abroad, with another four hundred thousand stuck at home, out of work. In July 2021, a quarter of a million workers were still stranded, with many of them laboring around the clock to maintain their vessels as crew changes continued to be restricted.

The ships themselves—particularly the older ones—didn't always make it through. Until early 2022, the *Salamis* languished, gathering rust in Limassol, as Salamis Lines sank into the red. Then, in February, she was sold to an Emirati company called Prime Spot Ship Trading LLC for $4.1 million, or $266 per ton.

Prime Spot had no intention of rehabilitating the old ferry. It renamed the *Salamis* the *Phoenix Titan*, reflagged her to the island nation of Saint Kitts and Nevis, and set her off across the Atlantic.

In March, a cruise ship influencer named Peter Knego reported seeing her at the Suez entrance to the Suez Canal. He uploaded a video to his YouTube channel bidding the old girl farewell, noting that she was the last of the five Soviet sisters to sail to her end.

The *Belorussia*, which had recently served as dockworker accommodations in Croatia, was in Aliağa, Turkey, in the process of being dismantled.

The *Azerbaijan* had been sold for scrap in 2020 but came loose from her anchor and broke in two off the coast of Mexico before she could make her last call.

The *Kareliya* had a good run as a floating Hong Kong casino until the pandemic. She was scrapped at Alang, in India, the world's largest ship graveyard, in 2021.

The *Kazakhstan* was long gone, having been recycled, also in Alang, in 2011.

Condolences poured in to the comments on the ship's Facebook fan page: from a sailor who'd joined the *Gruziya*'s crew in her first year of service; a photographer who'd documented her journeys in the 1980s; a tourist with golden memories from the 1990s; a port agent who had boarded her in the 2000s, when she sailed as the *Van Gogh*, and remembered marveling at the original Soviet furnishings her owners had somehow preserved. "The 5 sisters became successful cruise ships thanks to their intimate size and great maneuverability that made visits to less-visited ports in Europe possible," the port agent wrote. "I wish farewell to Gruziya and her beautiful sisters!"

By the time she exited Suez, the *Phoenix Titan* had changed state yet again. She was now the *Titan*, and she belonged to a second buyer, named Virna Maritime Corp. Virna's website lists a Dubai address and advertises all-inclusive ship-management services. Under the new guard, the vessel was reflagged to the Pacific nation of Palau and reported her destination as the Indonesian island of Batam, not far from Singapore. Vessel-tracking systems indicated that she was at that port in late April—the same time that an amateur photographer captured her mug shot as she ran up to Gadani Beach.

The *Titan* was at the gates. She'd been preparing to leave this world for some time. She'd said goodbye to her sisters, her country, her port; she'd repaid her debts and freed herself of worldly attachments. She had even separated herself from her hulking, rotting body: a transubstantiation, of sorts, at sea. By transiting through a tangle of companies, addresses, flags, and locations—some real, some fake, some somewhere in between—the *Ti-*

tan managed to evade European shipbreaking and waste-exporting regulations by becoming something else. As the Cypriot-owned *Salamis*, the vessel would have had to comply with European Union directives ensuring environmental and worker safety, as well as international agreements preventing ships from being broken down in unaccredited scrapyards. But as the Saint Kitts–flagged, Dubai-registered *Phoenix Titan*, or the Palau-flagged, Indian-owned *Titan*, she was not subject to these rules. Even though the ship herself remained utterly the same, from bow to stern, her jurisdiction had changed overnight. From then on, nobody could quite place her.

Prime Spot, which first took custody of the vessel, is a corporate entity with a name and address in Dubai's Burj Khalifa, the world's tallest tower, which happens to be built in the shape of a ship's sail. But to call Prime Spot a productive enterprise is a stretch: it does not appear to have ever done anything besides buy this one vessel once, which suggests it's a shell corporation set up to stuff paper between a ship, its seller, its buyer, and its demise. Virna, the next buyer, shares an address with an aptly named firm called Last Voyage, which specializes in buying vessels "as-is, where-is"—industry code for "cash, no questions asked"—and Best Oasis, a well-known cash buyer that arranges for condemned vessels "a perfect end to their magnificent journey." The companies are registered in Dubai's Multi Commodities Center, a free-trade zone focused on the exchange of commodities ranging from cocoa to metals.

Virna put yet another firm, BBN, in charge of her "single delivery voyage": a euphemism for when a ship needs to get from point A to point B with minimal crew, a skimpy insurance policy, and a new identity, preferably in a hurry.

In the shipping industry, these kinds of arrangements are common: according to one study, 90 percent of companies that own large ships own just one ship. The study's author, the French economist Guillaume Vuillemey, has shown how shipping firms use these tactics to insulate their assets—including their other ships—from potential creditors. (State-owned fleets tend to buck this trend. This is what had led to the *Gruziya*'s repeated and lengthy arrests in the 1990s: though she was technically held by a British Blasco subsidiary and flew a Liberian flag, it wasn't hard to show that her beneficial owner—not to mention the accountants it hired—were from the former Soviet Union.)

At the end of a ship's life, single-use LLCs will often trade in vessels for cash, hoping to make a profit off their worth in scrap metal. They are not selling full ships so much as trading commodities, and, crucially, shirking responsibility for any environmental damage they might cause. "If you had to comply with EU regulations about recycling, an old ship would need to pay in order to be recycled: the price to do it cleanly could be higher than the price of the raw materials," Vuillemey told me over the phone. "Reflagging and cash-buying practices convert something with a negative price into something with a positive price—positive only because they don't assume any of the environmental costs."

The *Salamis*'s owners could feign ignorance over the fallout, thanks to a carefully constructed corporate sandwich. Because the ship would not be docking in a country that had agreed to port state controls, pesky agents could not intervene. To be safe, ships sometimes even misreport their last port of call to muddle their morbid trajectory: the *Titan* had no business in Batam, Indonesia. And if her flag state ever intervened, its efforts would be for nothing.

Palau's flag registry claims to take its environmental responsibilities seriously. But the Pacific nation did not become one of the most popular funeral flags in the business by chance. With the help of foreign entrepreneurs aping Edward Stettinius, Palau and its peers in Saint Kitts, the Comoro Islands, and Cameroon have exploited international efforts to make shipbreaking more environmentally responsible by offering a way around increasingly stringent European and North American rules. Guillaume Vuillemey found that in the early 2000s, funeral flag nations barely had maritime registries at all. By 2019, more than half of all dying ships flew one of their flags.

Palau stands out even among this motley crew. Its registry makes up less than 0.001 percent of the world's fleet, but 59.5 percent of last flags. "In other terms, it is likely that this registry has been created specifically with the purpose of allowing shipping companies to evade end-of-life responsibilities," Vuillemey writes in a paper on the subject. (Curiously, Vuillemey also found that ship companies registered in common law countries are more likely to use a last-voyage flag, because "common law environments may lead to more attempts to conceal responsibilities via contracts that are mere veils.") Palauans themselves can hardly be blamed for this dirty business. The registry is run out of offices in the Woodlands, a planned community near Houston, Texas, and the Port of Piraeus in Athens. Its CEO is a businessman named Panos Kirnidis, who moonlights as the Pacific nation's honorary consul to Greece. To compete with other, more established flags, it makes transactions as quick and easy as possible.

The *Titan*'s next and final stop was Gadani: the world's third-largest shipbreaking facility, with 40 scrapping companies sprawled across 130 privately owned plots on six miles of tidal beachfront. Industry observers say Pakistan has shown little interest in improving environmental or labor conditions. "Gadani is the worst place to send a ship," a veteran shipbreaking consultant told me. "It's the one [yard] I've not been to. We aren't allowed into Gadani."

Videos from shipyards across the subcontinent give a hint of how hard the work can be. Against a stunning backdrop of clear waters and burnished sand, six thousand workers take apart around five million tons of scrap per year with cranes, chains, torches, wrenches, and their bare hands. The work exposes them, and their environment, to high levels of chemicals like mercury, asbestos, and lead, particularly when they deal with a ship as old as the *Titan*. Many have little to no equipment besides rags to protect themselves from the sparks and the flames, and when things go wrong, nothing seems to change. In 2016, a large fire on the decommissioned oil tanker *Aces* killed at least twenty-nine people and burned dozens more. No regulatory action followed. "They close for six months after an incident, and then start up again," the consultant said. "It just keeps happening."

It isn't clear who broke up the *Titan*, or how long it took. But she appears to have been beached on two plots, or subdivisions, of the beach for several months, getting smaller and smaller until little of her remained. The men who worked on her could not have been paid more than a few dollars a day in this sweatshop without walls, slowly, methodically, and dangerously picking apart some of humankind's biggest creations until all that was left was a carcass.

By the fall of 2022, the *Titan* had undergone her final transformation. She is classified as dead: no longer a ship, but a collection of parts sold off to build other, lesser machines.

Her body was broken: she had passed from rust to dust.

But the spirit of the thing—the fumes and fuel and fire that for half a century made her run—will live on forever: in the waters she sailed, in the people she saved, and in the bodies of the men who buried her and will someday too be buried.

9.

Excised

Here in this prison, everything is abnormal and different from
all the villages, cities and continents.

—BEHROUZ BOOCHANI,
FREEDOM, ONLY FREEDOM

Abdul Aziz Muhamat touched down at the Geneva airport on
February 11, 2019, with little besides a backpack and a clutch of
travel documents. It had taken four flights, two days, and a panic
at every stop to get there.

Aziz hadn't flown since he'd fled Sudan to escape political persecution
in 2013. After leaving home, he had tried to get to New Zealand via Indonesia by boat, hoping to claim asylum when he arrived. Instead, he was diverted to Manus Island, part of Papua New Guinea, by the Australian
authorities after his vessel failed in Australian waters. He languished on
Manus for most of his twenties. He'd committed no crime.

Manus, along with a second camp on the Pacific island of Nauru, were
Australia's answer to Guantánamo: hot, damp, secluded offshore prisons
where the nation warehoused asylum seekers until mid-2023. The extra-
legal entrepôts were part of a larger policy to limit migration, by turning
back boats of asylum seekers before they arrived and deterring them with
prolonged detention if they did happen to make it any farther. The schemes

were costly, unpopular, and widely acknowledged to be a humanitarian disaster. Still, Australian leaders pressed on, refusing to close the camps for years. It was a matter of protecting their borders, they said, invoking the supposedly immutable and sacred nature of sovereignty.

The captives, meanwhile, were treated like so much unwanted cargo. But the rank food and meager portions, the doorless toilets and inadequate ventilation, the subpar medical services that led to the deaths of more than a dozen detainees—those were not even the worst part.

It was the sense of placelessness—physical, temporal, spiritual, and legal—that drove so many to abject despair. "Being in perpetual limbo has so many destructive impacts on the mental health of every single person," wrote the Iranian Kurdish intellectual Behrouz Boochani, whom Aziz befriended in immigration detention. Boochani was referring to the Italian philosopher Giorgio Agamben's theory of the "state of exception"—when the state creates legal black holes in the name of emergency management. "Our legal status as individuals has been suspended and we become legally unnameable beings, transformed into animals devoid of dignity," he wrote.

Like Boochani and the 4,249 other refugees subjected to this treatment, Aziz had no idea when, how, or indeed whether he would be able to leave this man-made hell. To pass the time—and to preserve a sense of autonomy—he organized rallies, helped fellow refugees obtain medical care, and raised awareness about the squalid conditions, using a smuggled phone while guards, mostly Papuan locals, turned a blind eye. He corresponded with a Melbourne-based journalist, sending him recordings that chronicled the horrors detainees faced offshore, from boredom to riots. In the process, Aziz became one of the public faces of Australia's immigration crackdown and a nominee for a prestigious human rights award. That was what had brought him to Geneva that day.

Through the gap in the reinforced glass window at immigration control, Aziz slid a letter from the Martin Ennals Foundation, which had shortlisted him for the prize, along with a note from the Swiss government and a temporary travel authorization from Papua New Guinea. Aziz had no valid passport. His Sudanese one had expired years ago.

The border guard examined his papers and waved him through. The Swiss knew he was coming. At the gate, Michael Khambatta, the administrator of the prize, was there to greet Aziz. By his side was Michael Green, the Australian reporter who'd been chronicling Aziz's time on Manus Island for an award-winning podcast. Neither of them could quite believe Aziz had finally made it. There had been a number of hiccups along the way. Even with an official invitation from a well-known Swiss nonprofit, a Black African without a passport cannot make his way from Papua New Guinea to Switzerland without being questioned at every stop.

But here he was in Geneva's spotless airport, staring down ads for $50,000 wristwatches and bottles of duty-free Scotch. He'd traveled from one side of the hidden globe to the other.

For as long as Geneva has been a city of holes, it has also been a city of refuge. Geneva is the birthplace of international agencies and laws that are supposed to protect refugees like Aziz from places like Manus. It was also home to what the historian Quinn Slobodian calls the "Geneva School," a group of neoliberal economists made famous by Ludwig von Mises and Friedrich Hayek, who promoted an ideology of open borders for capital but not for people. While the internationalists of the 1920s dreamed up visions of a universal society on the banks of the Léman, these economists did, too, only their new world was organized around market competition, not democratic cooperation.

Geneva is full of such contradictions. Do conventions on war crimes absolve the city for its role in managing the wealth of war criminals? Do its summits on protecting the environment undo the damage wrought by its resident oil traders?

Perhaps I'm asking the wrong questions. These forces—not really opposite, not always equal—aren't separate at all, but contained within the same shell, like the two-headed tortoise born at Geneva's Museum of Natural

History in 1997. The tortoise, which was named Janus, has two heads, two hearts, two sets of lungs, and two personalities, but just one digestive system. In the wild, the creature would have quickly died—both heads can't fit in its shell at once to evade predators. But thanks to the care and patience of its minders, Janus, citizen of Geneva, is the longest-living such reptile in the world.

Aziz is one of ten siblings from a well-off political family in Sudan. His father was a successful livestock farmer. His mother, a community leader turned local politician, was a vocal supporter of Omar al-Bashir, the former military officer who ruled Sudan for thirty years before he was deposed in a 2019 coup.

Aziz didn't share his mother's politics, and he chafed against the factionalism and tribalism that he blames for Sudan's near-constant state of unrest—not to mention the civil wars that have killed tens of thousands of ordinary people. As a high school student in the early 2010s, he helped organize what he describes as a unity movement that rejected a divided Sudan and sought to bring citizens, regardless of their backgrounds, together.

If this sounds more or less anodyne, under Bashir's rule it was anything but—especially once Aziz and his classmates rejected the advances of established political groups they believed were trying to co-opt their movement. They had irked the establishment, and Aziz's family started to feel the heat—especially his uncle, who ran a successful business importing and exporting cars.

First the government took away the tax concession that had allowed his uncle to bring in the cars duty-free. Then they raised his taxes and started confiscating his property, Aziz recalls. Things weren't looking good for Aziz either. A student protest he'd been planning seemed to be gaining traction, and since he'd turned eighteen, his family began to worry that he would be arrested and tried as an adult. There was talk of his leaving, or at least hiding, until things calmed down.

It was the uncle who made the call in mid-2013: they should both go, and soon. "He understood the message, and he was like, 'Hey, whatever you want to do, I will always be behind you,'" Aziz recalls. "When things got bad, that's the time when he decided, let's leave."

So they dispersed: the uncle to Saudi Arabia, Aziz to Indonesia. His plan had been to continue his studies abroad, but shortly after the protests he'd helped organize took place back home, Aziz began to feel like he was being followed. He stopped showing his face in public, he said. He went out only at night. He heard of friends in Indonesia who'd been apprehended, harassed, even forced to travel home to face charges—"whether you are internal or external, as long as you are on the list, you will be hunted," he said.

So he decided to travel even farther, without leaving a trace. He couldn't renew his Indonesian visa for a third time without alerting the authorities to his whereabouts. And while he'd initially approached the UN's High Commissioner for Refugees to pursue an asylum claim, that didn't feel safe either. So Aziz did what more and more asylum seekers were starting to do: he went on Facebook to explore his options. That was how he wound up in the seaside town of Bogor, hitching a ride on a boat he thought was bound for New Zealand.

Aziz didn't exactly plan the journey. He stumbled his way into it after meeting a group of asylum seekers at an internet café—"They were supposed to leave, and I was there," he recalls. He paid around $500 to the smuggler, who probably figured he had nothing to lose by adding one more body to a vessel already teeming with them. The group of Afghans, Iranians, Syrians, and Aziz got in a minivan, drove to the shore, and crossed their fingers.

Their first attempt failed. Their second attempt failed. On their third try, they made it out far enough to get stranded, then spent three days on the water, wondering if help would ever come. Rescue came, but in the form of the Australian navy, which shipped them to Christmas Island and told them that they would never set foot in Australia, a policy governing all maritime arrivals that remains on the books. The women and children would be sent to Nauru, they were told, and the men to Manus.

Aziz was well educated and politically conscious. But he was also young and had only ever understood politics in the context of Sudan. He had no knowledge of his rights as an asylum seeker abroad, or as a subject of international law.

He was very good at asking questions, though.

On Christmas Island, Aziz asked one of the guards where, and what exactly, was Papua New Guinea. "She said Papua New Guinea is a country that was once part of Australia, so it's a history class. She gave us, like, a history class."

The guard had other stories too—ones that sounded more like mythology than history. He remembers that she called the island "a very bad place" and even mentioned cannibalism. (There are no cannibals on Manus, or anywhere in Papua New Guinea.)

"She said it has communicable diseases. So you cannot even shake hands with these people," Aziz remembered, still stunned at her outlandish assertions. "Sometimes I feel embarrassed to say what she said exactly," he went on, "but she said a lot of shit that actually terrified everyone."

It was a classic intimidation tactic, which Aziz understood: "The idea is, psychologically, I need to dominate [you], then send you there." More of that would be forthcoming.

As would be more questions from Aziz: Why, knowing these supposedly awful things, were the Australians sending them to Manus? How long until they got out? Where would they go next?

Aziz would soon learn that asylum seekers had been asking these questions since 2001, when a boat journey not unlike the one he took remade Australian history.

To this day, many will say that they have received no good answers.

. . .

On August 26, 2001, a maritime distress signal went out over the airwaves around Christmas Island, an Australian territory located about a thousand miles from the mainland: a fishing boat called the *Palapa* was on the verge of capsizing with 433 passengers on board. All but nine of the passengers were Afghans who'd run from Taliban rule. Many of them belonged to the Hazara minority, who were persecuted because of their religious practices. By plane, train, and automobile, they'd made their way to Indonesia, where they'd hidden from the police until the sea gods smiled. Then they'd embarked by boat for the last leg of their journey to Australia: a nice country, they presumed, that had signed all the right treaties and agreements, and that would respect their right to request asylum.

Almost immediately, the *Palapa* started breaking down: first, its engine gave out, then storms roiled the seas and the vessel took a bruising, leaving its passengers thirsty, seasick, and drifting. They managed to paint HELP on the roof, which prompted the Australian coast guard to send assistance. Luckily, a Norwegian freighter called the *Tampa* was on its way from Fremantle, Australia, to Singapore. Its captain, Arne Rinnan, sped to the *Palapa*'s rescue.

Rinnan reached the vessel eighty-five miles north of Christmas Island. The crew pulled the *Palapa*'s passengers aboard one by one. This was not an act of altruism, but a key stipulation of a maritime treaty signed by Norway, Australia, and dozens of other countries: that shipmasters have "a general obligation . . . to proceed to the assistance of those in distress." Moments after the last person was evacuated, they watched as the *Palapa* was engulfed by the waves. "There's no denying the sheer raw emotion of being saved," Abbas Nazari, who survived the wreck at age seven, told *The Guardian* years later. "Of climbing the stairs, catching your breath at the top and then looking down to see the *Palapa* fall to pieces. That doesn't need explaining to a child: a child can understand that."

The refugees were safe, but they were hardly sound. Over the coming months and years, their presence would unleash a series of diplomatic and legislative battles that would redraw the Australian map, redefine the form and function of its territory, and forever change the politics of global migration.

The trouble began right away. Rinnan, who had performed the rescue in Indonesian territorial waters, turned around to deliver the refugees to Java, as the Australians had requested. But like the Syrians aboard the *Salamis Filoxenia* who'd begged to be taken to Italy rather than Cyprus, his passengers pleaded with him to turn back.

Caught between commands from afar and an unraveling emergency, the captain considered what was before him: the young men and women who'd do most anything for a future; the tired, thirsty children; the mothers and fathers who'd risked the unthinkable just to get here, all of them preferring to tempt fate for a second time rather than turn back.

He thought about his responsibilities as a captain, as a man. On August 27, he returned to Christmas Island, stopping just short of the twelve-mile maritime zone encasing the territory.

The Australians were not pleased. The government threatened to prosecute Rinnan for people smuggling if he entered Australian waters, and Prime Minister John Howard announced that the *Tampa* would not be permitted to make land. Rinnan stayed where he was but requested that his passengers receive medical evaluations. By this point, fifteen people were unconscious, and dozens more were suffering from open sores, dehydration, stomach pains, and infections, but the ship was still not given the green light to enter Australia.

On August 28, the adult refugees began a hunger strike. Feeling he had no choice but to move, Rinnan entered Australian waters the next day. His welcome committee included forty-five members of Australian Special Air Service Regiment.

That same evening in Canberra, Prime Minister Howard introduced a law to allow the removal of all foreign ships arriving in Australia by the military, no questions asked. Howard made the law retroactive to nine o'clock that morning, just hours before the *Tampa* had arrived at Christmas Island. (Howard knew all about timekeeping: his great-great grandfather had been a convict deported to Australia from England after stealing a tortoiseshell watch.) That bill never passed, but over the next weeks and months, the contours of a policy known as the "Pacific Solution"—neither pacific nor a solution, refugee advocates like to say—would take shape. Directly inspired by U.S. interdiction operations in the Caribbean, according to the legal scholar Daniel Ghezelbash, Australia's plan to restrict migration relied on the heavy use of exceptions—spatial, temporal, and political—to shirk its humanitarian responsibilities. In lieu of Soviet ships and Cuban naval bases, it co-opted an archipelago of islands to serve as offshore detention facilities and rights-free zones.

The islands of Christmas, Ashmore, Cartier, and Cocos (which are today as Australian as Long Island is American), along with five thousand other islands and ports, went under the jurisdictional knife and were politically "excised" from Australian territory for the purposes of migration. What this meant is that these places remained under full Australian sovereignty, but that Australia's national migration laws—including the ones governing the country's international obligations toward migrants—were chiseled off from the social contract. People arriving by boat in excised territories were not considered legally "present" on Australian land, which made them ineligible to apply for a visa and gave Australia an out when it came to adhering to international treaties on human rights and refugees. (Lawyers dispute whether this is actually legal.) And because these were the places that most boat people landed, it was a convenient way to turn people away, even if their lives were at risk. Even when migrants detained offshore came to the mainland—for medical care, say—they traveled there "inside a legal bubble that sustained the fiction that they had not officially entered Australia, even if they were physically present in Australia for years," writes University of

California, San Diego sociologist David Scott FitzGerald in *Refuge Beyond Reach*. Their bodies, in other words, became encased in fictions.

This policy recalls an approach taken by the French in the 1990s as they were dealing with large numbers of people arriving at Paris's Charles de Gaulle Airport. Reluctant to admit the migrants without completing a full check on whether they qualified for refugee status, but unable under international law to simply send them away, the French authorities came up with an alternate plan, and created what are known as *zones d'attente*, or waiting zones, in the airport itself: duty-free law meets duty-free shopping. When detainees got sick, France designated ambulances and hospital rooms as "floating international zones" to keep up the charade.

Daniel Ghezelbash—himself the child of Iranian refugees in Australia—has a term for this overly literal, bad-faith use of extraterritorial space: "hyper-legalism." Hyper-legalism occurs when states exploit perceived gaps in the international system to get around agreements they willingly signed on to. "States have attempted to read down the extraterritorial scope of their international obligations," Ghezelbash writes in *The American Journal of Comparative Law*. "At the same time, they have developed legal fictions to allow them to treat certain asylum seekers who are physically present in their territory as not being present."

Ghezelbash wrote his paper with international refugee law, and Australia's behavior, in mind. But the concept can be understood more broadly. Hyper-legalism helps explain the animating logic behind the hidden globe: in much the same way that a Swiss millionaire can maintain fictitious residency in Singapore to save on taxes, or an unscrupulous shipbroker can book its vessel in Palau to get around environmental regulations, the state of Australia can lease part of another country to detain asylum seekers to shed itself of its legal and moral responsibilities. Hyper-legalism even explains the nonspace of a freeport originally intended to store perishable grain, now used to steal imperishable gold. It likewise allows governments (and the people they serve, be they citizens or foreigners) to have it both ways—to act callously but to appear outwardly moral, or at least lawful. "Because how bad can it be if it complies with international law?" Ghezelbash asks.

It might not even do that. By far the most controversial part of the Pacific Solution—one that has drawn near-universal condemnation from human rights lawyers—was Australia's use of two sovereign states: Nauru, where the passengers of the *Palapa* were sent, and Manus Island in Papua New Guinea, where Aziz landed.

Papua New Guinea is a nation of more than eight million people, eight hundred languages, and six hundred islands located between Indonesia and Australia that became fully independent in 1975. In the late nineteenth century, German settlers annexed parts of Papua, on the northern side of the country. The Dutch held west New Guinea, while Britain claimed the east, sharing administrative duties with the territories of Queensland, New South Wales, and Victoria. In 1906, control was handed over to the Australians, and during World War II they fought the Japanese occupation there alongside local and American troops. All this while some 750 distinct cultural or tribal groups carried on their own lives and rich customs.

Colonial administrators stuck around until the country's peaceful decolonization in 1975, but never fully thought of themselves as imperialists. (Weren't *they* the ones governed by the Crown from afar?) Yet to this day, Australia wields its influence on the country through trade, aid, and economic development schemes. Until 2017, that included building, funding, and staffing the Manus offshore detention facility for refugees.

If Papua New Guinea can trace a relatively straight line from more or less formal colonial rule to becoming an independent, more or less unified nation, Nauru's was defined by its continually ambiguous international status, per the Australian historian Cait Storr. The island—now the world's third-smallest sovereign nation—was never formally annexed as a colony by

Australia. Instead, it was exploited by trading companies and private firms acting with almost complete impunity.

Inhabited for centuries by Polynesian and Micronesian explorers, Nauru's destiny changed in 1888, when its twelve tribal leaders were rounded up, held at gunpoint, and told that their island would become part of Germany's Marshall Islands "protectorate." This legal category has meant different things in different places over the years, but it always involves a layer of outside control by a more powerful state. In this case, the arrangement ended up granting a German trading company control over Nauru's natural resources while requiring very little of them in the way of actual protection (unless banning alcohol, instituting strict dress codes, and shipping in Christian missionaries counts as "protection"). For the Germans, it was all gain, no pain. For Nauru, quite the opposite.

In 1900, British prospectors discovered vast reserves of phosphate, a powerful fertilizer, on the island. Mining operations began seven years later, and the British and the Germans split the profits, leaving locals with crumbs. The German firm then forfeited its stake to a British company, before Australian troops occupied Nauru during World War I. The occupation paved the way for Australia, Britain, and New Zealand to oversee Nauru as a League of Nations "mandate" between the wars. In theory, Nauru was a joint venture run by these powers. In practice, it was Australia and, more precisely, its phosphate interests, that ran the show.

World War II saw Nauru occupied by the Japanese, who deported twelve hundred people—two thirds of the native population—to work as laborers in Micronesia. Four hundred and sixty-three died. After the war, the United Nations assigned Nauru the status of a trust territory—again under the control of the Australians—before it finally achieved independence in 1968.

Rather than fitting into contemporary categories of state and nonstate, Nauru's shifting, vulnerable status enabled what scholars call extractivism: when "territories, populations, and animal and plant life [are] rendered into commodities for the taking so as to enrich world economic centers," as the anthropologist Julia Morris puts it. A rotating cast of foreign corporations strip-mined the island, decade after decade, with little regard for the native population. The phosphate raked in incredible profits and transformed Australia's agriculture sector, at an astonishing environmental cost.

"The island, it's like a big rock [made up of] stalagmites because they dug out all the phosphate," says John Pace, a human rights lawyer who visited Nauru's detention camps with Amnesty International in the months after the *Tampa* affair. "It was like being on the moon."

The miners had carried on with the explicit assumption that eventually the island would become uninhabitable. Because they weren't responsible for its people or its long-term health, it seemed like a good gamble. And while Nauruans benefited financially in the short term—phosphate revenues briefly made them among the richest citizens on the planet—a series of poor investment decisions and ecological negligence turned their brush with prosperity into a Pyrrhic victory.

By the 1980s, the phosphate was gone, and the island was again struggling. In 1989, Nauru sued Australia before the International Court of Justice for breaching its responsibilities as an administrator of the trusteeship, destroying its natural environment through overexploitation, and failing to rehabilitate the island. Australia paid AU$107 million in the settlement. But the 1993 payout also indemnified the nation against future lawsuits. Apparently undeterred, in the immediate aftermath of the *Tampa* affair, the Australians approached Nauru with a new proposition: prisons.

The camps at Nauru and Manus opened shortly after the *Tampa* affair, ostensibly to temporarily hold asylum seekers while their applications were being evaluated. The prisons were dismal proof that while Australia was not pillaging foreign land outright the way it used to, it would continue to squeeze every last drop of utility from its poorer, less powerful neighbors. That utility was Nauru's international status: the fact of being a state, in this

246 • THE HIDDEN GLOBE

case to take in unwanted people. "After the decline in phosphate revenue and the draining of trust funds, international status itself has become the resource the Republic seeks to rent," writes Cait Storr, of Nauru.

As we have seen, many countries commercialize their sovereignty, sometimes to absurd effect. But even former colonies' adoption of free zones were decisions made, if not from a position of outright power, then at least from one of choice. In the Pacific, the establishment of the camps follows a broad historical pattern defined by colonial exploitation. "It's states looking for opportunity . . . with little strong and sustainable economic opportunity," Damon Salesa, the vice chancellor of Auckland University of Technology, told me over Zoom. "And because they're small, they're more vulnerable to single points of capital and shifting political discussions."

Against this backdrop, Salesa nonetheless warns against painting Nauru and Manus with the same brush. "They're different and they're seen as different," he says. "Papua New Guinea is an independent functioning state, while Nauru has a deep history [of] dysfunction because of its origins and its key industry."

Even so: "Everyone in the Pacific sees the culpability as Australian."

The Australians' calculus was like that of the United States in Guantánamo: by moving people offshore, Australia could claim not to be responsible, or at least not completely responsible, for their fate. It could shirk its international responsibilities with this one clever trick.

But the practice "doesn't comply with international law, and it's not a shield for moral accountability," Daniel Ghezelbash told me, citing the UN's conventions against torture, the mistreatment of children on Nauru, and the basic tenets of the 1951 Refugee Convention, all of which Australia has flouted. "These are morally reprehensible acts." (Australia has not been sued in international court for violating these agreements.)

Australia's offshore detention policies took place in two parts: the first from the *Tampa* affair through early 2008, and the second, after a four-year reprieve, from 2012 to the present. Nauru, where the passengers of the

Tampa were sent, and the Manus camp, which was built on and around a former naval base, detained a total of 1,647 migrants in the early years; about half were resettled, mostly in Australia and New Zealand, and a handful went back home, apparently of their own accord. Both facilities were managed by the International Organization for Migration, a UN agency.

In 2008, the Australian government officially closed the camps. But in 2012, Prime Minister Julia Gillard's cabinet faced intense pressure from the right, and before long, the centers were back up and running. The subsequent administration, led by Kevin Rudd, banned anyone attempting to reach Australia by boat not just from residency but from ever entering the country. His successor, Tony Abbott, rebranded the policy as Operation Sovereign Borders and required families, women, and children arriving by boat to be sent to Nauru, as well as opening Manus again for adult men (though some teenagers wound up being sent there as well). All the while, several boats were towed back toward Indonesia by the navy, or forced to turn around on their own.

It was during the Abbott administration that Aziz became one of thirteen hundred asylum seekers sent to Manus. He recalls spending a lot of time waiting in lines for food, medical care, clothes, and time at the computer. He waited, too, for news of what would await him. But waiting aside, there was no such thing as a normal day on the island. The days, and weeks, and months felt arbitrary. "We are not in control of our routine," he recalled. "Someone else who's in control, someone else who's in charge, will tell you what time you sleep, what time you wake up, what you eat and when you will eat, and when and who you will see." Manus was not just a place where conventional logic was garbled: it revealed how incoherent the world order was, for its ability to create such a place at all. Even outside observers noticed. Madeleine Gleeson, a human rights lawyer at the Kaldor Centre in Sydney, called this weirdness "one of the few matters on which staff can generally agree." In her book on offshore detention, she speaks to a number of contractors who went to Nauru or Manus for work and were dumbfounded by how "nothing made sense but everyone was behaving as if it did."

"It's not something I can explain to my family or friends back home, so I end up having these weird, intense relationships with people on the island because we are the only ones who get it," one visitor told her. "I want to say it's like being in a war zone over there, but it's not, so I don't know why we are acting like it is. It's just so unhealthy . . . so artificial."

These testimonies echo other sense memories from offshore. On a visit to Guantánamo Bay, Jeffrey Kahn, the anthropologist, recalls how uneasy he felt navigating the naval base's "uncanny commingling of the old and the new." Cait Storr, who spent time on Nauru as a legal adviser to its parliament, remembers taking a walk on a beach in Nauru and losing her balance as she watched a container ship disappear over the horizon.

"In that moment, I realised I had not simply boarded a plane and shifted location in a fixed world; had not simply flown from one point to another," she writes. "Rather, the world itself unfolded differently from the point at which I stood. Standing on that beach, it no longer made sense to think of Nauru as an anomaly in the international order. As much as Paris and New York and London, as Japan and Germany and Australia, Nauru was what was. It was me that had it all wrong."

For children detained in such places, this awareness could even manifest itself through a set of physiological symptoms doctors have begun calling resignation syndrome.

The condition was first identified in a group of children facing deportation from Sweden in the early 2000s. The children entered a sort of waking coma: they stopped eating, speaking, moving, and going to the toilet. They fell ill for no apparent reason other than the stress of living in limbo for so long. In 2001, not long after Australia's crackdown on asylum seekers began, a young Iranian boy in an (onshore) Australian immigration prison displayed similar symptoms after watching fellow prisoners physically harm themselves. He went on to sue the state of Australia and received a AU$400,000 settlement.

The symptoms then reappeared in children held on Nauru, where in 2018, a teenage girl's condition deteriorated to the point that an Australian judge ordered her evacuation. The condition ultimately struck at least thirty Nauru children, with "pervasive uncertainty" and "lack of freedoms" as leading causes of their distress. The Australian Asylum Seeker Resource Centre notes that the condition tends to occur when patients are prevented from fleeing or fighting—both instinctual responses to intense stress—and have nothing left to do but freeze.

And yet time did pass. It always does. On Nauru, women had babies, and their children grew. On Manus, Behrouz Boochani wrote his novel, *No Friend but the Mountains*, one WhatsApp message at a time. A young Iranian woman who'd been stuck on Nauru since she turned eighteen improved her English to the point of fluency. In the process, she picked up an Australian accent. Where was she?

Aziz lived through hunger strikes, a prison riot found to have been instigated by the police, and the death of twelve of his friends. Weeks turned into months, months turned into years, and still his minders couldn't seem to tell him when he'd get out. Aziz was granted refugee status in 2015, which meant that the Australian government itself recognized he could not go home without risking persecution. But its policy toward the boats hadn't changed: it would deny all maritime arrivals the right to enter Australia, no questions asked. Until another country agreed to take him, Aziz would remain in limbo.

He coped by putting himself in the middle of the action: translating English and Arabic, giving language lessons, organizing, organizing, organizing. "Gradually I started just getting, like, more energy and more energy by doing that," he said. "I realized that I have a role to play and my role would be to speak out."

Aziz got hold of a cell phone—contraband, with the bills paid for by Australian volunteers. He began speaking to Michael Green, who documented his experience. He went on walks in the Manus jungle with Boochani. Inside and outside the camps, Aziz became something of a celebrity. Life, or something like it, went on.

Then, in 2016, Papua New Guinea's Supreme Court delivered a bombshell ruling: the camp at Manus was unconstitutional. At first, the men refused to leave: they wanted freedom, real freedom, not the fake freedom they would gain by simply leaving the confines of their prison complex and living in a town with no future. The standoff lasted twenty-three days. Then six hundred men were transferred to live in Port Moresby, the Papuan capital, where there was nowhere to go and nothing to do.

When Aziz found out he'd been nominated for the human rights award, he assumed he wouldn't be able to leave. Yet somehow, the stars aligned, and he secured the right documents he needed to leave Papua New Guinea, transit through Manila and Doha and Qatar, and arrive in Geneva, where he could stay for two weeks. Aziz knew he'd have to undertake the whole journey again in reverse two weeks later, but it was a rare chance to get his message across unmediated.

The trip to Switzerland was overwhelming. Aziz had spent almost seven years in near captivity with the same men in the same place. Suddenly, he was walking free in an airport, surrounded by all kinds of people from around the world. He froze, panicked, at his first layover in the Philippines. He remembers a security guard in Manila approaching him and giving him a hard time: Who was he? Where were his papers? Where was he going? Unsatisfied with Aziz's strange answers, the guard took him to his supervisor.

Now it was Aziz's turn to give the border guard a history lecture. "I'm coming from Manus, and I don't know whether you heard about the Australian immigration prison on Manus, but I was there for six and a half years," he said, explaining his situation as he held up his Swiss travel authorization.

"The guy went from being so pissed at me to being, like, quite helpful, which for them is just mind blowing," he recalls. "And I told them, 'I've never gotten used to seeing people, strange people. I only used to see people that I've known for years.'"

The guards—probably charmed by Aziz's winning smile and magnetic personality—did not just let him go. They escorted him by car to the terminal for his connecting flight to Qatar.

But there was another glitch: the airline wouldn't let him board.

"It was the same question. Who the hell are you? Where are you coming from?" he recalls. Aziz briefly considered complaining on social media, but, not wanting to attract more attention, decided to call his sponsors in Geneva instead. Michael Khambatta worked every connection he had to get Aziz to Switzerland. It was paperwork, but it felt like a hostage negotiation. "From a bureaucratic stage this was an absolute nightmare," recalls Khambatta. "He could have been sent back anytime."

The plane left without him, and Aziz found himself in a familiar predicament: a cell with a bed, a toilet, and a locked door. He couldn't believe it was happening again.

The next morning, though, Aziz awoke to find visitors from the airline at his door. "They came and then they started apologizing—'Sorry, we're not meant to do that, blah, blah, blah.' And I was just, I was over it. I was like, 'Hey, just get me out of here. I don't want to hear it.'

"So they took me from there and all the way back to the flight, and I found myself in Geneva. And then when I got out of the Geneva airport, that was the time when I realized that technically I'm out of Manus. But all the time, like all that time on the plane, it was all doubt for me. Just like a dream."

· · ·

Aziz's first day in Geneva was a blur. He had to return to the airport shortly after leaving it to fix an error in his immigration paperwork. He tried, restlessly, to get some sleep at the hotel. His acquaintances gave him a winter coat. He could not get over how cold it was.

Then he was shuttled to a press conference, where a roomful of activists, journalists, and humanitarians fairly mobbed him upon his arrival. "People asked me, 'How do you feel, you know, after, like, so many years in the prison, how does that make you feel? How do you see the contribution of the international community?'" he recalls.

"And I was just like, Why am I here? Why am I being asked all these questions right now? It was really messing with my head."

The junket was a taste of what would come. On the street in Geneva, Aziz would walk by posters with his picture, advertising the award. Not one week ago, he'd been living in a sweltering apartment complex, sharing a bathroom with nine people and being identified not by his name but by his prisoner number. Now he was getting recognized on the street in a city plastered with posters of his face. Michael Khambatta took a photo of him posing next to one.

Aziz got the good news that he'd won the award and would be delivering the keynote at the gala. In his hotel room near the train station, he fretted over his script, pacing around, revising.

For the gala, Aziz wore a cardigan over a red-and-white gingham button-down shirt and slacks. He stepped onto the stage and addressed the glamorous crowd. "It's my first time being in a cold place," he joked, visibly nervous. "I still feel like I'm on Manus. It's not, like, real." He started as he'd planned, by thanking the international community for the honor. But as soon as he'd dispensed with these formalities, he veered off script.

Aziz tore into the Australian government, accusing them of dehumanizing him and his fellow refugees, harassing them, locking them "like animals in a cage," showing complete disregard for their basic needs and rights. He talked about the twelve friends he'd lost—eleven of them to medical negligence. He and his friends were vulnerable people whose intention was only to seek protection. But Australia, he said, sent them to a place with none. "We are thousands of kilometers from Australia, but everything is being dictated by the Australian politicians or government. . . .

"You need to feel it, you don't need to think about this story," he told the audience. "Imagine putting innocent people who are vulnerable, putting them and exposing them to such cruel and inhumane conditions that make them lose faith in their existence, lose faith in God. I want to save these people. And all I hear from them is, 'You are a troublemaker, you are not supposed to be where you are. Why are you complaining? You come from a place with no safety.'"

Aziz ended his speech on a somber note: When his two weeks in Geneva were up, he would be returning to Manus. He was only a visitor, after all, with a visa that would soon run out and unfinished business that needed finishing. "That was the part of my speech that actually shocked people," he later told me.

It wasn't for effect. Under the terms of his travel pass, Aziz would have to return to the only place of residence he had: Manus. And he had every intention of going back.

But in the coming weeks, his life would take another turn. Aziz would end up staying and making a life in Geneva.

I met Aziz one August day outside a Geneva University building, smack in the middle of a historic heat wave, after being introduced by Madeleine Gleeson. But like many encounters in the parallel universe of the hidden globe, our acquaintance felt fated. After I'd arrived in Geneva at the end of July, a friend from Brooklyn wrote to say he was in town visiting an old colleague. I went over for a drink and, within minutes, learned that his host, Mike Flynn, ran the Global Detention Project, the nonprofit where Aziz worked.

"Do you know Aziz?" I asked him.

"Everyone knows Aziz!"

It was true. Classmates, the cafeteria staff, a janitor all greeted him by name as we walked. Aziz was cramming for exams he'd deferred from the spring, but he looked the opposite of a disheveled student. Tall and muscular, with a sweet smile and an intense gaze, Aziz is a sharp dresser. ("He likes his bling," Flynn had told me.)

Aziz seemed surprised to still be in Geneva. He insisted again that he'd never planned on sticking around. "I wanted to show that I was a man of my word," he says of his intention to return to Manus. The idea kind of crept up. First, he extended his visitor visa. Then he did it again. At a certain point, he realized that to return to Manus would be to risk his life a second time over. The UN Refugee Agency had deemed Papua New Guinea an unsuitable place to resettle asylum seekers, on account of high levels of violence and few immigrants. He had few prospects, economic or otherwise. Besides, in 2019, Aziz was only twenty-six years old. He'd missed out on so much life, and he didn't want to throw the rest away.

First, he thought about moving to Canada as a refugee but was informed he'd have to try his luck first with the Swiss. So he put in his request for asylum in Geneva, and spent weeks being shuttled around Switzerland to different migrant centers, living once again in semiconfinement, seeing the world through the lens of paperwork, interviews, paperwork. He repeated his story more times than he can recall. It was boring and upsetting at the same time. One thing about the process managed to surprise him. "In the interview, they were not asking me any longer about Sudan," he said. "They were asking me about Australia"—that is, the hardships and persecution he'd faced not from the Sudanese authorities, but from the Australian ones.

Aziz was initially offered only temporary protection. He refused, appealed, and was granted permanent status in June 2019. Just when he'd gotten settled in his new apartment, the COVID pandemic shut down his new city, his new country, and his new life. One kind of lockdown gave way to another kind of lockdown, in another country, in another language but, this time, without all his friends. Time stopped making sense again. Life went on in a room, on social media, through his phone.

"I was one of the people that was told that I will be the last person, that I would die on Manus," Aziz went on. "That is something that I accepted. I forced myself to take it in and live with it.

"For me, it's just the recall of something that I'd been through," he said. "So I'm not unfamiliar with the situation. You have to find an alternative to live with."

Aziz felt lucky that he'd left temporary housing by then and moved into his rental flat between the train station and the UN. He spent the lockdowns attending Zoom school—mainly auditing Geneva University courses and working on his French. When we met, he was studying for exams that he hoped would land him a scholarship for graduate school. He passed and said he would begin a master's degree in international relations in late 2024.

Aziz and I also spoke about the hidden globe. I told him how my own experience of Geneva made me understand Manus Island and Nauru as a continuation of other kinds of offshore activity: if not morally equivalent, then party to the same logic, and certainly complicit in helping nationalist ideologies thrive in a globalized world. (One difference is that offshore financial centers do, occasionally, cave to pressure and close loopholes. No state has yet been formally reprimanded, let alone sued in international courts, for detaining people offshore in this manner.)

Ever critical, Aziz grappled with whether I was making a false equivalence—even downplaying or sanitizing what he and his fellow detainees had gone through—by connecting commercial and financial loopholes to physical and psychological abuse. And he had a point. Of course Geneva is not Manus Island. Of course a work of art in a climate-controlled box in an impenetrable freeport does not cause the same harm as being trapped in a legal abyss.

But wasn't that also the point—the abstraction, the obscuring, the loophole of deniability, the amoral equivocation? Geneva, for one, exemplifies how a haven for money and wealth and things can also be a haven for people and justice and order; how these forces are not mutually exclusive, but sometimes even sustain one another at the expense of the world that surrounds them.

Samuel Moyn, a professor of law and history at Yale, is the author of several books about the relationship between human rights and capitalism. He's come to see the two as mutually reinforcing. "Capital is cosmopolitan—Marx uses that word in *Communist Manifesto*—and in a sense, it's the victorious cosmopolitanism of our time," Moyn told me, noting that Geneva's human rights institutions aren't designed or intended to dismantle nation-states and the capital that sustains them. On the contrary: "It seems like other cosmopolitanisms so far have had to live in capital's world."

Small, neutral, and wealthy, Geneva is a microcosm of this universe. "There are well-meaning people in Switzerland rubbing shoulders with the powerful bankers," Moyn says. "They aren't the same people, but the first set of people is living in the world created by the second, and don't really face that fact or challenge the relationship, which is not one of complicity but one of forced companionship. So you begin to ask, 'How can you begin to have a different cosmopolitanism than the one in which capital wins?' And I don't think the Swiss are going to be the ones that help answer that question."

Aziz—who will likely become a Swiss citizen someday—is trying. He'd like to finish his studies, find work, maybe even move on entirely. But refugees keep trying to move, and countries keep trying to block them. And having apparently learned nothing from Australia's debacle, some states are even entertaining new offshore fantasies of their own.

The United Kingdom has pledged many times over to "stop the boats" of asylum seekers crossing the English Channel. In 2022, it came close to deporting a planeful of asylum seekers to Rwanda, thanks to a refugee resettlement deal former prime minister Boris Johnson had struck with President Paul Kagame in 2022. An order from the European Court of Human Rights prevented it from taking off at the eleventh hour. The following year, when a British appeals court ruled that the deportations would violate the UK's international legal obligations because Rwanda was not considered safe, the UK made plans to put migrants on a cruise ship instead. And until the Tories—and their migration plan—were defeated in July 2024, former prime minister Rishi Sunak insisted he would find a way to make the expulsions happen. (Sunak happens to be a big fan of Paul Romer's. He first encountered the economist's work on growth during a lecture as a Stanford MBA student; he went on to author a 2016 white paper advocating for freeports in Great Britain. The admiration is apparently not mutual, though: when I mentioned the Rwanda scheme to Romer, he sounded a little horrified.)

The European Union—with an assist from consultants at McKinsey—has been paying the Libyan and Turkish authorities what amounts to hundreds of millions of dollars to stop migrants from leaving their territory to begin with. The EU's coast guard, known as Frontex, has been responsible for some of the most egregious pushbacks, with thousands dead at sea. Frontex is supposed to follow international and European laws assuring asylum seekers a safe place to land, but on at least one occasion, involving Hungary, the European Court of Justice has ruled that the agency violated these charters.

"Despite all the evidence we have, people, like in Europe here, are looking at offshore detention as a model, you know, and they are even, like, proud to say in their own speech that, like, this is what we'd like to have," Aziz lamented. "So I feel like there's still so much to be done."

And then there's his own life. Aziz is outgoing and strong; he probably has more friends than most people. But the other men and women from Manus and Nauru have found new homes, mostly in the United States, under an agreement reached by the Australian and American governments.

Their resettlement, while difficult and traumatic, was part of a formal process; his was idiosyncratic, and lonely, and it never let him forget where he
came from. It has been exceedingly difficult to leave the past behind.

"I'm living this normal life. But still, just like I said, it's still alive. When
you are done [resettling], you think, now is the time where you can restart
and reshape your life, you know? But for me, I still haven't gotten to that
point.

"Hopefully, maybe, by end of this year," Aziz continued. "I'll graduate
and then from there will be the next step. The real life step will start."

10.

Laos Vegas

Fictive lots on fictive streets in fictive towns became the basis
for thousands of transactions whose only justification was a
dubious idea expressed on an overly optimistic map.

—WILLIAM CRONON, *NATURE'S METROPOLIS*

It is customary for journalists to begin stories with a place, a time, an action, and a subject: *At 9:12 a.m. on Monday in Manhattan, a piece of scaffolding fell from the side of a building and injured a pedestrian.* Openings like these establish four of the five *W*s—who, what, when, and where—before beginning to explain why. I spent years composing ledes like these, and I have chosen to start several chapters of this book that way too.

Still, there are limits to the convention—limits I confronted while visiting Boten, a new city in a special economic zone on the border of Laos and China.

I embarked on this journey because I had read that Boten was not just your average free zone, but one so dominated by Chinese businesses that it had pushed its clocks forward by an hour to better suit Beijing. That, to me, seemed to exemplify the hidden globe's capacity for manipulating time, be it in a warehouse, in an offshore prison, or on the wall behind a hotel's reception desk. In Boten, I'd hoped to observe how the vagaries of clock time affected daily life: how ordinary people lived with one foot in one zone and one in another.

It turns out that Boten exists in two temporalities, simultaneously inhabiting Laos and China, the old and the new. Where and when the following story takes place thus depends on who you are, what country you think the city belongs to, and which clock you consult.

There was even more to Boten's connection to time than that. The city's main selling point is a brand-new railway that serves as its link to the rest of the world: a technology that, fittingly, has had a profound historical impact on the setting of time, and which promises to project this sleepy rural enclave into the future. And for me, the experience of traveling from Michigan to Laos and back in the span of a week presented its own circadian conundrum. The jet lag was out of this world.

Time—the kind measured in minutes, by clocks and phones and watches—is necessarily a construct, and a relatively recent one at that. But it reaches deep into our lives. The power of measured time is why there are no clocks in casinos, or in solitary confinement. It is why we feel rich when we "gain" an hour in the autumn and confused and cheated when we "spring forward" in March.

Now imagine existing permanently in this state of mild dislocation: of having to add or subtract an hour to make plans, meet a friend, catch your train.

That's what it's like to be in Boten. You're never sure quite where or when you are. You can almost think that you're seeing double.

When I awoke in Vientiane on the second Sunday of May 2023, my phone informed me that it was four thirty in the morning. Back home in the United States, it wasn't yet dinnertime yesterday. I had already missed two dinnertimes just getting here, skipping forward more than half a day and losing a whole night to a layover in Seoul.

Jet lag—also known as desynchronosis—is the animal opposite of technology: it reminds us to the minute where, exactly, we are not. And in Vientiane, I needed some reminding.

The evening prior, I'd met some friends of friends for dinner around the corner from my hotel. The restaurant's decor was a hodgepodge of vintage signs, Italian moka pots, and framed photos of cobblestones and dried pasta: images to signify "Italy" to a clientele of tourists, expats, and well-off locals in Southeast Asia. But halfway through the meal, I spotted a familiar image in the mix: a close-up of an oversize black chess piece—the queen—standing on a painted board in a leafy park with a wooden bench in the background.

I knew this chessboard. I knew this park. I knew its benches and leaves and chestnut trees. Across the street, in my mother's apartment in Geneva, there is a framed photograph of me, taken by my father, playing there with a white knight and some black pawns. I'm wearing a flannel shirt, white socks, and jelly sandals, and I am standing a head taller than the knight, looking pleased. On the other side of the lawn is a wall with a row of sullen Protestant Reformers carved into it. Below the Reformers may have been some ducks in a shallow pool. Behind me was the restaurant where I celebrated my fifth birthday. There are photos of that day too.

For as long as I lived in Geneva, those chessboards were part of my habitat. A few years after he took the photo, I played against my dad (he let me win). Some years after that, a drunk friend showed up at a house party straddling the white knight (I made her bring it back). I passed the giant chess set in the park wherever I went: school, sports, babysitting. There is a hole in my head the size and shape of that picture, and it burrowed back in as deviously as an old lover.

There was an explanation, of course, for the photo on the wall—the Swiss mother of one of the proprietors had taken a picture of the chess set, as do many people who visit the park. Still, seeing it there in my desynchronized state made my head spin. I was in Laos. There I was.

I began the final leg of my journey to Boten that next morning, chessboards still on my mind. To get there, I'd take the brand-new Laos–China Railway northwest for almost four hours, until I arrived just shy of the Chinese border. I'd hired a guide, T., and two interpreters, V. and P., to accompany me. T. spoke English and Lao. V. spoke English and could help convey the nuances of the northern Lao dialect. P. spoke Lao and Mandarin, which we'd need to get around Boten, but no English at all. It was a complicated setup, arranged from afar, and for a reporter less than ideal. But our group, motley as it was, could pass for very clean backpackers, and that turned out to be a good thing. The Democratic People's Republic of Laos is a single-party state with no press freedoms and a track record of arresting dissidents: not North Korea, but not North America either.

What's more, Boten's indeterminate status and the even thornier subject of China's influence here put people on edge. The likelihood of anyone speaking freely, with or without translation, was remote, and I had agreed not to identify my companions in whatever I ended up writing before they agreed to show me around. My reporting would consist of blending in, gleaning bits of information, and corroborating it as best I could against other sources when I got home.

At around eight that morning, we hailed a taxi and drove down the capital's main boulevard to a dusty suburb where the brand-new train station stood tall. It was hard to miss, with its brick-red roof, gleaming marble floors, lotus-like latticework decorating the ceiling, and rows of seats without so much as a scuff.

Security was tight, with two identity controls, a ticket scanner, and an X-ray for luggage. During a body check conducted by a guard with a wand, T. had his vape confiscated. We waited until check-in, presented our ID and tickets again, and stepped aboard. Immediately, I sensed in our compartment an air of triumph: this was not a commute, but a celebration.

A train might not seem like such a big deal these days, but the Laos–China Railway, or LCR for short, made history for being the country's only existing train, and for all intents and purposes, its first. (French officials had built, then abandoned, a 4.7-mile rail line near the colonial capital, Luang Prabang.) The LCR turned a daylong journey along bumpy roads into a cool and comfortable jaunt, with assigned seating and announcements in Lao, Chinese, and English. I could not help but think it made Amtrak feel shabby in comparison, but then again, most trains do.

The train was also symbolic of the Chinese state's increasing influence in the region. The railway was built by Chinese contractors, financed by Chinese capital, governed by Chinese technical standards, owned in majority by Chinese firms, and conceived under the auspices of China's Belt and Road Initiative (BRI), a global development-and-infrastructure plan that aims to connect the European and African continents to Central Asia, and the rest of Asia to China. The LCR now runs all the way from Kunming in southwest China to Vientiane and back—a trip that takes ten and a half hours each way, including customs inspections on both sides. A southern extension to the railway is planned, too, stretching all the way to Singapore via Thailand and Malaysia.

The line I boarded ended in Boten. Chinese and Lao officials hope the train and the free zone it stops in will together open the remote area to commerce, trade, agriculture, and industry. The Boten SEZ is not just intended for bookkeeping and tax dodging; nor is it a simple depot for storage or a center for manufacturing. In its developers' eyes, Boten will be something else: a place for living.

Railways have always been a form of frontier making. It's easy to see similarities, however crude, between the railways built in service to Americans' westward expansions in the nineteenth century and this one, the product of Chinese geopolitical ambitions in the twenty-first.

Both were built and financed not solely by the state, but also by those standing to gain from the faster movement of merchandise: in the United

States, grain and meat companies, and in Laos, Chinese logistics and import firms moving goods like rubber and bananas. Both systems turned physical things into homogenized abstractions: apples into pallets, land into track. Railways exploit a vast geography of in-betweenness, putting new cities and landscapes (not to mention their resources) on the map. Before I left for my trip, my research assistant told me about a Chinese expression that translates to "When the train runs, there will be gold." How American is that?

Only there's another force at play here. Critics of the project worry that Laos is becoming an "external province" of the People's Republic of China (PRC) because of China's expansionist ambitions. The Laos–China Railway, they argue, primarily serves Chinese interests by facilitating the movement of goods from China to Laos and beyond. Considerably less freight is going in the other direction, from Laos to China, and it is almost all from Chinese companies (there have even been reports that non-Chinese businesses are unable to get access to the freight line). Laos, the critics contend, is being literally bulldozed into compliance by its more powerful neighbor, with severe environmental and social costs.

The railway's financing is likewise perceived as coercive: the threat of "debt-trap diplomacy"—of the PRC's seizing control of critical foreign infrastructure it helped finance if its loans aren't repaid—bolsters these skeptical perspectives on the BRI. Indeed, Laos owes more to Beijing relative to its GDP than any other country—122 percent, to be precise— which helped plunge the nation into an economic crisis. China reportedly also controls part of the Lao electrical grid as compensation for unpaid debts.

But the geographer Jessica DiCarlo, whose dissertation is all about the railroad, argues that there's more to the arrangement than the desire to wield power. Of course Chinese firms and the state that backs them are acting on their long-term interests. And of course they'll seek returns on these risky gambles. But DiCarlo contends that the intention isn't to colonize foreign assets through hypothetical foreclosures so much as to find space to invest excess Chinese capital. Moving money abroad allows it to accrue interest in a new arena and pushes its devaluation further into the future. The key here is not just foreign land, but foreign time. "We must think of capital temporally," DiCarlo writes. "Beyond expanding across space, it also expands into the future. The deeply intertwined relationships between finance, debt/credit, and railways alongside China's current crises of overaccumulation reveal that the railway and other large BRI initiatives are intended to sidestep domestic devaluation of capital."

The LCR's completion was hard won. Not only was the work interrupted by the COVID-19 pandemic; its architects also had to carefully dodge unexploded land mines, bombs, and rockets—a grim legacy of Henry Kissinger's aerial bombing campaign of the Ho Chi Minh Trail during the Vietnam War. The railway displaced some residents, who told DiCarlo that they had not been adequately (or punctually) compensated. And to clear the train's path through the Lao countryside, engineers had to cut down rainforests and bore tunnels into karst—forested peaks of soluble rock that are home to bats, rare orchids, geckos, and other flora and fauna—as well as construct hundreds of bridges over waterways.

From the café car, I looked out the window to see how these changes might have damaged Laos's landscape. A route that, not so long ago, must have borne the wear and tear of a massive engineering project—exploded rock, drained rivers, paved-over grass, barren fields—looked as smooth and seamless as the views from the trains I grew up riding in the Swiss countryside. We sped through hills and valleys and rivers, villages with soccer fields, chicken farms, and warehouses, and hundreds (if not thousands) of navy-blue Chinese freight cars on a parallel track. Rice paddies turned into forests, which turned into pasture where buffalo and goats grazed.

This is the image that train boosters—from the Chinese contractors building it to the international financial institutions tracking its impact—want to cultivate. They contend that the LCR will turn Laos from a "landlocked" to a "land-linked" region full of potential: that it will transform trade,

tourism, industry, and development and unlock the country's abundant agricultural and mineral resources. Karl Marx famously theorized about the
"annihilation of space by time": the tendency of capitalism to destroy spatial
barriers to its expansion with inventions like the railroad or the telegraph. He
would have felt vindicated in Laos. The World Bank projects up to 21 percent
growth in Lao GDP as a result of access to the Belt and Road network (admittedly, a long way away). According to the railway, more than 23 million
passengers and 27.8 million metric tons of goods have been transported by
the Laos–China Railway to date.

In our car, Lao families, arms laden with snacks and babies, sat beside
Chinese tourists, a small number of European and Australian backpackers,
and us. It was a smooth ride, half through dark tunnels and half in the
bright-green open.

As we neared Luang Prabang, now the country's tourism center, a young
female rail employee approached me holding a printed piece of paper. This
was the first and only time during my trip that a stranger would come up to
me for anything. The woman pointed to the page, grimacing. It was an an-
nouncement, but there was a word in it that she couldn't pronounce. The
word was "temporarily."

We practiced three, four, five times until she wrapped her tongue around
her r's and l's.

Save for its scheduled stops, the train halted—yes, temporarily—just
once, to let another train out of the tunnel. The pause did not result in significant delays.

By the time we arrived in Boten at 1:00 p.m., the train had emptied out.
The air was noticeably cooler on the platform—a relief from Vientiane's
stifling heat—and outside the station, informal shuttle buses were lined up,

ready to take travelers onward to the Chinese border. The four of us piled into a minivan with three other people and drove the five miles up a wide paved road lined with Chinese and Lao flags limply hanging side by side.

Moments later, we arrived at a large, gilded gate modeled on Vientiane's holy Pha That Luang stupa. It was the border. Most travelers got out of their vans and walked through the gaudy checkpoint to enter China and continue their journeys north. We took off on foot in the other direction to find a hotel.

Boten was all around us, incoherent: a hypothetical city trying to convince the world it was really happening. We walked a few hundred feet past several construction sites, each encircling a tower in a different stage of completion: some skeletons, others near-finished condos, all charmless, all empty. Cranes and tractors seemed to outnumber people in Boten, and the clang of construction animated the otherwise quiet midday. "This doesn't feel like Laos. This is China," V. immediately remarked, noting the license plates (all Chinese), the height of the buildings (orders of magnitude taller than in Vientiane), the cops (in black Chinese uniforms), and the snatches of Mandarin we'd overheard in the van.

Arriving at the town's main drag, we found a two-block stretch of restaurants and convenience stores, with a few people in them eating lunch. Around the corner was a hotel: a towering structure flanked with palms, a murky pool, and six white-and-gold elephants carved from stone standing at the entrance. It was obvious from the decor that the Jing Land Hotel had had a previous life.

Three women stood behind the front desk. One of them informed us in Mandarin that the hotel did not accept the local kip, only Chinese yuan and, at an unfavorable exchange rate, U.S. dollars. A digital clock flashed above their heads. The time it displayed was an hour ahead: Beijing.

This was Boten's most peculiar quality. Special economic zones have always traded in the fictions of space and time—recall the indefinitely transitory status of Yves Bouvier's freeport Rothkos, and of indefinite tax "holidays" in offshore factories (Marx might have dubbed this "the annihilation of time by space"). But rarely do these enclaves change their clocks to match another country's. In fact, the very pretense of a free zone—the reason they have been made palatable to regimes across the ideological spectrum—is that they proffer a place devoid of politics.

Clocks, on the other hand, can be overtly political. To lose agency over one's time signals a much deeper capitulation than the temporary waiving of a customs fee. And China takes national time seriously. The PRC has just one official time zone, spanning from where we stood in the lobby of the Jing Land Hotel to the outer edges of the Mongolian steppe. This projects the illusion of one billion people waking, breathing, working, and sleeping in step. (Singapore, meanwhile, has changed time zones on six occasions in the past century to accommodate occupiers, neighbors, and the sun.)

Unified time is supposed to make things easier, in theory at least. Before the 1830s, American towns set their clocks based on the position of the sun at high noon. It wasn't until trains began linking East and West that America adopted four formal time zones delinked from dawn and dusk. The objective was predictability. "Railroad schedules redefined the hours of the day," writes the environmental historian William Cronon in *Nature's Metropolis*. "Sunrise over Chicago would henceforth come ten minutes sooner, and the noonday sun would hang a little lower in the sky." Time zones divided territories and erected borders to make capitalism (and its trains) run more smoothly.

In Boten, though, we discovered quite the opposite.

Most of the clocks we saw—at the hotel, the real estate developer's showrooms, the local investment office—were indeed set an hour ahead, as news reports have noted for more than a decade. But not everybody behaved as though that were the case. My cell phone, for instance, stayed on the Lao network, so the clock in my pocket didn't budge. The hotel workers seemed to use the local time, too, even as the time displayed behind them—and on their timesheets, most likely—were an hour off. We navigated the world a little disynchronously: When was checkout? What time was breakfast? An hour is a long time without coffee in the morning.

My body, meanwhile, was still a world away. I did not need lunch at whatever hour it was. I needed a nap.

Fighting sleep on one of the twin beds in my room, I looked out the window. Over the hotel parking lot, I saw the city, its cranes, and beyond it, a thick rainforest. I took a shower and put on a pair of papery yellow slippers. Our hotel was called the Jing Land, but its branding was a work in progress, and my slides still bore the logo of its predecessor, the Bodhi.

The whole hotel, and the city around it, was likewise a palimpsest of lives and logos, papered over like the lingering smell of a thousand cigarettes that must once have been permitted but were now loudly verboten. It, too, lived in two times. I could smell old smoke on the bedframe, on the curtains, in the hall. In my room's green dresser drawer, I found investment pamphlets dating back to 2019 that somebody must have left behind before the pandemic. They were prospectuses from Boten's real estate developer, the Yunnan Haicheng Industry Group, outlining another city the company was building in a neighboring Chinese province.

Haicheng isn't just the only game in town. It has been both game and town since it signed a ninety-year lease in 2016 on the land Boten occupies, according to Chinese state media. The firm enjoys the usual concessions of a SEZ: the freedom to register a company without a Lao partner, exceptions from duties, and so on.

But it's only here because its predecessor went down in infamy.

For much of its human history, the inhabitants of what is now Boten lived quite statelessly in a highland region known as Zomia. Zomia is a heterogeneous territory the size of Europe, covering the highlands of Laos, Vietnam, Thailand, Myanmar, and Cambodia, as well as four provinces in China. For the Yale anthropologist James Scott, Zomia also represents a distinct way of life for a diverse array of peoples who, Scott argues, fled to higher ground in part to avoid being folded into state-centered societies. Rather than submitting to taxation, conscription, and a sedentary agrarian lifestyle, Zomians opted out and, despite their ethnic and cultural diversity, found common ground in their material circumstances. Scott likens Zomia to a "pervasive Switzerland without cuckoo clocks"—"a mountain kingdom at the periphery of Germany, France, and Italy that itself became a nation-state." Zomia reminds us of the newness of modern nations, of their coerciveness and their dispensability.

When Scott published *The Art of Not Being Governed* in 2009, there were still communities in Zomia functionally living without a central state, but their days were waning. "Gone, in principle, are the large areas of no sovereignty or mutually canceling weak sovereignties. Gone too, of course, are peoples under no particular sovereignty," he wrote. Nation-states had begun "establishing armed border posts, moving loyal populations to the frontier . . . clearing frontier lands for sedentary agriculture, building roads to the borders, and registering hitherto fugitive peoples."

Boten knew all about it.

In the 1980s, the town had little but a wooden pole and a rickety customs house for a border crossing. Those were hard times. Lao society was still recovering from a brutal civil war that lasted from around 1959 to 1975, not to mention the millions upon millions of bombs the U.S. military had dropped between 1964 and 1973. Like their Chinese neighbors, Lao people were hungry, poor, and falling behind other Asian states when it came to urbanization and development. So when free zones appeared to offer easy solutions north of the border, it made sense for the government in Vientiane to consider them too.

As we've seen, the idea of these zones had been percolating in the international community for some time, and Chinese nationals had been well represented on the scene. Early on, entrepreneurs from China opened factories in SEZs in Mauritius to exploit the export quota loophole and sell their goods in Europe. Chinese officials, including future president Jiang Zemin, had participated in the three-week course on zone management run by UNIDO in Shannon, Ireland, in 1980.

Simultaneously, Shenzhen was starting to show the world just how much and how fast a free zone could grow, even though the factors that contributed to this growth are still misconstrued. "The idea that Shenzhen is a replicable model reinforces the assumption that cities can be politically planned and socially engineered from scratch," writes Juan Du, the architect, warning that displacing native populations, relying on top-down directives from developers, putting too much faith in the power of tax concessions, and casting aside local culture can have "devastating consequences."

Nevertheless, the takeaway from abroad was that China's new zones were allowing the communist-run state to have it both ways and create a refuge for business, often at the expense of labor, in an otherwise tightly controlled political economy. In Laos, which opened its economy to foreign investment in 1986 and established diplomatic relations with China in 1989, foreign economic consultants got to work planning ways to boost cross-border trade. This continued through the 1990s as the Chinese and Lao states grew more interested in the region. In 2003, the Laos government designated Boten as a special economic zone. This corner of Zomia—once a territory of free people—would become an enclave for free (or at least, freer) money. Lacking the resources to go it alone, though, the Lao state granted a Chinese businessman named Huang Mingxuan (who sometimes goes by the alias Wong Man Suen) a concession over the land, which at the time was mostly jungle.

By 2011, Huang had reason to be bullish on free zones: at fifty-six, he was part of a generation raised on the mythology of Shenzhen. Originally from Fujian, he'd done business in Hong Kong and dabbled in gambling projects in Myanmar. Huang told *Forbes Asia* that he'd been "talked into the idea" of running Boten by high-ranking Lao officials. Whatever form these negotiations took, the final arrangement granted him an unusual amount of autonomy—a move analysts have likened to the state outsourcing its economic development, as well as control of its borderlands, to foreign business.

Under the agreement, the Golden City would be run not by a local municipality but by a committee headed by Huang and paid for by Huang's firm. For a time, the company reportedly controlled everything from cultural education to policing. In exchange for a yearly concession fee, it could collect taxes, enact legislation, issue license plates, and hand out ID cards separate from those administered by Laos. According to *Forbes*, Huang paid the Laos government between $700,000 and $2.4 million a year for this kingdom. His company, Fuk Hing Travel Entertainment Group, called the shots from Hong Kong. It was a form of governance that recalled dystopian science-fiction plots. It also looks a little like Próspera Honduras: a corporate statelet defying socialism with outsized ambitions, conceived by a wealthy few.

The initial rendering of Golden Boten City was a suburban idyll: golf, condos, shopping malls, glimmering lakes and lagoons, all grafted onto six square miles of raw jungle. To make space, the residents of Boten—a village of a few hundred—were paid to move to a place now called New Boten, a few miles away. But only a fraction of the development was completed, and it could not have been a secret that Huang had planned to sustain his empire with casinos all along.

Gambling on China's periphery was all the rage at the time. The territory of Macau started granting concessions to casinos in 2002, and across the next decade the industry grew to outearn the Las Vegas strip many times over. Singapore legalized the practice not long after, with Cambodia and Myanmar joining in after that (though some of these countries grant only foreigners access—citizens are not allowed). These jurisdictions gamed the asymmetry between mainland China's ban on gambling and its nationals' appetite for it, much like the way American citizens patronize casinos on Native American reservations.

Our hotel, I learned, used to house a casino. So did a gem shop across the street. A Haicheng office on the main drag was home to Fok Hing's Royal Jinlun Hotel and Casino, Boten's party central, where busloads of Chinese revelers came each day to get their kicks visa-free. For a while, the customs checkpoint even moved a few miles south, which for the purposes of duties and immigration turned Boten into the open-air equivalent of an airport or freeport, a zone between one state and the next.

Most of the clients were professional gamblers "equipped with headsets for receiving instructions from their bosses based in China, who could follow the game on the internet," wrote one observer—no time-zone math required. They could have been in Macau, or Singapore, or Vegas, for all they cared. And even after hours, they were resolutely not there to play golf.

"A dozen lingerie shops catered to battalions of Chinese prostitutes, with the finest choice of stiletto heels in Laos," *Forbes* reported. "Pharmacies stocked sex potions alongside racks of X-rated DVDs and containers of bile from black bears fresh from a hilltop factory and used in traditional Chinese medicine. Next door to the factory was a massive pink entertainment hall that boasted transvestite shows. The ladyboys [their preferred label] hailed from Thailand but everything else came from China: the beer, the police and practically all the dealers, even the currency that made it all possible."

Boten's peculiar form of governance was catnip for scholars interested in the mutable nature of state sovereignty. Pal Nyiri, a history professor at Vrije University in Amsterdam, noted in a paper that the zone could be likened to China's treaty port system in the nineteenth century, during which foreign powers came to control (often by force) enclaves on Chinese territory and impose their own laws, courts, and customs on their expatriates living there. "Although [the zone] model seems to fit with the neoliberal approach to the global economy," Nyiri wrote, "the Chinese state in fact plays a major role in the establishment and operation of these zones . . . just as Western powers did in the operation of concessions."

In her important work on free zones in East Asia, the UC Berkeley anthropologist Aihwa Ong coined the term "graduated sovereignty" to describe the multiple layers of control (or lack thereof) in places like Boten. The idea of one nation, one government, one set of rules, and one population did not hold up in places like these, she argued, because "shifting relations between market, state, and society have resulted in the state's flexible experimentations."

Kearrin Sims, an Australian scholar at James Cook University, has visited Boten regularly over the years. He's also conducted fieldwork in other gambling enclaves in the region, like the Golden Triangle, where the borders of Laos, Myanmar, and Thailand meet. (Thibault Serlet, an economic zone consultant, calls the Golden Triangle "the worst SEZ in the world": "The zone was built on stolen indigenous land, workers are routinely unpaid and forced to work against their will, and the zone regularly dumps toxic waste into local streams," he writes in a report that calls the area "an embarrassment to the global SEZ industry.")

Sims became fascinated by the criminal elements that these zones attracted—not just the gambling, but wildlife trafficking, prostitution, online scam rings, and armed gangs that flocked there and were often left undisturbed. Did the zones court crime, or did crime find the zones? It was a chicken-and-egg question.

"Free zones are established to create wealth and transnational wealth, whether that's a tax haven or a freeport," Sims told me over Zoom. "You have Nike, Apple, the multinationals looking for tax exemptions, but also all these other people looking to hide money, move it, find investments for a quick buck." In other words, the point of a zone is money—and it's no mystery that crime loves money. Crime, then, is both a feature and a bug: it's not the be-all, end-all of a free zone, but it does tend to come with the territory. After all, these are places that the state itself sets apart—"The role of the state is important in supporting all of them," Sims says—and when the state is complicit in the criminal elements, or simply unable to stop them, the oulaws will naturally thrive. In these enclaves, much like on the high seas, the line between the legal and the illegal—or at least, the enforced and unenforceable—is wobbly: not for a lack of laws on the books, but because of the pervasiveness of corruption, and the government's inability, or unwillingness, to make it stop.

There is evidence that SEZs encourage certain kinds of criminality: according to the Organisation for Economic Co-operation and Development, the addition of a special economic zone in a country increases the average value of counterfeit exports by 5.9 percent. Again, smuggling and fraud can occur anywhere, but because these places are often defined by the lack, or laxity, of regulation and their locations at ports of entry, they "act not only as the ideal locations for tax evaders to place high-end commodities in duty-free transit, but also as a means of concealing and smuggling illicit goods," notes *The British Journal of Criminology*.

In its heyday, Boten exemplified this laxity and lack of state control: even the police were privately hired. Its lawlessness quickly spiraled out of control, and reports of unsolved murders, debt-related suicides, kidnappings, armed gangs, and street violence began multiplying. In 2011, Chinese officials deemed that things had gone too far and intervened by cutting Boten's power and shutting down its phone lines from over the border. The Lao government closed the casinos and started requiring visas of Chinese visitors.

The party was over. The real state had arrived.

Over the ensuing years, Boten's population dropped from ten thousand people to about five hundred as shops and restaurants went out of business. It became a ghost town: Kearrin Sims recalls visiting Boten after it had emptied out and encountering a few small-time gamblers playing slot machines as cows grazed outside abandoned casinos.

The jungle began creeping back, leaf by leaf, branch by branch. But this was no return to nature. Far from it.

. . .

Our first stop in town after we arrived was to find lunch on the main drag. We settled on a Thai place called Bangkok; my Lao companions, unsettled by how very Chinese Boten was, preferred not to patronize the offending establishments. (Never mind that Thailand is also not Laos. This grudge was purely bilateral.) Still, a Chinese man, very drunk, sat down with us and blabbered nonsensically over beers and fried rice. We could not make out why he was here and what he was doing. We would run into him a number of times throughout the day. He never seemed to get any more sober.

After eating, we set off to explore town, or what was left of it. Besides eateries and a rubber manufacturer that would not let us in, the only open businesses were linked to the city's developer, Haicheng. In a showroom adorned with large photos of Chinese and Lao officials, we visited model condo apartments that, we were told, would soon be real units in the building across the street.

A Lao woman in a silk skirt with a black bow in her hair walked us through the flats, priced at $27,000 and up. It felt like being in an IKEA showroom calibrated to the aesthetic preferences of the ascendant Chinese middle class—all white and gold and a little chintzy, Mickey Mouse in the children's room, fake flowers in the kitchen, a principal bedroom opening onto the balcony, a hanging chair from which to enjoy the view.

As she went over a 3-D model of the city's master plan, the saleswoman explained that while Lao people could own the units outright, Chinese nationals would be leasing them for seventy years: time-shares, really, that expired with Haicheng's lease. According to the saleswoman, nine out of ten units had already been sold, four fifths of them to Chinese buyers, with the rest going to the odd Lao and foreign citizen. This meant that the very foundation of the city was set to turn over in two generations—that the three hundred thousand people that Zhou Khun, president of the Haicheng group, anticipated would move there would be temporary residents. How could this ever be a home?

Pointing a laser at the golden border crossing, she added with some confidence that the border would eventually move south to meet the train, making the journey for Chinese customers as seamless as crossing into a neighboring province. It was a return to Boten's freewheeling days as a no-man's-land, only a sanitized version: condos, not casinos. I felt my companions flinch at the suggestion. Boten had already made a mockery of its host nation: linguistically, financially, culturally, horologically. You could not so much as buy a local beer using Lao kip. Moving the checkpoint would be saying the quiet part out loud.

We saw much the same at the city's "urban development" office—really, another hall of advertising for the Haicheng Group. Filling the entire ground floor of the opulent golden building that was once the Royal Jinlun Hotel and Casino, the venue looked more suited to a wedding, what with its fake flowers, crystal chandeliers, and white furniture. The former gambling hall was now plastered with propaganda: maps, prospectuses, models of the city-to-be centered around gigantic twin Buddhas, one facing China to the north, the other smiling upon Laos to the south. He pointed out the different areas that would be home to schools, banks, logistics companies, medical services, and tourism offices. More than a billion dollars has been invested in Boten, China's Xinhua New Agency reported in 2019; the total cost of the project, if completed, will likely top ten times that.

Using a translation app on his phone, a salesman told me about excursions visitors would enjoy to Boten's outskirts: "scenic spots, duty-free shops, elephant camps, and shooting ranges with real guns." An entire wall was covered in glowing brand logos of Swiss watches and high-end cosmetics—companies, the young man explained, that would soon be opening stores in Boten. This, I realized, might have been a misunderstanding: the logos were from products on sale at the duty-free mall across the street (a shop that, in the vein of Geneva's diplomatic store, sold a baffling selection of gummy candy, enormous jugs of Hennessy, Japanese thermoses, and cans upon cans of Spam).

Next, I walked past a cavernous gem store—the converted casino—and went inside to explore. I walked through at least four different rooms filled with cases of jade jewelry, Buddhas, and trinkets. It was an impressive display, but the young woman who worked there said she hadn't sold a thing in weeks.

In the evening—7:00 p.m. Laos, 8:00 p.m. Boten—we went back out and wound our way through an informal night market near the main road. It was dark and smelled of chicken three ways: dead, live, fried. Dance music briefly pulsed through the walls of a two-story building, then stopped as abruptly as it had begun. Puppies splashed around in a puddle. We saw what appeared to be a pharmacy and went in so I could buy painkillers for my throbbing head, but I didn't recognize the packages and was suspicious of the unmarked pills the man behind the counter told me to take "before bed." On my way out, empty-handed, I noticed two cots tucked into a dark corner and, in front of them, a glass cabinet filled with "France"-themed sex dolls and a stack of dildos.

This was the only remnant of Boten's insalubrious past that we saw in the open. Despite prepandemic reports of illegal wildlife products like bear bile on sale, and a 2019 *Outside* article describing elephants being smuggled into China via Boten, these businesses are believed to now be in the Golden Triangle—a place where caged tigers are reportedly kept in the open, scam call centers lure poor young girls from their homes with the promise of good jobs, and a paramilitary mafia rules the streets.

Up a steep hill from the night market was the Eccellente Cabaret, where two dozen or so Thai ladyboys performed nightly for Chinese tour groups and curious onlookers. Later in the evening, back at the Café Bangkok, we encountered the performers, who confirmed our hunch: there was nothing, and they meant *nothing*, to do in Boten. The delegation of performers—all of them transgender, between the ages of around twenty and forty—had come from Thailand and worked on six-month contracts with no days off, explained a performer with an exquisite figure who went, onstage and off, by the name of Irene.

Chinese visitors loved the ladyboy shows, Irene told us, so business had been decent since the border reopened in January 2023. Still, the work was hard: hours of rehearsing, no time off, a nightly show. Irene's boss at the cabaret was Chinese, his employees were all Lao, and the dancers were clearly at the bottom of the food chain. She insisted that she was happy: "I love it, and this is my family," she said. She sounded sad, but wouldn't elaborate, and urged us to come watch them rehearse the next day.

Then a police car pulled up with four cops dressed in black, and the real song and dance began.

The policemen hopped out of their car and made some noise in Mandarin about the volume of the music. Its pulsing beats felt wildly out of place— Ibiza, this was not—but the track did bring this carcass of a city to life for a moment. The girls sashayed up to the cops and blew kisses; the cops blushed and got back in their car; and the strip went quiet again as the car pulled away.

The cops in Boten are still Chinese. They wear black uniforms with the word SWAT printed on the back in English. They ride motorbikes and cars around town and can be seen hanging out on street corners. They don't seem to get too involved in anyone's business—certainly not enough to prevent dozens of young Lao girls from posting up in storefronts come nightfall and waiting around for someone to call.

In Vientiane, I learned from my guides, this sort of thing is unheard of—sex work happens, of course, but not like this. Here, though, it was all fair game, and happy endings were advertised as liberally as the condos down the street. THERE IS NO AND [SIC] TO HAPPINESS flashed a neon sign down the way.

After dinner, we dropped by an open clothing store, also Chinese, to see what had brought this seemingly wholesome business to town. Its young male proprietor told us he used to work in a restaurant in Hunan province. He'd moved to Boten just three days ago, after seeing posts about it on Tik-Tok. He hadn't come to strike it rich; he was here, he said, to find a wife, because getting married in China was hard, and he'd heard Lao women were beautiful and easy. (This, my Lao companions said, was a relatively common perception, and one that is growing. Indeed, the U.S. State Department noted in a report that "brokered marriages between rural Lao women and [Chinese] men employed at SEZs known for trafficking vulnerabilities . . . increased during the pandemic.")

The young man tried to sell us clothes but ended up refusing payment for a pair of gold and green earrings. "Take them, take them!" he said as we extricated ourselves from the conversation. He seemed lonely and bored. He was the only person besides the drunk who wanted to keep talking.

At breakfast the next day, I struck up a conversation with a Chinese tourist who spoke impeccable English and said her name was Mandy. She was part of a large group I'd spotted that morning from my window practicing tai chi in the parking lot, and they arrived at breakfast game and glowing. Mandy worked for a company that made ball bearings for vehicles in Fujian province and often traveled the world for work. But she was here in Boten for a three-week course in personal development based in part on the Rhonda Byrne book *The Secret*, about the (pseudoscientific) "law of attraction." The hotel owner's wife was teaching the course, she said—that was the only reason why it was being held here. She didn't think much of the place besides that.

Little came otherwise of my hope to learn what it was like to live, really *live*, in Boten. Perhaps our awkward three-way interpretation system—English to Lao to Chinese and back—put people off from talking. But it was also true that almost no one seemed to live in Boten for more than a few months at a time. Staff turnover at the hotel was high, business was shaky, and the people who came to seek their fortunes seemed only to be passing through.

I decided, then, to see what the tourists saw, and booked a tour through the hotel. A young Lao man with pretty eyelashes drove the four of us around in a golf cart–like vehicle—to the border, down the main drag, and by the various buildings in progress. On the way back, he took a sharp turn and charged our little cart toward the mountain, past construction-worker housing, past piles of rubble and dirt, and up a forested road.

I relaxed a little as the nature grew more lush. I saw taller and taller trees ahead, their trunks braided together like thick rope. I stared down at a still salt lake and a large, languid fish biding his time just beneath the surface. I saw beautiful black birds with a fan of red in their tails, squirrels, bees, and butterflies abuzz.

It was only then that I fully understood something important: Boten really *had* sprung from the jungle. Every inch of land cleared by the developers for their buildings—first Fuk Hing's casinos, and now Haicheng's condos—had been cleared intentionally, with a purpose, by workers toiling away in the heat. It is easy to forget the scale of labor that a project like this demands, especially when the results are so disappointing.

As we climbed the hill that took us deeper into the jungle, the silhouette of the city came into view, and I finally had a sense of why we were where we were.

Some people had decided to start a new city in what they deemed was a good location—a crossroads, if you will, on a new silk road. They brought other people there by permitting certain things, sinful things, that would not pass muster elsewhere: a temporary draw that flamed out and took the city down with it.

But the seal was broken; they had gotten a taste of what could be. So they built and planned, and planned and built, and would not, could not, stop building. There was nothing organic about this city, nothing human and alive and animate.

In our golf cart, we passed a little checkpoint, where we bought tickets to proceed along the road up the hill. Moments later, a tidy little village came into view. It looked to be traditional: huts with straw roofs, a woman sitting by a silk loom, cats and chickens running amok. We all noticed a striking tree in the background and wondered what kind it might be. It looked like a pine amid the vines: pale, sparse, and different. When we stepped out of the car, we realized it was not a tree but a telephone pole that somebody had dressed up in Christmas camo.

Right on cue, six women appeared on a low platform and began performing a dance, which I was told was more or less traditional. The dancers were all employed by Haicheng, the hotel guide told us, and they did not live in the village but in the worker dorms behind our hotel. They reverse-commuted to dance for tourists making the same trip.

Confusingly, there were also "real" villagers living there, but they came from different cultural or ethnic groups who, pre-zone, would not have lived together in this particular place. Haicheng apparently considered them interchangeable enough to put on a show for its clientele. The village, in other words, was part of the spectacle. The village and its inhabitants all worked for the Boten SEZ.

The more we looked, the more we found evidence of this artifice. Haicheng had added stones to the village floor, installed a boccie court, and erected a swing that looked suspiciously like it was put there for social media photo ops. The developer had even built a toilet that mimicked the village style from the outside but was by far the biggest structure there, with highly nontraditional drainage.

Where were we?

What time was it?

We got back in the golf cart, a little deflated. So much for the jungle.

Then our guide took us to another worksite, down the hill and around a sharp bend.

Surrounding a large fake lake—it had been excavated and filled with river water—stood the carcasses of more condos. Closer to us was a strange little restaurant built in the style of a Greek island taverna, white and blue and airy. Mykonos! Three women were hanging around on the tiled terrace waiting, it seemed, for something. There was a power outage. Nothing to do. Nobody was quite sure when the lakeside properties would be finished.

We turned back, bewildered. Before we reached our hotel, the driver pointed out a strange, steep hill with a tree sitting on top. Its trunk was a tangle of smaller trunks, and it stuck out amid its denuded, flattened surroundings. Local folklore had it that the tree was home to ghosts and spirits—spirits that the developers had laughed off until a worker died clearing the area. After the incident, they decided to play it safe and left the tree on its hilltop in peace.

As they dug up everything around it, the little tree lorded over the city, sovereign, timeless.

I was in Boten barely thirty-six hours, but it felt interminable, and by our final morning, I was desperate to leave. The train wouldn't depart until afternoon, though, and I was up early so I went for a last walk around. To my surprise, I saw signs of life. At a small street market, merchants sold fragrant herbs, fruits, vegetables, and cuts of meat from the backs of pickup trucks. They'd come from the neighboring village—New Boten—to sell their goods. Their presence made the older, newer, other Boten feel alive. It felt almost like a city.

I turned a corner to see toddlers playing in a storefront day care. The only children I'd seen thus far had been small babies strapped to their parents. A Chinese-language school was advertised in the lobby of one of the condo buildings, but it had no students yet. The doorman said classes would begin in the fall.

I went in search of coffee and found a tea shop off the main drag. The shopkeeper—who also sold herbal supplements and stacks of blood pressure cuffs—told me the coffee he brewed was only for men. I lied and said it was for a friend, and he handed me a cup.

Then he explained, using a translation app on my phone, that he'd come from China with his wife after they retired from their jobs at a hospital (which explained the cuffs). Boten was relatively cheap, the weather was all right, and the business was a way to pass the time. His son had inquired about joining them, but he'd told him not to bother. It was too boring here. No place for young people.

I walked a block before trying the coffee and spitting it out. It was not coffee. Or maybe it *was* just for men. I did another loop, looking for something, anything that might help me understand the city I was in. Could this really all be an elaborate plan to park Chinese cash? Did anyone believe in the promises that Haicheng was making? Did Haicheng really think that if they built it, the people would come? And did the Chinese state care enough about *this* piece of land to encroach so flagrantly on Lao sovereignty, to bend not just space but also time in an untested quasi-expansionary experiment?

The answer, I realized, was probably not a simple yes, but a *yes enough*. I found a convenience store and pleaded for them to accept my Lao money in exchange for another attempt at coffee. It was fine. Coffee enough.

Back at the Boten train station, I walked across the main road to what looked like a truck stop, along a muddy path, past parked vehicles, and between stacks of large blue shipping containers. It smelled like livestock and damp exhaust. I arrived at a checkpoint. Where a jungle once stood were signs for plant quarantine.

I was at the Lao customs border: the place where goods went to change state. The human border, for immigration to and from China, was on the other side of town. Divorcing these lines had made Boten what it was: a place free of duties, a place in between.

It is the decoupling of people and capital—the fiction that you can have one without the other—that for centuries has animated so many freeports and free zones and other strange jurisdictions. But if the Haicheng representatives we'd spoken to were well informed, the human border could soon move here too. It would give up its spot by the golden stupa to make it easier on Boten's Chinese clientele, who could visit their Laos condos and explore the Laos jungle and swim in a fake Laos lake and watch Lao performers sing and dance, all without crossing into Laos—at least not fully.

The two borders—the one for things, and the one for people—would reunite here at the train. It would be so convenient to have them back in one place.

11.

Terra Nullius

Remember that I am thy creature, I ought to be thy Adam,
but I am rather the fallen angel whom thou drivest from joy
for no misdeed. Everywhere I see bliss from which I alone am
irrevocably excluded. . . . The desert mountains and dreary
glaciers are my refuge. I have wandered here many days. The
caves of ice, which I only do not fear, are a dwelling to me, and
the only one which man does not grudge. These bleak skies I
hail, for they are kinder to me than your fellow beings.

—MARY SHELLEY, *FRANKENSTEIN*

When you land in Longyearbyen, the largest settlement in the
Norwegian archipelago of Svalbard, you can step out of
the plane and just walk away. You might hitch a ride into the
town, or walk through ice and snow to a nearby campsite by the bay. Wherever you go, there will be no passport control to submit to, no armed guard
retracing your steps, no biometric machine scanning your fingers—just an
airport terminal about the size of a school gym, whose most memorable feature is a taxidermied polar bear bearing a sign with Svalbard's most famous
bylaws: To venture beyond the town's borders, you must respect nature, notify the government, and carry a gun.

Svalbard—also known as Spitsbergen—has lots more laws. You cannot
be born there. Nor are you supposed to die: because permafrost covers the

entire island, your buried body will never decay, and, after seasons of melting and freezing, it may rise back up, as though from the dead.

The building code of Svalbard is strict for much the same reason. There are draconian quarantines for plants and animals.

What Svalbard does not have is borders—at least not the kind we speak of farther south. As long as you can support yourself, you can live there footloose and visa-free, no matter where you come from.

That doesn't make Svalbard an egalitarian place. Commercial flights currently transit through Oslo or Tromsø, so travelers must obtain transit visas and wait in lines there instead. Svalbard provides minimal social services, so it won't attract the world's tired, poor, and weary. When in 2015 a right-wing Norwegian politician offered to send refugee families north rather than accommodate them on the mainland, it was not meant as a kindness.

Still, Svalbard is the only place in the world where anyone, from anywhere, can live: a free zone for people, not just commerce, taxes, or things. In 2019, I went there to find out what we could learn from this twenty-three-hundred person community a few hundred miles from the North Pole. I found, in this frigid extremity of the globe, no linear explanation for how it got to be that way, but a fortuitous brew of historical contingencies, human egos, and environmental hindrances.

As climate change renders large swaths of the globe hostile to human life, the nations of the world must make choices about how to accommodate those left behind. One option is to throw up walls and keep newcomers out. The other is to tear them down, let them in.

Svalbard teaches us something else: that in the cracks of the nation-state system, we might find more space than we think possible.

If you ask a diplomat to whom, exactly, Svalbard belongs, they will confidently repeat that the territory belongs to Norway, which writes the laws, enforces order, builds infrastructure, and regulates hunting, fishing, and housing. In 2018, when a Russian man was caught trying to rob a bank in town, a Norwegian judge sentenced him under Norwegian law to a Norwegian jail. During the pandemic, comings and goings from the island were monitored stringently by the Norwegian authorities. (The virus didn't care, and came anyway.) Svalbard's governor is Norwegian. So are its schools.

But Norway's control over Svalbard comes with obligations outlined by an unusual 1920 treaty, signed as part of the Versailles negotiations ending World War I.

Written at a time when the world was still rife with what we now consider territorial anomalies, the Svalbard Treaty is both of its time and light-years ahead of it. In the aftermath of the Great War, the treaty's architects stipulated that the territory could not be used for belligerent purposes. In a flash of foresight, they included in its text one of the world's first international conservation agreements, making Norway the steward of Svalbard's natural environment. The treaty also insists that the state must not tax its citizens more than the minimum needed to keep Svalbard running, which today typically amounts to an 8 percent income tax, well below mainland Norway's 22 percent.

But most radically, the Svalbard Treaty's architects held Norway to what's known as the nondiscrimination principle, which prevents the Norwegian state from treating non-Norwegians differently from Norwegians. This applies not just to immigration but also to opening businesses, hunting, fishing, and other commercial activities. While sovereign, Norway can't deny someone the right to live and work there on the basis of their citizenship. The combination of state control with genuine freedom of movement for individuals represents a radical way of thinking about sovereignty, territory, and migration.

Other countries cannot lay formal claims to Svalbard—but their people and companies, which are foreign by no real fault of their own, should suffer no disadvantage. If Nauru's semistateless status during most of the last century was designed to put an Australian mining company's property rights above its native population's right to self-government, then Svalbard's arrangement flipped the script: in a place overseen by Norwegians, the sovereign power was compelled by international law not to play favorites.

Svalbard never had an indigenous population, which meant that there were no people to exploit, no settlements to displace, no culture or human history to run roughshod over. This lack of locals was undoubtedly a great simplifier, and a great equalizer too: it was about as close as you could get to the imperial fantasy of tabula rasa, or blank slate. Still, its fate was not predetermined. Choices were made. The settlement could have become fully absorbed by Norway, split in two with Russia, overseen by an international mandate or protectorate system, or left stateless forevermore.

Instead, it ended up with one of the more distinctive forms of governance in existence today.

Scholars have proposed, with little evidence, that seafaring Vikings first spotted Svalbard around 1200. But Willem Barentsz, a Dutch explorer, is credited with its discovery, during his 1596 expedition to find the Northeast Passage to China at a time when maritime embargoes blocked Dutch ships from much of Southern Europe. A decade later, on one of his trips in search of the Northwest Passage, Henry Hudson noticed pods of whales swimming off the archipelago's coast. His observations helped to spur the development of a whaling industry, and as foreigners clamored for ambergris, oil, and whalebone, Svalbard's wildlife suffered. At the end of the seventeenth century, the Dutch fleet alone killed 750 to 1,250 whales a year. By the 1870s, overexploitation had taken its toll. The legal scholar Christopher Rossi describes the remains of butchered whales lining the coasts even as the industry declined: "Denuded of its cetological economy, human interest in Spitsbergen was swept away, along with the detritus left by flensers at the water's edge." Those slaughtered whales are said to haunt Svalbard's bays and beaches to this day.

In the late nineteenth century, Sweden and Norway—until 1904, one nation—tried to assert their sovereignty over the archipelago. But Russia, then a monarchy, objected. Through an exchange of diplomatic notes, Russia and Sweden–Norway reached a compromise, declaring the archipelago *terra nullius*. This meant that it "could not be the object of exclusive possession by any State."

So, until 1919, Svalbard was officially a no-man's-land, one of the world's last. But that didn't mean there were no people there. Thousands of miles from the halls of power, a very small, very cold cadre of entrepreneurs wrestled with fundamental questions about property, sovereignty, and statehood at a time when all these definitions were very much up for grabs.

The conflict began, as many such conflicts do, with land—or, rather, what lay beneath it. At the turn of the twentieth century, prospectors from England, the United States, and Norway found coal seams buried deep in Svalbard's ice and jumped at the chance to start mining. Coal production and export quickly became the archipelago's main (and only) viable industry. Only a few dozen men lived there at a time, and their output was modest and seasonal. But for a certain kind of person, the Arctic was full of potential: a new frontier.

In the early years, coal companies competed against one another for land, resources, and labor in an essentially lawless environment, hammering stakes into the frozen ground to mark their possession. Altercations were rare, but before long, the lack of any kind of official oversight became a nuisance to mine owners. When workers went on strike, no one knew to whom to appeal. At one ill-fated coal operation, named Advent City, English managers tried to petition the Royal Navy to intervene in the unrest. Later, disgruntled Norwegian workers complained to their government about how an American boss was treating them, objecting in particular to the food. In neither case did the governments do much to help.

Still, the nations of the world kept an eye on what was going on in this northernmost place. They started paying it particular attention after the arrival of an American businessman named John Munro Longyear.

Longyear, now the Arctic city's namesake, was thirty-six years old and recently married when he began making sea journeys from northern Michigan to Svalbard in the early 1900s. The son of a district court judge, Longyear was handsome, rich, rugged, and determined: after a childhood of near-constant illness, he'd regained strength as a young man and found great pleasure in the outdoors.

There was plenty of that in Svalbard—and in Marquette, a small town in Michigan's Upper Peninsula, where Longyear was a boy. On a frigid day in early 2023, I visited Longyear's archives there. Looking out over Lake Superior as the sun rose behind the town's massive iron ore docks, it struck me that Longyear must have felt right at home on Svalbard, and that he'd likely feel that way still were he around to visit today. The shade of the water, the sharp whip of the air, the aurora borealis that electrifies the winter sky: these two places are of a kind, and their inhabitants of a rugged and congenitally libertarian type.

Longyear first visited Svalbard (then known as Spitsbergen or Spitzbergen) in 1901 as a tourist, with his wife and children. Two years later, he returned for a thirty-six-hour pit stop to check out his business prospects. There couldn't have been much to see besides this desolate, sublime landscape and the odd whaling hut made of wood. But he was in his element and had a hunch that there were fortunes to be made. Even better: nobody quite knew what to make of the place. To Longyear, that was not a deterrent, but an invitation.

In 1904, Longyear wrote to the U.S. State Department inquiring about the islands' status under international law. In response, Secretary of State John Hay informed Michigan senator Russell Alger of his constituent's "inquiries with regard to the Spitzbergen Islands." The secretary erroneously replied that "it is this Department's understanding that the Spitzbergen

Islands are claimed by Russia." In fact, as Longyear discovered, the lands were still *terra nullius*, which presented an even more enticing prospect. Without a state, there were no taxes levied on the islands. And without taxes, he could make himself rich.

Longyear got straight to work. With his American associates, he bought up land and tools from some embryonic Norwegian mining operations. Over the next few years, he took regular trips to Svalbard, claiming more and more tracts of land to build up his own. These investments were incorporated in Virginia as the Arctic Coal Company in 1905, and with a few hundred Scandinavian and English men on the ground, the firm established a thriving company town that was operational year-round.

Before long, Longyear City became home to these men, but also to horses, cows, pigs, and chickens. According to Longyear's correspondences archived in Marquette, illnesses were rare, and even a woman could live there comfortably if she was "of cheerful disposition." "The temperature does not get as low as it does on the Masabe Range in Minnesota," he told a prospective employee who'd inquired about bringing his wife. "But the long absence of sunlight is probably the most difficult matter to overcome. This darkness of course is relieved part of the time by wonderful moonlight, and I have photographs taken in mid-winter by moonlight, which indicate a brilliancy almost equal to sunlight."

As the Arctic Coal Company grew, Longyear, who split his time between the Arctic and Michigan, began to regard himself as a kind of polar emperor, bragging about being the "King of Spitsbergen." The company hired hierarchically, with English and American managers and poorly paid Scandinavian and Nordic workers, who often threatened to strike. It had problems with employee retention: many men left after a season. Still, the more money Longyear poured into his creaky mines, the more entitled he felt to political control, and the more of his time he dedicated to ensuring that the company's holdings would be protected.

This was no Wild West, but a painstaking, deliberate, and stultifying bureaucratic process of accounting and documentation. From the moment he arrived, Longyear was advised by his lawyer in Washington, D.C., Nathaniel Wilson, to keep careful records of his possessions, and to mark and measure the "facts by which you show your occupancy and ownership." Soon, Wilson warned him, Norway, Sweden, and perhaps Russia would enter serious discussions about the status of the archipelago—and "when that moment arrives, it will certainly be desirable that your rights be in the protection of the United States." The first of these conferences on Spitsbergen was due to take place in Christiania (now Oslo) in 1910.

The Americans in Svalbard had already been dogged by petty land disputes that, in the context of sovereign claims, took on an outsize political dimension. Longyear's nemesis, a Norwegian explorer, geologist, and patriot named Adolf Hoel, was hell-bent on his country's asserting its sovereignty in Spitsbergen, and in turn appealed to his government to complain about the Arctic Coal Company's encroaching enclosures. "A number of the districts marked on the map by the Americans are by no means 'no man's land' [but] unquestionably older titles," wrote Hoel's associate to the Norwegian department of foreign affairs, citing claims made as early as 1900. "The Americans have simply taken possession of these . . . as if the owners had never existed."

Longyear and his associates contended that Hoel and the Norwegians in his delegation were not businessmen but government plants. "The Norwegian government . . . had engaged an agent in the northern part of the country all the autumn and winter in hunting up Norwegians who could make any claims whatever on Spitsbergen and persuading them to file their claims," he wrote.

Longyear had a point. Hoel was a legitimate geologist—he'd undertaken voyages with the great Norwegian explorers Roald Amundsen and Fridtjof Nansen, the latter of whom would go on to win a Nobel Peace Prize for his advocacy on behalf of refugees. But what animated Hoel was his love of country. In Greenland, Hoel's trading company built trapping

huts, surveyed land, and explored little-known regions in the 1920s in an unsuccessful attempt to establish Norwegian rule; Hoel was also behind Norway's claim over an Antarctic territory named Queen Maud Land, as well
as its present-day possession of Svalbard. Hoel was so nationalistic that during World War II, he was persuaded to join the Norwegian Nazi Party after its leader promised to put the colonization of Greenland on its agenda.

Hoel, in other words, was even more brazen than Longyear—so in the
run-up to the long-planned international conference on Svalbard's future,
Longyear defended his turf aggressively and shamelessly, with yearly reports, maps, and correspondence filed to Washington.

In a letter to Senator Henry Cabot Lodge, Longyear asked the State Department to expand a piece of legislation called the Guano Islands Act to
cover "coal and other minerals." This would allow him to put the archipelago
under American jurisdiction during their occupancy, just as Congress had
allowed U.S. citizens to claim uninhabited islands with reserves of precious
phosphate. "There would probably be no objection to such an amendment, as
there is no possible reason why, if such protections should be extended over
the guano industry, it should not be likewise extended over any other legitimate enterprise," Longyear insisted in a letter to Lodge in October 1909.

Lodge—a committed anti-internationalist who blocked his country's bid
for membership in the League of Nations—was sympathetic, and put the
amendment before Congress, writing to Longyear in early December, "You
may be sure that I have the matter constantly in mind and am doing what I
can." The amendment was read twice in the Senate and referred to the
Committee on Foreign Relations, but it did not pass.

With this defeat, Longyear began worrying openly about the prospect of
living under Norwegian laws: the high taxes and countless church holidays
that prevented men from working "would be disastrous in the very short
season if enforced on Spitsbergen." Most of all, he feared the possibility that
trespassers would take his land and that the United States, still largely un-
willing to involve itself in foreign affairs, would leave him high and dry.

Longyear did not mind if Norway extended its police jurisdiction and criminal laws over Spitsbergen: with the right rules, a police force could help protect his property. It was the civil and regulatory meddling the American businessman did not care for. After eight years of hard work, he'd sunk a fortune into the project. This was no vanity show. It was his calling.

So he appealed to anyone who'd listen. In a letter to a major shareholder of a competing Anglo-Norwegian coal firm, Longyear tested a strategic alliance of business owners, telling the executive that he suspected Norway was interested in "securing of the valuable properties to Norwegians, regardless of the claims of people of other nationalities." Longyear also protested the idea of Norwegian taxes, which he believed "should be so limited that it would not be possible to drive people other than Norwegians out of the field." The rate he proposed in the letter was to pay 2 cents per ton of mined coal, in lieu of any Norwegian tax on business.

In yet another letter, to shareholders of an English trading company in Sheffield with Arctic interests, Longyear said he suspected that Norway would argue at the proposed conference that "being a No Man's Land, there are no titles on Spitsbergen. This, of course, would deprive your Company and ours of all title to the properties on which we have spent our money, and I am writing to you to suggest that, if possible, you secure instructions from your government to its representative to the conference to insist on the recognition of such titles by occupancy, development work, etc., as can properly be proven by British subjects."

When in 1909 Norwegian and Swedish diplomats made a proposal to ban firearms and protect wild animals on the islands, Longyear and his partners objected vehemently. They needed guns to hunt game. They needed guns to protect themselves.

Longyear went so far as to propose his own zany governance plan—a kind of charter city, really—to the U.S. government: that the region be run by a private corporation, registered in the United States or Britain and capitalized with a combined $10 million from interested countries. Naturally, he, his business partners, and their Arctic Coal Company would control a combined one third of the stock. Under his plan, the territory would remain open to all nationalities, and the corporation would oversee government functions like regulating hunting and fishing, managing prisons, administering land and real estate, and limiting the sale of booze (to deter the miners from getting drunk and working less).

Longyear's lawyer was more circumspect in his response. He pointed out that should shareholders opt to liquidate their assets, another country could easily seize control. Also, the company could purchase a majority of the shares, turning Svalbard into a corporate dictatorship overnight.

Norway, meanwhile, was inching closer to asserting political control. It built the first telegraph station in Svalbard in 1911, establishing control over crucial telecommunications infrastructure; two years later, a papal decree combined the archipelago "with the Apostolic vicarate of Norway," suggesting an entitlement of a more divine provenance.

Negotiations at Christiania came and went without a final decision, but the White House began to take Longyear's overtures more seriously. In his 1912 State of the Union Address, President Taft referred to the situation, noting that "the great preponderance of American material interests in the sub-arctic island of Spitzbergen . . . impels this Government to a continued and lively interest in . . . the political governance and administration of that region."

Emboldened, Longyear showed up at the talks (to which he was not invited) and hung around the lobby of the delegates' hotel. In a last-ditch effort, he invited the diplomats on a yacht tour of Spitsbergen to show them what they were dealing with; they declined, and he was privately relieved: "To think that taking a lot of sybaritic diplomats on a cruise in the Arctic Ocean on an old whaler might have put them in a frame of mind to 'soak' the company," he wrote.

But before anyone could decide anything, war broke out. Among other things, exporting coal became more complicated, as the supply and safe passage of ships was unreliable. It was also nearly impossible to buy dynamite, replacement parts for German and English machines, and certain foods.

In 1915, a German torpedo sank the tourist ship *Lusitania*. On board was Scott Turner, the Arctic Coal Company's secretary, who was on his way to Spitzbergen. Turner miraculously survived, treading water for hours, and later making light of his "rather rough experience." In letters, he seemed unduly concerned with having lost his company's "private records, notes, and memoranda." In September of that year, the Arctic Coal Company halted operations, and an exhausted Longyear walked away after digging 217,000 tons of coal out of the frozen ground.

After some back-and-forth with potential buyers, Longyear sold the Arctic Coal Company to a Norwegian company, Store Norske Spitsbergen, for $2 million in 1916. "In the future, the writer will miss the frequent trips to Norway but will remember the pleasant business relations with you," he wrote to his banker in Trondheim. Politically, Svalbard remained ungoverned until the Paris Peace Conference, when the Allies accepted Norway's bid to become the archipelago's official and full sovereign.

It was not a tough negotiation. Even the newly empowered Bolsheviks played ball; they were apparently so desperate to establish their own sovereign legitimacy that they ceded the land in the hopes of extracting diplomatic recognition from Norway. The treaty went into effect in 1925 and, over time, forty-six countries signed on—notably, North Korea in 2016.

Today, the Svalbard Treaty is celebrated for its longevity, its spirit of cooperation, and its inclusivity. This is all for good reason: in the world we live in, it is a miracle that there exists a place where everyone can go.

But to regard Svalbard's anomalous governance as a triumph of internationalism is to ignore Longyear's influence on the foreign policy of the United States, even as he abandoned the place himself. American diplomats arrived at peace talks determined to achieve two things: one, to avoid any fiscal or political responsibility for the islands; and two, to ensure that private U.S. interests would be respected and their property defended, no matter what administration took over. This happened to be exactly what Longyear wanted. The businessman's recommendation—"that the only interest of the U.S. is to see that the interests of its citizens are properly protected etc."—was adopted.

In a letter sent from the Château de Crillon, Paris, on November 19, 1919, Fred Kenelm Nielsen, the U.S. representative at Versailles, told Nathaniel Wilson, Longyear's lawyer, that his delegation had finally put the matter to bed. "In case the interests in Spitzbergen which you protected were still American-owned, I think they would have been thoroughly safeguarded by the Annex of this Treaty," Nielsen wrote. "I am hoping to get away from this place in about two weeks."

Longyear's successors would face no barriers to opening a business on Svalbard. They would not pay high taxes or have their property seized for coming from the wrong place. They could—they *had* to—bring their guns. And for once, everyone else would benefit from these privileges too.

A treaty between states is no simple matter. It absorbs a whole world of contingencies. The Svalbard Treaty was undoubtedly a product of its time and its place, but also of the ambitions of a rugged, stubborn Michigander determined to protect his property: in other words, full of the messy realities that govern our world still.

So, far from casting a shadow on the tiny miracle that Svalbard represents, I have chosen to be encouraged by the story of how a company town can turn into an open community.

I have spent much of this book documenting how consultants, lawyers, financiers, and other white-collar mercenaries have carved out physical and virtual space above, below, and between nations so that businesses can cloister themselves and grow in ways inimical to human thriving.

Svalbard suggests that out of that darkness, we might coax some light: *post tenebras lux.*

. . .

I landed in Svalbard for reasons quite unlike Longyear's. A college friend and his partner were visiting from Boston, and after listening to me complain about my difficulties in applying for a U.S. green card—the interminable paperwork, the agonizing delays, the black box of U.S. Citizenship and Immigration Services, and, most of all, the feeling of not quite belonging in the place I have called home since I turned eighteen—my friend asked if I'd heard of Svalbard.

I had, but it had never fully registered as a real place where people actually lived. My friend's partner joked that I should consider relocating, as had a friend of his from high school.

I read Wikipedia, skimmed an academic paper or two, and glossed over a couple of articles about a doomsday vault on the islands that holds specimens of nearly a million seed varieties. I assumed it would be like Werner Herzog's portrayal of Antarctica in his documentary *Encounters at the End of the World*: governed by an international treaty system but closed off, full of scientists, and home to at least one gay penguin. (Spoiler: there are no penguins north of the equator.)

Still, I put off going. I've never thought of myself as a polar kind of person. That seemed to me to be a different sort of animal—ruddy, straightforward, strong of nerve, and keen to endure physical challenges. Australian, perhaps, and on the taller side. Bearded, if male. Probably blond.

I—small, dark, often anxious, and usually cold—have few of these polar qualities. But I was restless for adventure, and when my green card finally arrived, I applied for an art residency to sail around Svalbard for two weeks.

We departed from Longyearbyen, which was nothing like what I expected. The town, perhaps obviously, has lots of normal things: roads, a supermarket, museums, a veterinarian for all the sled dogs. Its center is a small strip of shops and colorful prefabricated buildings. Longyearbyen was unremarkable—ugly, even—save for the dramatic backdrop of mountains with names like Sukkertoppen, Gruvfjellet, and Trollsteinen. It looked like Marquette, Michigan—or was it that Marquette looked like it?

Evidence of Svalbard's open-border policy is solid, but subtle. At the time of my visit, there were people of fifty-three nationalities living there, including a significant Thai and Filipino population and lots of younger backpacking types (seemingly all polar) from around the world, who showed up mainly to work in the tourism industry. According to Svalbard's governor, 37 percent of Longyearbyen's population at the time was foreign. That's less than Geneva's, or Dubai's, or even Singapore's proportion of foreigners. But when you consider what it takes to go to Svalbard and make a living, it feels like more.

The leader of our traveling expedition—let's call her Anna—was exactly as I imagined a polar person to be. Fair and agile, with sun-seared cheeks and eyes as blue as glacier ice, she spends much of her time on ships, passing the northern summer months in the Arctic and the southern summer in Antarctica—a migratory pattern comparable to that of the Arctic tern, a bird that traverses the globe to chase the sun. Our ship was the *Antigua*, and it was where we slept, worked, and ate. Mealtimes, regular to the point of being military, kept us on a schedule in the endless daylight. We quickly learned that the experience of visiting the Arctic depends overwhelmingly on the season, the weather, and the thickness and thaw of the ice, which can immobilize waters for months at a time.

Far from a frigid monochrome, the landscape can be varied and full of life. Our first stop was Gnålodden, a landing spot in Hornsund, a fjord where we anchored after a queasy day at sea. A Zodiac boat took us to shore at the foot of a mossy mountain, where small white gulls called kittiwakes chattered over waterfalls and crackling ice. There was no discernible smell other than an occasional whiff of loam. The ground under my hiking shoes felt damp and squishy, with snowmelt trickling its way through rocks and clusters of purple flowers.

Back at sea, we were well within Svalbard's territorial waters and, a century on, fully subject to the 1920 treaty. But beyond twelve nautical miles from the coasts, in what would ordinarily be Norway's exclusive economic zone, governments don't all agree on how Norwegian—or not—the waters and their contents are. Maritime regulations can be complex, but disagreements, not unlike those over the U.S. Constitution, are essentially over whether the Svalbard Treaty is a living document. The Norwegians contend that any area not explicitly mentioned in the treaty defaults to ordinary Norwegian sovereignty. Critics like Russia and Spain say the spirit of the treaty, namely the nondiscrimination principle, should prevail.

The reason this is more than an abstract dispute is that in 1969, Norway discovered oil in the North Sea. More recently, snow crabs, escaping warming waters, migrated north, bringing renewed attention to the Svalbard Treaty. In January 2017, the Norwegian Coast Guard held a Latvian trawler, the *Senator*, in Svalbard's port for setting out twenty-six hundred crab traps. The ship claimed to have obtained a permit from the European Union, but Norway insisted that only it had the jurisdiction to hand out licenses. The case made it to the Norwegian Supreme Court, where all eleven of the judges ruled in favor of Norway and against the trawler.

The case wasn't just about shellfish, though. Snow crabs are sedentary species, unlikely to move far during their short lives. That means they're regulated not like fish but like minerals. Snow crabs were a proxy for oil.

The case is settled, but perhaps not for long. Since the ruling was a domestic court case, it leaves open the possibility of another state's suing Norway in international court over who can claim ownership of Svalbard's resources.

All this as John Munro Longyear turns over in his grave.

In the modern world, the concept of state sovereignty governs how we govern. It is a human invention—the setting of borders, the wielding of power, the deciding of who belongs. But in the Arctic, as in any remote place, it's obvious that we're not actually in charge. We carry no special privileges or diplomatic immunities in spaces where nature makes the rules.

It feels especially absurd to impose the construct of the nation-state, what with its laws and regulations, on something so wild, so unruly. Svalbard's landscape disregards any concept of national borders, of industrial time, or of politics as we know it. We aren't its citizens, residents, or denizens. This far north, we are all at its mercy. We are its guests.

Svalbard has always been a place for superlatives. It was the site of the northernmost battle of the Second World War, after which much of its population was evacuated. Today, Svalbard boasts the world's northernmost pub, northernmost wine cellar, northernmost alternative weekly newspaper, and northernmost jazz festival. A performance artist once traveled here to make the world's northernmost piece of toast—a metaphor for climate change, or capitalism, or something.

Svalbard is also home to the northernmost statue of Vladimir Lenin: a symbol of faded Soviet ambitions as well as the nondiscrimination principle at work. Norway owns all the real estate in Svalbard, except for the settlements belonging to a state-owned Russian coal company, Arktikugol. The treaty granted the Soviet Union (and now Russia) the right to maintain a commercial presence on the archipelago as long as it abided by Norwegian law; because the USSR could not colonize a town outright (due to Norway's now internationally recognized claim), it asserted itself with state-owned industry instead.

The presence of Russians has been contentious since the seventeenth century, when Russian hunters, known as Pomors, lived alongside Dutch whalers, settling for months at a time and returning home to sell their fox, reindeer, polar bear, and walrus hides. More recently, Russians almost tested the openness of Svalbard's airspace when Andrey Yakunin, the son of a close associate of Vladimir Putin, was arrested for flying a drone over the archipelago on a 2022 polar yacht trip. As part of a sanctions package against Russia following the invasion of Ukraine, Norway passed a law prohibiting

Russian citizens from flying drones in its airspace; Yakunin, who has dual citizenship, claimed he was not acting as a Russian citizen but as a Brit. The case was ultimately dismissed because the rule did not apply to drone hobbyists like Yakunin, who filmed himself sailing, hiking, and mountaineering. In December, Yakunin was declared a free man and returned back home—to Italy.

Meanwhile, a small number of Russians and Ukrainians populate Svalbard's ex-Soviet settlements, living side by side as their compatriots drop bombs. One Arktikugol company town, Barentsburg, was founded by the Dutch and sold to the USSR in 1932, destroyed by the Nazis in 1943, then rebuilt in the 1970s. Today it has a population of roughly 450 and a sputtering mining sector. Barentsburg is just thirty-five miles from Longyearbyen but is accessible only by boat, snowmobile, or helicopter. In 2014, *The New York Times* described it as "grim," and a decade earlier, a Norwegian court sentenced a murderer there to just four years in prison, reasoning that conditions provided "mitigating circumstances in favor of the convict." We did not visit Barentsburg.

Pyramiden, on the other hand, has none of these problems: it has been practically a ghost town since 1998. We arrived there about twelve days into our voyage, and it was the first sign of human life we'd seen since departing on the *Antigua*, save for some run-down trapper cabins, one of which had been destroyed by a polar bear. When I stepped onto the decrepit pier, a rotting wood plank collapsed, nearly claiming my ankle. In the distance, coal tunnels raised above the permafrost snaked their way up the peak for which the town is named, passing by the words "Mirni Mir" (Peace on Earth) painted in white Cyrillic letters on the side of the mountain.

These days, Pyramiden—or Pyramida, as the Russians call it—has only a handful of residents, but for decades it was a thriving Soviet town. Between the crumbling remnants of its mining infrastructure, the classic Soviet architecture, and some surprisingly resilient monuments (including Lenin), you can see clues as to how it prospered. Unlike other settlements on the archipelago, Pyramiden boasts grassy lawns, with soil the Soviet government shipped in from the mainland. The town has an old greenhouse where tomatoes, cucumbers, and greens once grew; a barn for imported livestock; a playground; and workers' dorms, where iceboxes still sit on windowsills.

Over the years, mismanagement and dwindling coal reserves—not to mention the fall of the USSR—caused residents to trickle out. Then a plane crash in 1996 killed more than one hundred residents, pushing more to move away. Most didn't bother to take their belongings, so it looked as if the people of Pyramiden had evaporated, leaving their furniture, clothes, books, and tools behind. The most unsettling thing about Pyramiden today is the massive colony of kittiwakes that have taken up residence in the ruins and shriek at all hours as they build nests and feed their young.

Under their din, the town was experiencing the beginnings of a revival. As I wandered around the nearly abandoned Soviet recreation center, complete with a basketball court, a movie theater, and music rooms with untuned pianos, broken drum kits, and Russian sheet music for songs from Paul McCartney's band Wings, I encountered four young men in skullcaps. I asked them in Russian how they got here; they replied that they were builders from Tajikistan who arrived on a charter flight from Moscow that flies every few months (thus avoiding Norwegian transit visa requirements). They were hired to restore a few of the buildings. It's lonely here, one of them said.

The builders lived alongside a small group of entrepreneurial Russian hipsters who lead tours trying to capitalize on Pyramiden's Soviet kitsch and spooky ghost-town appeal. There is a hotel, Tulpan (Tulip), with a bar that serves Negronis (the world's northernmost) and vodkas infused with local cowberry, ginger, and horseradish while screening black-and-white footage of the town from decades past. It's easy to picture boatloads of tourists filling Pyramiden, or at least this bar, ready to let loose, as we were, after long days at sea. It's hard not to resent them in advance for ruining something so perfectly ruined.

. . .

A few days before our journey's end, our expedition landed at Sarstangen, a sliver of a beach jutting into a glassy sound with a blurring palette of blues and whites—sea, ice, clouds, and sky—stretching out to the horizon. If it hadn't been for the stench of a nearby walrus colony, it was like a cartoon of heaven. But then I looked down; the ground was covered in trash.

The refuse of humanity came in all shapes, colors, and textures—yellow fishing nets, rusted tin cans, pink candy wrappers, a black TV. We picked up as much as we could, filling white bags that we dragged back across the sand to our Zodiacs so we could drop them off in Longyearbyen. It was so distracting that we couldn't look up. Even without the spectacle of Arctic garbage, we encountered human damage at every stop—glaciers calving as though losing teeth, their shorelines receding like sickly gums.

Some of the garbage came from fishing boats, or from elsewhere. But the problem of overtourism in Svalbard is well known. These days, travelers from around the world go to Svalbard for what has become known as last-chance tourism: the desire to see polar bears, glaciers, and icebergs before they disappear. Until 2024, when legislation capped the number of people allowed on cruises at two hundred, passengers would descend upon Longyearbyen, sometimes doubling the town's population in a matter of hours. In their wake, they left a trail of trash.

Tourism, like whaling and coal before it, is a lucrative industry that can't continue growing indefinitely. Only this time, instead of frontiersmen acting largely alone, decision-making happens by a great many people. Svalbard might appear to be a libertarian fantasy of open borders, self-sufficiency, and low taxes, but managing such a society requires a surprising amount of government.

The highest authority on the islands is the *sysselmesteren*, or governor, of Svalbard, who is appointed by the central government in Oslo. The job—a combination of police chief, spokesperson, and consul general—is a bit like being a sheriff in the Wild West. "I never thought I'd have to learn to use a rifle and a satellite phone for my job," Kjerstin Askholt, then the governor, told me as we walked down the halls of her office (per local tradition dating to coal-mining days, I took off my shoes upon entering and thus conducted the interview in Hawaiian-print socks).

She said her office managed search-and-rescue operations, arrested drunk drivers and snowmobilers, and occasionally officiated at weddings. She also expelled people to the mainland three or four times a year if they were homeless, ill, or broke. "This is not a cradle-to-grave society," one of Askholt's colleagues told me.

In Longyearbyen, there's also a democratically elected mayor and community council, chosen by residents, who oversee the school, roads, waste management, and other town affairs. Askholt said the governor's office was working with the council as well as with tourism companies to make recommendations to Oslo on how to manage the crush of arrivals, but the final decision got made on the mainland. Her immediate concern was that there is little regulation about who could lead tours. "A few years ago, six Saudi tourists hired a guide who took them out with a weapon but no real license," she recalled. "They thought they saw a polar bear, but because the guide wasn't certified, he tossed the weapon, left, and told them all to run for their lives." She added, "We found six very cold Saudi tourists a few hours later. This is the sort of thing that needs to stop." Askholt did not criticize Svalbard's diversity, but she did note, referring to a government white paper, that making sure Norwegians aren't outnumbered here is a national priority. Norway clearly wants to avoid ruling over a community made up mostly of nonnationals. "What matters the most to us is to protect the wilderness and maintain the Norwegian community in Svalbard," she said.

In a free zone for people, crafting incentives is complex: If you make life on Svalbard appealing—with good schools, for instance, or better housing—there's no way to guarantee that it will be Norwegians who come. At the same time, Svalbard can accommodate only so many people. The result, which can easily be justified with the treaty's mandate of low taxes, is that the Norwegian government provides as little as possible: unlike the mainland, the islands have minimal welfare benefits. And that, in turn, shapes Svalbard's spirit—for better or for worse. "A lot of people are coming here with different kinds of dreams and visions, and it's not always a success for them," Askholt said. "When you can come from so many countries, to come up at all says something about the kind of person you are. You have to have something in you."

Or maybe Svalbard is where you go to find it. On midsummer, my shipmates and I stripped down and jumped into the ocean from the side of the boat. The water is not like other cold water—not the chilly North Atlantic, not an icy shower, not even the cold pool at a Russian bathhouse. It is so cold that it does not register as having a temperature at all. Swimming in the Arctic is senseless. It makes you feel weightless, like you were born anew. When you leave the water, you feel different: polar.

When I boarded the *Antigua*, there were a few important things I did not yet know.

I did not know that six months on, the prospect of being crammed onto a small ship with a dozen-odd artists would seem inconceivable (not to mention unhygienic). I did not know that because of that, I would end up writing and reporting much of this book quite extraterritorially, from the depths of my couch.

I also did not anticipate that during this period, I would inhabit various states of liminality: before, during, and after the birth of my two children, born two years apart during the pandemic. During these years, time was bent, boundaries banished, space redrawn, and the rules of ordinary life suspended. There was something liberating about this life: not freedom by any stretch, but some kind of reprieve from the routines of the everyday.

Another thing I didn't know: Mary Shelley had based the opening letters of Frankenstein on the accounts of polar explorers chasing the very same "eternal light" that I basked in that summer on the deck of the *Antigua*. Though it's hard to know for sure, some scholars think it was the journey of Constantine Phipps that informed Shelley's writing the most. Phipps had taken a trip to Spitsbergen to find the Northwest Passage and study terrestrial magnetism. That was in 1773: long before Svalbard was Norwegian, before Norway was its own state at all.

Frankenstein; or the Modern Prometheus is an epistolary novel told through the letters of the polar explorer Robert Walton. Walton (a failed writer, I should note) is working on a ship that finds her journey interrupted when she is immobilized by pack ice. Large sheets of ice "closed in the ship on all sides, scarcely leaving her the sea-room in which she floated," Walton writes, in a letter to his sister. "Our situation was somewhat dangerous, especially as we were compassed round by a very thick fog."

The same happened to the *Antigua* near the end of our trip. My shipmates and I hung around the deck for a few hours. When it became clear that the ship could not move any farther, we set off on Zodiacs. I admired Arctic ducks and the glittering blue landscape while my colleagues filmed performance art and studied the structure of icebergs.

Then our captain changed our itinerary, and we headed south. In the novel, Walton's captain decides to wait it out instead. That's when the ghost story begins.

From the deck, Walton spots in the distance a stranger approaching on a low sled pulled by dogs. The crew members want to catch his attention, but before they have a chance to, he disappears into the bright polar expanse. The next morning, another sled appears pulled by a lone dog on a large, broken ice fragment. The passenger, Walton recalls, was not "a savage inhabitant of some undiscovered island" like the first figure they'd spotted. It was Victor Frankenstein, the monster's creator, and he was emaciated, frozen, and half mad.

Recognizing him as a fellow traveler nonetheless, the crew invites him on board, and after regaining some strength, Frankenstein tells them the story of his feverish descent into creation and regret: of his idyllic upbringing on the banks of the Léman and his beloved family; of the monster's birth, and its subsequent disappearance; of his own return to his hometown of Geneva; and of his last encounter with the creature on the Mer de Grace (sea of ice) beneath "the supreme and magnificent Mont Blanc." Victor Frankenstein dies on board Walton's ship, exhorting his host to finish the job and kill the monster. He is stuck in a death loop of his own making.

The second half of the book tells the same story from the creature's perspective: from his birth in Frankenstein's student quarters in a small alpine town near Geneva, where he haunts his creator's family, all the way to the North Pole. There, he breaks into the ship, visits Victor's body, expresses regret for his murders and mistakes, and states his intentions to take his own life by fire and "exult in the agony of the torturing flames."

I first read *Frankenstein* in middle school. I remember learning of Shelley's preoccupations: of the dangers of knowledge and the impulse to play God; the Romantic fixation on the sublime; the critiques of colonialism, modernity, and masculinity. I remember our Australian teacher telling us to look out the window at the mountains that inspired the action and the lake from which the monster's image sprang. It was a curiosity at the time, meaningful only within the confines of English class.

Rereading the book at the end of my own journey through the hidden globe, it occurred to me that *Frankenstein* is as much a book about places that don't quite fit. The novel, if you'll recall, was written on the eerie banks of Lake Geneva. Its protagonist, Victor Frankenstein, keeps his secrets close and loses his mind as a result. His creation—the source of all his woes—is comprised of body parts that came from different people and places; he's a stranger, an immigrant, stateless, unwanted. And from the laboratory where the monster was conceived to the ship he crossed in his final hours, his pit stops correspond to the philosopher Michel Foucault's idea of a "heterotopia":

"a floating part of space, a placeless place, that lives by itself, closed in on itself and at the same time poised in the infinite ocean."

There's more. Shelley makes it clear that this monster is not, as many would have it, an evil creature. Nor is he particularly good. Frankenstein's creation is just like him: a man seeking a friend and a place to call home, only coming up short again and again through no fault of his own.

Like the monster, the places I have traveled to are composites. And like the monster, they are a product of colonialism, capitalism, technology, megalomania, and a pinch of alchemy. Taken together, these places are much more than the sum of their parts. They can't be entirely reduced to single policy decisions, or individual people, or clear ideologies. I don't think they can be definitively written off as all good or all evil. Like the visible world of flesh and blood and bone, they just are what is.

What these places do offer is an alternative way of seeing—and a fresh understanding of why and how we built the world the way we did, in whose image, and with whose rules. In revealing themselves as exceptional, these chimeras push us to question what, really, is so normal about everything and everyone else.

It is no coincidence that I began my explorations in a city of refuge and a city of holes. And it is no coincidence, either, that this quest led me all the way to the High Arctic: a place that belongs to us all. Frankenstein's monster traveled this path after the city of refuge, and the world around it, cast him away. Then and now, it is the only place left for him to go.

Acknowledgments

I couldn't have pulled this off without Joe Bernstein: #1 dad, husband, friend, editor, and stand-in shrink (sorry). I love you. Special thanks to my mother, Irene Abrahamian, for Geneva, and everything else.

I am so grateful for Kian and Adi, and to all the people who cared for them—and us!—over the years: Irene Abrahamian, Stephanie Bernstein, Henry Winokur, Melyne Tcha, Mihran Abrahamian, Ellie Payne Smith, Matt Berry, Sarah Bernstein, Ervand Abrahamian, and Molly Nolan. Thanks also to the teachers at CDC-Forest in Ann Arbor and to the staff of Le Paradis des Anges day care in Park Slope, Brooklyn. Writing without childcare is hard; international reporting is impossible.

Thanks to Sarah Leonard and our continued collaborations (and trips). To Caroline Bankoff, Kate Duguid, and Jason Holloway, the pandemic pod that never split. To Katie Baker and Max Strasser, for your friendship and for holding down the fort when we were away. To Lynette Clemetson, the Wallace House staff and all the 2022–23 Knight-Wallace fellows at the University of Michigan for a transformative year, and the late Alice Simsar, who we were so lucky to have as a neighbor on Baldwin Place.

Thanks to the Whiting Foundation, the Robert Silvers Foundation, and New America for so generously supporting this project, as well as the Arctic Circle fellowship for the unforgettable trip to Svalbard. Thanks to the Potato Barn and anyone who ever lent me a desk, and to James Ryan and NYU's Kevorkian Center for helping me secure library access.

Double thanks to Linda Kinstler and Don Herzog, my first readers. I knew you'd get it. Thanks to all the academics I spoke to but especially Jatin Dua, Sam Weeks, Patrick Neveling, and Dara Orenstein, who were incredibly generous with their time and knowledge. And thanks to the editors I've worked with on stories that led to this book: David Wolf and Jonathan Shainin, who took a chance on a weird pitch about Luxembourg for *The Guardian*; David Marcus, Chris Shay, the staff and interns at *The Nation*, and Katrina vanden Heuvel, for giving me the time to travel to Svalbard and the space to write long; Emily Greenhouse and Andrew Katzenstein at *The New York Review of Books*; Michelle Legro, Jillian Goodman, and Suzy Hansen.

Thanks to all my friends—you know who you are—and especially to Marc da Costa, Jessica Loudis, Madeleine Schwartz, Elvia Wilk, Andreas Petrossiants, Moira Weigel, Meehan Crist, Aelfie Oudghiri, Hicham Oudghiri, Sam Hinds, Anna Louie Sussman, Katrina Forrester, Jamie Martin, David Levine, and Zara Mirza, who listened patiently as I talked (and talked, and talked) about weird jurisdictions.

Thanks to Mel Flashman and Becky Saletan, and everyone at Riverhead, for their unfailing and enthusiastic support. My fact checkers—Isabel Cristo, Thea Smith, Alma Beauvais, and Noah Rawlings—saved me from untold embarrassment. Maya Perry, Youyou Zhou, Gor Barsegyan, and Lydia Emmanouilidou helped me fill in the gaps.

Finally, thanks to all the people who spoke to me for this project. There would be no book without you!

Notes on Sources

1. City of Holes

This chapter is largely a product of my personal experience growing up in Geneva and returning to the city as an adult to explore it with fresh eyes. I found literary inspiration in Italo Calvino's *Invisible Cities* and Mary Shelley's *Frankenstein*. Jon Halliday's article "Switzerland: The Bourgeois Eldorado," published in the *New Left Review* in 1969, helped me see my hometown in a new light. Had I not stumbled across it at a used bookstore in DUMBO in 2008, I might never have written this book.

Data on commodities trading from the Swiss accountability nonprofit Public Eye was crucial in helping me understand Geneva's spectral economy. Special thanks to Adrià Budry Carbó and Agathe Duparc for their insights over lunch. Marcia Ristaino's book on Father Jacquinot was instructive, and V. G. Kiernan's and John Caspeari's histories helped me understand the political economy of mercenaries from a period I knew little about. Quinn Slobodian's writing, and his book *Globalists* in particular, helped me connect Geneva's ideological past with its present (and likely future). Vanessa Ogle's work on tax havens and decolonization is among the most riveting scholarship on the subject out there.

This chapter would not have been possible without the contributions of Swiss historians—Bernhard Schaer, Christophe Farquet, and Marc Cramer in particular—working on their nation's troubled history and a non-Swiss, Jonathan Steinberg, whose *Why Switzerland?* asks, and answers, a very good question indeed.

2. Good Fences

To report this chapter, I read many of Ziegler's books, most notably *The Swiss, The Gold, and the Dead* and *Switzerland: The Awful Truth*. I spent time interviewing Ziegler at his home and spoke to him on the phone on two occasions before that and read his former student Jürg Wegelin's biography in French. I watched many videos of Ziegler on YouTube, from student seminars to UN conferences, to get an idea of how he presented himself in public. Jürg Wegelin's biography of Ziegler was critical in helping fill in the biographical gaps, and articles by Christophe Farquet and Peter Hug on Swiss tax and bank history helped me corroborate some (but not all!) of Ziegler's invectives. Gor Barsegyan tracked down details about Che Guevara's guns, and Noah Rawlings fact-checked the chapter.

I also consulted reams of articles in publications ranging from swissinfo.ch to the *Los Angeles Times*, particularly on Ziegler's run-ins with Swiss defamation law and his activism around the so-called "Nazi gold" scandals of the 1990s. Finally, records from the Geneva City Council shed light on Ziegler's dispute with the university faculty.

3. White Cube, Black Box

I owe a great debt to journalists who have covered the Bouvier affair over the years—in particular Antoine Harari, whose book *The Fox and the Oligarch* helped introduce me to Bouvier's modus operandi and ultimately led to my meeting and interviewing Bouvier at his Geneva office in October 2021. Bouvier, in turn, connected me to his rather muscular public affairs team, who helped confirm details about his business; Rybolovlev's team did much the same. Sam Knight's *New Yorker* story on Bouvier, and Alexandra Bregman's *The Bouvier Affair: A True Story* were both fascinating reads. I relied on *The New York Times*'s coverage of Bouvier's and Rybolovlev's litigation by Graham Bowley, as well as articles in *The Wall Street Journal* and *Swissinfo*, to summarize the men's conflict.

Peter Watson and Cecilia Todeschini's *The Medici Conspiracy* helped me summarize the Geneva Freeport's first scandal. I also learned a great deal from my copresenters at a panel on the uses of offshore techniques within global art markets, organized by John Zarobell and Samuel Weeks for the 2019 American Anthropological Association meeting in Vancouver. Oddný Helgadóttir's paper on the subject was of particular interest. Georgina Adam was a great help (as was her excellent book *Dark Side of the Boom*) when I began looking into freeports in 2016.

Freeports have recently piqued the interest of global historians, and I'm incredibly grateful to the scholars who shared and discussed their work with me: Koen Stapelbroek, Dara Orenstein, Corey Tazzara, and the journal *Global Intellectual History*, which dedicated a whole issue to the subject.

I've been obsessed with Singapore since I visited the city-state in 2014. That trip, together with Lee Kuan Yew's writings and John Curtis Perry's *Singapore*, informed my view of the state.

Alma Beauvais was the fact-checker on this chapter. Lon Fuller's *Legal Fiction* is one of the foundational texts for *The Hidden Globe*. I return to it often.

4. In the Zones

To tell the story of special economic zones in terms that nonexperts can understand, I relied primarily on interviews with a dozen or so people who worked in the business. Among them are Claude de Baissac, Jean-Paul Gauthier, Michael Castle-Miller, Thibault Serlet, Edouard Dommen, Andreas Baumgardner, Chuck Heath, and the World Bank's Douglas Zeng.

Patrick Neveling's scholarly work has been absolutely vital in helping me understand the political dimensions of free zones, their spread after decolonization, and their use in Mauritius especially. Neveling's mordant commentary over the phone was greatly appreciated. Reading Adom Getachew's *Worldmaking after Empire* gave me a new perspective on the ambitions of anticolonial nationalist leaders. Daniel Immerwahr's wonderful *How to Hide an Empire* is a fascinating look into American overseas territories.

Christian Poncini, Alfred's grandson, helped fact-check information about his predecessors. For material on Richard Bolin, I interviewed his son, Doug, and spent a day at MIT examining his and ADL's archives.

I used UNIDO and UNCTAD reports and data on the spread of EPZs. Much of this data also appears in Keller Easterling's *Extrastatecraft*, an important book that helped me grasp the connections between law and infrastructure.

For background on Puerto Rico, I relied on news reports and Ed Morales's *Fantasy Island*. Kojo Koram's *Uncommon Wealth* taught me about Jamaica and answered my questions about the IMF.

5. Hacking the World

For this chapter, I interviewed Paul Romer on Zoom in early 2024 after having read his work from over the years—by no means all of it, but enough, I hope, to get a sense of how he sees the world. Romer is a rare economist who writes for mortals, and that is a gift to us all.

That conversation was the last of dozens, possibly hundreds, I've had about charter cities and related projects, beginning in 2012. These discussions took place at conferences, through phone calls and Zooms, and during in-person interviews around the world. I'm particularly grateful to Joseph McKinney, Thibault Serlet, Katarina Serlet, Joe Quirk, Patri Friedman, Michael Strong, Randy Hencken, Kurtis Lockhart, Mark Lutter, the Charter Cities Institute, Gustavo Lacerda, Michael Castle-Miller, Jorge Colindres, William O'Shea, Joel Burke, Nick Dranias, Humberto Macias, and all the Próspera publicists I've ever known for taking the time to talk to me about their project, as well as everyone else I met through the seasteading/charter cities universe. We may not always agree on how the world should be, but at least we agree on what it is.

Ray Craib, Isabelle Simpson, Beth Geglia, and Quinn Slobodian helped me think through the ideology of "freezoning." Greg Lindsay brought the gossip, Dug Song the humanist techy perspective. Alexander Betts and Paul Collier's work illustrated the real world applications of some of these ideas. I also relied on Juan Du's and Taomo Zhou's important correctives to the "Shenzhen myth." Interviews with Lan Cao and Tom Bell helped me understand what friendly lawyers see in charter cities.

Dara Orenstein provided the missing piece for this chapter, and really the entire book, when she generously shared her unpublished paper on "freeports for refugees." And Sebastian Mallaby's *Atlantic* article about Paul Romer set me on the path to writing *The Hidden Globe* by blowing my twentysomething mind apart. It's worth rereading.

6. The City and the City

Interviews with Mark Beer on Zoom and in person laid the foundations for this chapter. A trip to Dubai in November 2021 gave me a feel for the city (and the city) and gave me the opportunity to meet Amna Al Owais, whom I spoke to on-site. I spent a lot of time wandering the DIFC mall and watching You-Tube videos of legal proceedings at the DIFC courts.

In my yearslong quest to wrap my head around the DIFC court system, I also asked every lawyer I met over the course of three years if they had heard of such a court. Most hadn't, and I began to wonder if I was losing my mind. Fortunately, I found scholarship by Pamela Bookman and Katarina Pistor that, in addition to teaching me about law, made me feel less crazy. Jayanth Krishnan's monograph on the DIFC court, *The Story of the Dubai International Financial Center Courts: A Retrospective*, provided crucial insight into the court's beginnings. Lauren Benton's work on legal pluralism and colonialism helped me understand the foundations of these courts.

The National (Abu Dhabi) was a reasonably reliable source of news from the UAE and the Gulf region, as were Simeon Kerr's expert reports for the *Financial Times*. Information about Kazakhstan is mostly from news clips unearthed by Maya Perry. And while I struggle terribly with science fiction, China Miéville's *The City & the City* is so brilliant that it transcends genre.

7. Ad Astra

This chapter is based in part on an article I published in *The Guardian*'s Long Reads section in 2018. I followed a delegation from Luxembourg on their tour of California, where they pitched their country as a home for "space resources" with the help of the royal family. Through that trip, and subsequent events organized by the Luxembourg Space Agency, I got in touch with and interviewed all the people quoted in this chapter, most important among them Georges Schmit and Etienne Schneider. Luxembourg, I should note, is still putting these events on around the world. I also met the American entrepreneurs I quote in the piece, and the NASA visionary Pete Worden. I visited Luxembourg in the spring of 2018.

I had inspiring conversations with scholars of space and its resources over the years: Haris Durrani, Tamara Álvarez Fernández, Rory Rowan, and Jessy Kate Schingler all helped me get a sense of the (long) stakes of the issue. Sam Weeks will forever be my authority on all things Luxembourgeois. Cris van Eijk alerted me to the existence of a wealth of incredible UN speeches, notably Fernando Belaúnde Terry's.

I also learned a great deal from lawyers Gunjan Sharma and Florentine Voss through their firm Volterra Fietta's Zoom sessions on space law. Gabriel Zucman's insights into offshore money flows informed all of this book, but particularly the Luxembourg sections. Bernard Thomas is an indefatigable chronicler of his country's machinations. And Oliver Bullough's work on tax havens and offshore finance over the years taught me that these topics aren't just possible to understand but can even be interesting in the right writer's hands.

I could not track down Mats Nilson (and heaven knows I tried) to get his side of the Tonga affair. I did speak to his erstwhile business associate, James Simon, over the phone in 2022. Most of the sourcing around Tonga's satellites comes from papers by Anthony van Fossen and news clips from the time that I found on LexisNexis and JSTOR. It was a big story about a not-so-small place.

Paul Stimers' *Wall Street Journal* op-ed on John Locke and outer space capitalism turned me on to the subject in 2015. I think about it almost every day.

8. Titanic

I was pleasantly surprised to learn that ships have avid fan clubs on the internet. To begin to tell the story of the *Gruziya*, I spent countless hours on Facebook messaging former passengers, crew members, and cruise ship aficionados. I also looked at videos, photos, menus, and cruise itineraries, a few of which have since been taken down (I regrettably did not save it, but I assure you that that rendition of "YMCA" was spectacular). I trawled these forums for so long that I forgot I'd never been on board myself. I'm biased, but the *Gruziya* was a special vessel.

Every ship has a unique seven-digit number, assigned to it by the International Maritime Organization, that remains the same through changes in flags and ownership, until it is scrapped. This identifier helped me follow the *Gruziya* from cradle to grave. The Robin des Bois shipbreaking newsletter provided the ship's last sightings, and the NGO Shipbreaking Platform educated me about the practice as a whole and led me to the consultants who explained the conditions at Gadani. The ITF and UNCTAD publish data on flags of convenience and labor.

Rodney Carlisle remains the authority on sovereignty at sea thanks to many books and papers, most important among them *Sovereignty for Sale*. We also spoke on the phone twice in 2020. Much of the information on Stettinius, Panama, and Liberia, as well as my understanding of the *Muscat Dhows* case, comes from Carlisle's work.

Jeffrey Kahn's *Islands of Sovereignty* was an invaluable resource, as were conversations with Kahn himself. News clips and White House press conferences helped me reconstruct what the *Gruziya* did and didn't do during its stint working for the military. My phone interviews with Alexander Bout filled in some blanks, as did archival documents shared by the Naval Historical Center. Conversations with Laleh Khalili, Jatin Dua, and the AnthroHistory seminar at the University of Michigan deepened my understanding of shipping, trade, and globalization.

Articles in *TradeWinds*, an industry paper about maritime affairs, provided a wealth of information about the *Gruziya*'s various run-ins with the law and changes in ownership. Juergen Maly and Michael Kolesnichenko recounted the Wilhelmshaven episode to me on Zoom, which I supplemented with local news reports. Archives from local Montreal papers, and a very generous librarian, helped me collect enough to reconstruct its time in Canada.

Harold Koh and Michael Ratner's legal advocacy for Guantánamo detainees was a vital resource for understanding interdiction and Gitmo's status under U.S. law. Subsequent U.S. lawsuits—namely *Sale v. Haitian Centers Council, Inc.*—solidified that. Lydia Emmanouilidou tracked down the survivors of the *Salamis* rescue and summarized Cypriot newspaper articles. Itamar Mann's writing, and his book *Humanity at Sea* especially, were helpful to my understanding of interdiction and offshore detention.

To get to the bottom of who bought the *Titan* in its final days, I turned to corporate databases from Dubai's Ministry of the Economy. Peter Knego confirmed having spotted the ship on its way to Gadani, and a Facebook post in a shipbreaking affinity group reported its arrival at the beach with a photo. Guillaume Vuillemay shed light on funeral flags and Palau through his remarkable study and a phone conversation.

B. Traven's *The Death Ship* is the third most important novel about the sea, after *The Odyssey* and *Moby-Dick*. You should read it.

9. Excised

This chapter was reported from Ann Arbor, Michigan, and Geneva, Switzerland. Aziz's story was reconstructed through interviews with him and the excellent podcast *The Messenger*, as well as conversations with producer Michael Greene. Michael Khambatta corroborated information and shared photos of Aziz's first days in Switzerland. Behrouz Boochani's novel and essays set the scene in Manus in a way nothing else quite could.

The Guardian was the most complete and compelling source of daily news on the Australian offshore immigration regime, while the Kaldor Centre was indispensable when it came to the nuances of the actual law. Madeleine Gleeson and Daniel Ghezelbash illuminated the issue through books, papers, and Zoom conversations, along with Graham Thom, who's been following the issue for decades with Amnesty International. As one of the few outsiders allowed to visit Nauru, John Pace shared fascinating insights into the island's early years. He also attended my birthday party in the park with the chessboards when I turned five. The globe may be hidden, but the world is still very small.

Cait Storr's book on Nauru, *International Status in the Shadow of Empire*, and her generous insights over Zoom were beyond helpful in understanding Nauru in a historical legal frame. Damon Salesa provided a view of the detentions from the Pacific, while David Armitage's Harvard seminar on Pacific history gave me a bibliography to begin to understand the bigger context.

10. Laos Vegas

I traveled to Boten, Laos, in May 2023. Most of the chapter consists of my recollections and conversations with people I met along the way—in particular, people working in showrooms for the Haicheng real estate group. Fixers translated some of these conversations. Google Translate picked up the slack.

William Cronon's *Nature's Metropolis* (which I read on the Laos–China Railway) helped situate railways in the context of frontier making and time shifting. By far the most informative source on the LCR today was Jessica Di-Carlo's wonderful dissertation. I was also informed by the photographs of Ore Huiying, who has been traveling to Boten for years and documenting its rise and fall and (potential) rise again.

To prepare for the trip, I spoke to or corresponded with Will Doig, Sebastian Strangio, Pal Nyiri, Shibani Mahtani, and Kearrin Sims. YouYou Zhou assisted with Chinese-language research. Quinn Slobodian put me in touch with Hadji Bakara, who introduced me to the person who would introduce me to my fixer and take me out to that weird Italian dinner. I also returned to James Scott's *The Art of Not Being Governed* for background on Zomia.

11. Terra Nullius

I reported this chapter in two parts. It began as a story for *The Nation* in the summer of 2019, when I traveled to Svalbard for the Arctic Circle Fellowship, observed the landscape for many hours, and interviewed a handful of people on the ground, including the then governor. But after spending time in Longyear's archives in Marquette, Michigan, in early 2023, I realized there was much more to the story. That was where I found Longyear's correspondence, notes, and other documents (some of which I had previously encountered in Nathan Haskell Dole's *America in Spitsbergen*).

More recent news on the snow crab case and the Russian drones, and other mentions of Svalbard, come from *The Barents Observer*, Mark Sabbatini's *Icepeople* (RIP), and more mainstream publications, such as Reuters and the *Financial Times*.

I've been particularly inspired by the academic work of Surabhi Ranganathan on this subject (and other extraterritorial delights) for years, as well as papers by Elizabeth Nyman and Rachel Tiller. Christopher R. Rossi's *Sovereignty and Territorial Temptation* answered many of my questions, and confirmed some hunches too.

Stephanie DeGooyer's chapter on *Frankenstein* in *Before Borders* unlocked the connection between Geneva and the High Arctic. Finally, portions of this chapter were fact-checked by Kadal Jesuthasan at *The Nation*, but Isabel Cristo handled the bulk of the checking for this chapter and the entire book. Knowing Isabel was on the case helped me sleep.